Adorno's Negative Dialectic

Studies in Contemporary German Social Thought (partial listing)
Thomas McCarthy, general editor

Theodor W. Adorno, *Hegel: Three Studies*
Theodor W. Adorno, *Prisms*
James Bohman, *Public Deliberation: Pluralism, Complexity, and Democracy*
James Bohman and William Rehg, editors, *Pluralism and the Pragmatic Turn: The Transformation of Critical Theory*
Craig Calhoun, editor, *Habermas and the Public Sphere*
Jean Cohen and Andrew Arato, *Civil Society and Political Theory*
Pablo De Greiff and Ciaran Cohen, editors, *Global Justice and Transnational Politics: Essays on the Moral and Political Challenges of Globalization*
Jürgen Habermas, *Between Facts and Norms: Contributions to a Discourse Theory of Law and Democracy*
Jürgen Habermas, *The Inclusion of the Other: Studies in Political Theory*
Jürgen Habermas, *The Liberating Power of Symbols: Philosophical Essays*
Jürgen Habermas, *Moral Consciousness and Communicative Action*
Jürgen Habermas, *The New Conservatism: Cultural Criticism and the Historians' Debate*
Jürgen Habermas, *The Philosophical Discourse of Modernity: Twelve Lectures*
Jürgen Habermas, *The Postnational Constellation: Political Essays*
Jürgen Habermas, *On the Pragmatics of Communication*
Jürgen Habermas, *On the Pragmatics of Social Interaction: Preliminary Studies in the Theory of Communicative Action*
Jürgen Habermas, *Religion and Rationality: Essays on Reason, God and Modernity*
Jürgen Habermas, *The Structural Transformation of the Public Sphere: An Inquiry into a Category of Bourgeois Society*
Joseph Heath, *Communicative Action and Rational Choice*
Axel Honneth, *The Critique of Power: Reflective Stages in a Critical Social Theory*
Axel Honneth, *The Struggle for Recognition: The Moral Grammar of Social Conflicts*
Tom Huhn and Lambert Zuidervaart, editors, *The Semblance of Subjectivity: Essays in Adorno's Aesthetic Theory*
Elliot L. Jurist, *Beyond Hegel and Nietzsche: Philosophy, Culture, and Agency*
Cristina Lafont, *The Linguistic Turn in Hermeneutic Philosophy*
Jeff Malpas, Ulrich Arnswald, and Jens Kertscher, editors, *Gadamer's Century: Essays in Honor Of Hans-Georg Gadamer*
Larry May and Jerome Kohn, editors, *Hannah Arendt: Twenty Years Later*
Christoph Menke, *The Sovereignty of Art: Aesthetic Negativity in Adorno and Derrida*
Shierry Weber Nicholsen, *Exact Imagination, Late Work: On Adorno's Aesthetics*
Claus Offe, *Modernity and the State: East, West*
Claus Offe, *Varieties of Transition: The East European and East German Experience*
Kirk Pillow, *Sublime Understanding: Aesthetic Reflection in Kant and Hegel*
William E. Scheuerman, *Between the Norm and the Exception: The Frankfurt School and the Rule of Law*
Albrecht Wellmer, *Endgames: The Irreconcilable Nature of Modernity*
Rolf Wiggershaus, *The Frankfurt School: Its History, Theories, and Political Significance*

Adorno's Negative Dialectic

Philosophy and the Possibility of Critical Rationality

Brian O'Connor

The MIT Press
Cambridge, Massachusetts
London, England

First MIT Press paperback edition, 2005

© 2004 Massachusetts Institute of Technology

All rights reserved. No part of this book may be reproduced in any form by any electronic or mechanical means (including photocopying, recording, or information storage and retrieval) without permission in writing from the publisher.

This book was set in New Baskerville by Integra Software Services Pvt. Ltd.

Library of Congress Cataloging-in-Publication Data

O'Connor, Brian 1965– .
  Adorno's negative dialectic : philosophy and the possibility of critical rationality/ Brian O'Connor.
    p. cm.—(Studies in contemporary German social thought)
  Includes bibliographical references (p.) and index.
  ISBN 978-0-262-15110-8 (hc: alk. paper), 978-0-262-65108-0 (pb.)
  1. Adorno, Theodor W., 1903–1969. Negative Dialektik. 2. Philosophy. 3. Dialectic. I. Title II. Series.
B3199.A33N4365 2004
193—dc22

                                                                                        2003060613

The MIT Press is pleased to keep this title available in print by manufacturing single copies, on demand, via digital printing technology.

For my mother and in memory of my father

Contents

Preface	ix
Acknowledgments	xv
Abbreviations Used in the Text	xvii
Introduction	1
1 The Role of German Idealism in the Negative Dialectic	15
2 The Structure of Adorno's Epistemology: The Priority of the Object	45
3 The Structure of Adorno's Epistemology: The Role of Subjectivity	71
4 The Critique of Kant	99
5 Adorno on Husserl and Heidegger	127
Conclusion	165
Notes	175
References	193
Index	201

Preface

Adorno's negative dialectic, the name he gives to the purely philosophical parts of his work, often appears to be quite remote from the concrete business of a critical theory of society. Indeed, Adorno's philosophy remains remarkably close to what might be considered a traditional concern of "pure" philosophy: the structure of experience. Furthermore extensive criticisms of seemingly esoteric parts of modern philosophy—particularly of modern German philosophy from Kant to Heidegger—are interwoven with arguments presented in support of a particular account of experience. In contrast, critical theory is supposed to be a consciousness-raising critique of society in which empirically specific aspects of society are examined.[1] Adorno himself, however, urges us to think of his apparently theoretical work as intimately connected with the "concrete" aims of critical theory. In the preface to *Negative Dialectics* he writes: "[T]his largely abstract text seeks no less to serve authentic concretion than to explain the author's concrete procedure" (*ND* 9–10/xix). But what can "concretion" amount to in a discussion of abstract philosophical problems?

I suggest that the answer to this question is to understand the negative dialectic as the theoretical foundation of the sort of reflexivity—the critical stance—required by critical theory. In the negative dialectic we are offered ways by which, for instance, we might question "the given" or recognize distortions of experience. These theoretical issues are painstakingly developed by Adorno, but not because he wants to add one more theory of knowledge or experience or whatever to the history of philosophy. Rather, he wants to demonstrate that there are radical alternatives—supported by philosophy—to how we take our reality to be; that it makes sense, simply, to claim that reality is available to us in ways which go beyond appearances. This is both an abstract philosophical exercise and one which lays the foundations for the applied "concrete" critique of appearances—for critical theory itself. Philosophy, then, not only exemplifies the critical attitude, it also, in fact, demonstrates that it is possible.

It can only be because Adorno is committed to the "concretion" of philosophy—that is, to developing a philosophy which lends itself to the task of criticism—that he is concerned with responding to the charge that philosophy "had merely interpreted the world" (*ND* 15/3). For him, "inadequate interpretation" and inadequate philosophizing lie behind the failure of the traditional Marxist program of praxis. What is required is not simply an adequate interpretation of the world but reflection on what philosophy thinks it is doing when it thinks it is criticizing. Adorno's relentless critique of key modern German philosophers is ultimately conducted in the name of this reflection. He gives particular attention to the subject-object relation in philosophy. This relation must take a particular form, Adorno believes, if critical theory is to be possible. After all, if objects, for instance, can be nothing other than what they are determined as being by subjectivity then there is no philosophical basis to the effort of critical theory to correct the misconceptions of the false consciousness of subjectivity. As Adorno writes: "The subject is the object's agent, not its constituent; this fact has consequences for the relation of theory and practice" (*SO* 752/146).

Given the tight connection that Adorno makes between "abstract" philosophy and the task of concretion it is surprising to find that the negative dialectic has been somewhat neglected in considerations of his work. No book-length examination has yet appeared in English on the subject, and those in German have tended to interpret Adorno's philosophical work through the framework of his writings on aesthetics and sociology. Of course reading Adorno's philosophy through other parts of his writings is a perfectly permissible way of thinking about his work, although it comes with the built-in disadvantage that it does not address the purely philosophical justifications that Adorno actually gives for the various claims made in his negative dialectic. Although Adorno sees the negative dialectic as the route to concretion he is quite determined to conduct philosophy in a rigorous and internally rational way: that is, philosophical arguments are by no means bent to the needs of a theory of society. Rather, the more rational philosophy is, the more it supports the development of the critical stance. To examine Adorno's negative dialectic *on its own terms* then, to treat it in its purely theoretical expression, is actually to carry through on Adorno's idea of concretion. For that reason I think that it is important to consider Adorno's negative dialectic in isolation from the sociological specifics of his critical theory. In this book I want to do just that. I will explore the structure of Adorno's dialectic, its key concepts, and its historical influences. I will show also that Adorno's philosophy, although sometimes flawed, contains concepts and arguments that are philosophically valuable. In particular, I want to point out how Adorno's philosophy offers us challenging ways of thinking about certain problems in epistemology and the philosophy of the subject, not necessarily because Adorno always has superior alternative theories within these areas of philosophy, but because his contributions in these areas remind us of what it is that philosophy is to do if it is to play a role in the development of critical rationality. It will become apparent, in this regard, that Adorno's philosophy is a "transcendental" one, something which has not previously been appreciated. It is strongly committed, I will show, to a connection between experience and rationality, claiming no less than that philosophical positions that fail to recognize the structure of experience (as Adorno will describe it) will deprive themselves of the ability to express themselves rationally.

Certain difficulties stand in the way of the examination I propose here. First, and perhaps most obvious, is the complex style used by Adorno to present his arguments. His way of putting things demands a great deal of the reader, though it is important to know that Adorno painstakingly defends the stylistic aspects of his philosophical writings.[2] Unfortunately, he has not persuaded very many of his readers. His texts are labeled variously as pompous and pretentious. Maybe so, but he is not, I think, impenetrable. With some patient restatement of Adorno's ideas, clear lines of thought can be revealed. A second difficulty for the interpretation of Adorno's work is the change in philosophical circumstances since the time in which Adorno wrote. His key works, as far as this examination of his work is concerned, are the *Metacritique of Epistemology* of 1956 and *Negative Dialectics* of 1966. These works are hardly ancient, yet the theoretical framework that can make sense of much of their content is no longer familiar to a great many of Adorno's readers, in particular to readers who think of philosophical problems through the prism of the linguistic turn. Although by no means reducible to German Idealism, much of what Adorno has to say is cast within the concepts of German Idealism. Reading Adorno's work involves taking a tour through the entire tradition of modern German philosophy, from Kant to Heidegger. Inevitably, unfamiliar and obscure terminology will lead to some confusion. Little wonder, indeed, that, as Rüdiger Bubner remarks, "*Negative Dialectics* remains a book whose seals are in no sense all entirely broken."[3] A key objective of this book will be to explicate the context in which Adorno's philosophy operates. Much space will therefore be given to considerations of the ideas of the major philosophers with whom Adorno is in debate.

I have set out this examination of Adorno's philosophy in the following way. In the introduction I shall give a historical account of what Adorno himself saw as the key problems of contemporary philosophy. What contemporary philosophy cannot do, he argues, is explain experience. Its failure to do so is connected with the inadequacies of the various methodologies it employs, methodologies which actually inhibit the development of criticism. I will introduce the notion that Adorno's philosophy is a philosophy for modernity by examining the influence of Georg Lukács's protocritical theory (with particular attention to Lukács's account of the relation between philosophy and socially sanctioned forms of rationality.) In chapter 1 I shall read through various selected parts of Kant and Hegel since those parts, I argue, are appropriated in various ways by Adorno in order to enable him to construct an alternative model of philosophy (one that in explaining experience would avoid precisely those difficulties identified in the introduction). That model will be based on a particular theory of subject-object interaction. In chapter 2 I look at Adorno's theory of objects—their role in experience, the part they play in subject-object epistemology and the manner in which they are misrepresented by noncritical philosophy. Chapter 3 will examine the role of subjects. Chapters 2 and 3, then, will give us the essential arguments of Adorno's philosophy. Adorno's philosophy, however, achieves great precision in the criticisms it makes of other philosophies; that is, in the application of the principles we will have seen in chapters 2 and 3. Criticism of other positions enables Adorno to demarcate the limits of his own commitments. For that reason the remaining two chapters will deal with the most significant of Adorno's critiques: chapter 4 is concerned with the critique of Kant, emphasizing what Adorno sees as the excesses of Kant's theory of subjectivity, and chapter 5 turns to phenomenology. Phenomenology is a particularly important position in Adorno's view since Husserl, in some places, argues for a version of objectivity which, like Adorno's position, aims to avoids subjective reductionism, whereas Heidegger explains experience by means that seem to undermine Adorno's subject-object theory. The conclusion offers a closing defense of Adorno's position. There I will argue that two key objections regarding the fundamental coherence of Adorno's position can be answered, provided we properly contextualize the problems with which Adorno is concerned.

Acknowledgments

I have been very fortunate to receive the help and advice of so many during the time in which I prepared this book. Rüdiger Bubner and Michael Inwood with their comments on and criticisms of an early version gave me the confidence to pursue it further. Michael Rosen read through seemingly innumerable drafts. His belief in the project, his philosophical acuity, and his generosity with time and thought were simply indispensable in getting me to this point. My colleagues and students at University College, Dublin have given me a constant supply of suggestions. In particular, Louise Campbell and Jim O'Shea—both staunch defenders of some of the things against which I want to argue—read through various sections and provided me with plenty of challenges. Ger Casey, Dermot Moran, and John Mullarkey offered sensible advice. And Tim Mooney, with whom I discussed virtually every idea contained in this book, was a spirited interlocutor. Here, I think, is a good opportunity to thank Liberato Santoro, my first Adorno teacher, who shared with me his extraordinary learning and enthusiasm. My most recent debt is to all of those who were instrumental in the publication of this work with the MIT Press: two anonymous readers, whose critiques of an earlier version of this project were enormously significant for the final shape of the book, and Tom McCarthy, the series editor, who supported the project since it first hit his desk.

The generous support of The Principal and Fellows of Hertford College, Oxford, the British Academy, the National University of Ireland,

and the Deutsche Akademische Austauschdienst allowed me to pursue much of my research in the most congenial of circumstances.

My wife Eileen Brennan has been my constant philosophical companion, always a rich source of ideas, and a totally giving reader of my work. I cannot find words of thanks adequate to her kindness. With good humor and love she and my daughters, Jane and Anna, have allowed me to absorb myself in this project. Finally, I thank my parents who in their different and profoundly loving ways have encouraged and inspired me throughout my life. I dedicate this book to them.

An earlier version of part of chapter 5 of this book appeared in *Philosophy and Social Criticism*, volume 24 (1998).

Abbreviations Used in the Text

Books by Adorno

Reference is given first to the original German text then, after the '/' symbol, to the indicated translation (where one exists). Translations have been slightly emended in some instances.

AP   "Die Aktualität der Philosophie," *Gesammelte Schriften*, volume 1 (Frankfurt am Main: Suhrkamp Verlag, 1973)/"The Actuality of Philosophy," trans. Benjamin Snow, *The Adorno Reader*, ed. Brian O'Connor (Oxford/Malden, Mass.: Blackwell, 2000).

BU   *Der Begriff des Unbewußten in der transzendentalen Seelenlehre*, *Gesammelte Schriften*, volume 1.

DA   (with Max Horkheimer) *Dialektik der Aufklärung: Philosophische Fragmente*, *Gesammelte Schriften*, volume 3 (1981)/*Dialectic of Enlightenment*, trans. John Cumming (London: Verso, 1979).

DSH   *Drei Studien zu Hegel*, *Gesammelte Schriften*, volume 5 (1970)/*Hegel: Three Studies*, trans. Shierry Weber Nicholsen (Cambridge, Mass./London: MIT Press, 1993).

EF   "Der Essay als Form," *Gesammelte Schriften*, volume 11 (1974)/"The Essay as Form," trans. B. Hullot-Kentor and Frederic Will, *The Adorno Reader*, ed. Brian O'Connor (Oxford/Malden, Mass.: Blackwell, 2000).

IN   "Die Idee der Naturgeschichte," *Gesammelte Schriften*, volume 1/"The Idea of Natural History," trans. Bob Hullot-Kentor, *Telos*, no. 60 (1984).

KK   *Kants "Kritik der reinen Vernunft," Nachgelassene Schriften*, section IV, volume 4 (Frankfurt am Main: Suhrkamp Verlag, 1995).

ME   *Zur Metakritik der Erkenntnistheorie*, *Gesammelte Schriften*, volume 5 (1970)/*Against Epistemology: A Metacritique*, trans. Willis Domingo (Oxford: Basil Blackwell, 1982/Cambridge, Mass.: MIT Press, 1983), referred to in this book as *The Metacritique of Epistemology*.

Abbreviations

MM *Minima Moralia, Gesammelte Schriften*, volume 4 (1980) / *Minima Moralia*, trans. E. F. N. Jephcott, (London: New Left Books, 1974).

ND *Negative Dialektik, Gesammelte Schriften*, volume 6 (1973) / *Negative Dialectics*, trans. E. B. Ashton, (London: Routledge, 1973).

PT *Philosophische Terminologie (1)* (Frankfurt am Main: Suhrkamp Verlag, 1973).

SeF "Soziologie und empirische Forschung," *Gesammelte Schriften*, volume 8 (1972) / "Sociology and Empirical Research," trans. Glyn Adey and David Frisby, *The Positivist Dispute in German Sociology* (London: Heinemann, 1976).

SO "Zu Subjekt und Objekt," *Gesammelte Schriften*, volume 10.2 (1977) / "Subject and Object," trans. Andrew Arato and Eike Gebhardt, *The Adorno Reader*, ed. Brian O'Connor (Oxford/Malden, Mass.: Blackwell, 2000).

Other Authors

BT Martin Heidegger, *Being and Time*, trans. J. Stambaugh (Albany, N.Y.: State University of New York Press, 1996). References are to the English marginal pagination.

CPR Immanuel Kant, *Critique of Pure Reason*, trans. Norman Kemp Smith (London: Macmillan, 1927).

EL G. W. F. Hegel, *The Encyclopaedia Logic*, trans. T. F. Geraets, W. A. Suchting, and H. S. Harris (Indianapolis, Ind.: Hackett, 1991). References are given to Hegel's paragraph numbers.

HCC Georg Lukács, *History and Class Consciousness*, trans. Rodney Livingston (London: Merlin Press, 1971).

LI Edmund Husserl, *Logical Investigations*, trans. J. N. Findlay (London: Routledge and Kegan Paul, 1973).

PhS G. W. F. Hegel, *Phenomenology of Spirit*, trans. A. V. Miller (Oxford: Oxford University Press, 1977).

Introduction

A unique feature of Adorno's commitment to critical theory is his view that the achievement of a critical rationality—the aim of all versions of critical theory—is an epistemological task. Adorno develops an account of the subject-object relation that he believes can justify the claim for an alternative and nonreductive rationality, one that allows relations "between persons in which the one accommodates to the other, identifies with the other, empathizes with the other," as Jürgen Habermas describes it.[1] Adorno develops this account of rational experience through a critique of the epistemological models available in modern philosophy. His approach to epistemology is, as Adorno himself liked to term it, as a metacritique of epistemology. The motivating idea behind the metacritique of epistemology is that every epistemology is determined by a normative commitment to how the world *ought to be*. Epistemologies thus work within rationalities that defend particular pictures of the subject-object relation, of relations in the world. The description of the subject-object relation is therefore never a neutral report of purely natural responses.

There are at least two senses of this epistemological normativity in Adorno's discussion. First, there is a *normativity of correctness*, such as Frege proposed in his claim that logic is the discipline of *how we ought to think*. Second, there is a kind of *goal-directed normativity* in which a philosophy envisages a goal or desired outcome: hence philosophy contributes to *the way things ought to be*. Through his view that the negative dialectic accounts for experience in a way that is uniquely consistent with rationality Adorno seems to operate with a normativity of correctness: in order to get experience right this is what one must think. The sense of a goal-directed normativity is, I think, attributed to other positions by Adorno. (Indeed it is this thought that enables him to charge other positions with ideology: they operate under conditions of what kind of world they would like.) The insight about the implicit normativity of philosophy can be traced back at least as far as Fichte who argued that the decisive factor in our choice of a philosophical account of the subject-object relation lies in a deeper commitment to a particular worldview. But in Adorno's case this insight is supplemented with various recognizably Kantian and Hegelian concepts that enable him, he thinks, to settle the matter of a choice of philosophy in a nonrelativistic way: it is the case that for Adorno the kind of philosophy a person chooses depends on what kind of person they are, but it is also true that there are, philosophically speaking, wrong sorts of persons, persons who are produced within, as Adorno puts it, "the ontology of the wrong state of things" (*ND* 22/11). The products of the "wrong state of things"—individuals and their intellectual efforts—can only be but wrong too.

So what can Adorno offer that is actually "true"? Contrary to a conventional line of thought on Adorno, that his position has no positive contribution to make as it is purely negative and critical, we find a comprehensively if not systematically stated account of the subject-object relation in his work.[2] This position emerges as a direct implication of his metacritique of epistemology. The metacritique is not merely negative. Were it so it would be nothing more than skepticism. What the metacritique sets out to achieve is to bring us to a rationally articulable account of experience. Adorno sets out by a variety of means to reveal an underlying yet never acknowledged version of experience. Chief among these means is the transcendental approach. In this approach he holds that what he regards as the truth of experience—his own account of the subject-object relation[3]—is an implicit assumption of the positions he criticizes. For Adorno, experience is the process in which ideally, that is, in its fullest possibility, one (a subject) is affected and somehow changed by confrontation with some aspect of objective reality (an object).

Introduction

Experience has, in a sense, a structure of reciprocity and transformation. Were this ideal to be realized we would have, as Adorno puts it, "nothing but full, unreduced experience in the medium of conceptual reflection" (*ND* 25/13).[4] Adorno sees it as his task to establish a form of philosophy that through a metacritique of epistemology will be capable of rescuing the idea of experience from a range of basic philosophical assumptions to be found throughout a spectrum of positions within modern philosophy.[5] The problem for these positions is that they in some sense assume what Adorno outlines as the essential structure of experience despite offering, officially, an account of experience which is quite at odds with those assumptions. The result of this is incoherence. But this incoherence is instructive: in pointing to the failure of the false constructions of philosophy the metacritique opens the way for the "truth of experience," that is, to give philosophical articulation to the essential structures of experience. The Kantian influence is evident here, I think, in that Adorno's transcendental critique of philosophy relies on a notion of experience that exclusively is consistent with the rational expression of philosophy. (We will see more of the basis of this in the following chapter.)

However, Kantian optimism about the power of rationality to redirect the course of philosophy is no longer possible. If individuals really are the products of "the ontology of the wrong state of things" it cannot be assumed that there is a persuasive account of the incoherence. Persuasion relies on a shared sense of rationality. But for modernity, rationality is a problem. Modernity, Adorno holds, is marked by a dominating version of rationality that, isomorphic with the economic structure of society, informs all critical enquiry and ensures that the enquiry falls short. So the metacritique of epistemology operates within a context in which truth is not necessarily efficacious. For that reason, the metacritique of epistemology is implicitly a critique of models of rationality that render truth inefficacious.

In this introduction I want to look at how Adorno initially came to think of philosophy in this way, that is, as both a critique of philosophy and a critique of rationality. For that reason I will examine his inaugural lecture, "The Actuality of Philosophy," and then the influential contribution of Georg Lukács. What both of these examinations can give us is the sense that Adorno had that the philosophy of experience of his time fell short of the implicit commitment to experience, and why (following Lukács) the idea of a transformed or corrected philosophy might be inhibited by the prevailing rationality of the time.

1 The Problems of Philosophy

With a certainty and self-assurance that was to characterize him throughout his career Theodor W. Adorno took to the lectern in 1931 to deliver his inaugural lecture (at the University of Frankfurt). This was a programmatic and polemical enough paper. In it he surveys the state of contemporary philosophy with one probing issue in mind: by what means do the various available philosophical models attempt to explain experience, and what lies implicit in the failures of their explanations? It is worth noting that Adorno restricts his enquiry to *contemporary models* of philosophy. He was concerned, even then, with the critical theory question of how a model of rationality valid for today could be articulated through philosophy.

Experience in its ideal realization is for Adorno, as I have mentioned, an open and reciprocal relationship between subject and object. The cardinal error of philosophy, he contends, is to simplify this relationship of reciprocity by assuming that the object in its *totality* can be encapsulated—mastered to put it in Adorno's emphatic way—by a subject. The totalistic aims of philosophy are not consistent with the sense of reciprocity implicit in ideal experience. Adorno writes: "Whoever chooses philosophy as a profession today must first reject the illusion that earlier philosophical enterprises began with: that the power of thought is sufficient to grasp the totality of the real" (*AP* 325/24). This is a foundational belief of Adorno's understanding of the possibility of philosophy; for him there can be no *total philosophy*. The ambition of revealing the rational structure of the world—as, say, Spinoza or Hegel might have attempted—is undermined by the complexity of the object, the world itself. However, Adorno does not draw the skeptical conclusion that knowledge of the object is impossible. Rather, a kind of knowledge of the object compatible with the reciprocal structure of experience has to be defended. This, then, will be a nontotalistic knowledge that excludes the assumption that knowledge means total encapsulation by the subject of the object. Adorno notes: "[O]nly polemically does reason present itself to the knower as total reality, while only in traces and ruins is it prepared to hope that it will ever come across correct and just reality [*richtige und gerechtige Wirklichkeit*]" (*AP* 325/24).

The notion of a philosophy that can account for a nonreduced experience, then, is proposed in this early lecture. Adorno's way of illuminating the need for such a philosophy is through an analysis of the failure of modern philosophies to deliver coherently their versions of experience. Hence the survey of contemporary philosophy offered by Adorno in "The Actuality of Philosophy" is important to our understanding of what it is that Adorno requires of philosophy. And because, as it has often been noted, Adorno was consistently committed to certain principles throughout his career with no significant difference between the younger and older Adorno, the programmatic nature of "The Actuality of Philosophy" is remarkably useful to us. Adorno's consequent program of philosophy is defined and limited by his apprehension of the debates current in these early years.

"The Actuality of Philosophy" surveys the most influential schools of contemporary philosophy, pointing out what Adorno sees as their inability to explain the reciprocity that is characteristic of experience. In effect, the main positions in philosophy have emphasized the role of either the subject or the object, but never both as a relationship of reciprocity. I want to concentrate on the four most significant of these schools, and I measure their significance in terms of the strength of challenge Adorno, here and elsewhere, felt they posed to a philosophy of nonreduced experience. (1) Heidegger (fundamental ontology) is accused of attempting, in the ontological project, to reduce reality to the meaning constituting activities of *Dasein* or, in effect, ourselves. Adorno claims that the influence of Kierkegaard lies behind this Heideggerian move in that Heidegger commits himself to an existentialist "subjective ontology" (*AP* 329/27). By pursuing that course, Heidegger, Adorno thinks, can be accused of a totalistic tendency: "The fullness of the real, as totality, does not let itself be subsumed under the idea of being which might allocate meaning to it" (*AP* 325/25); "[The idea of being] is lost for philosophy, and thereby its claim to the totality of the real is struck at its source" (*AP* 325/25). Heidegger, then, contributes, it seems, to a new idealism by reducing reality to ontological categories. Adorno's point is that these ontological categories *prestructure* the object and thereby cannot account for the reciprocal quality of experience. This is clearly controversial, and I shall address the question extensively later on in the chapter on phenomenology (chapter 5), but the important point for present purposes is to see just what Adorno saw as those self-defeating limitations in philosophy.

Adorno also questions (2) the coherence of Marburg neo-Kantianism. Marburg neo-Kantianism must be defined, according to Adorno, as system driven in that it attempts to establish a method based on rational consistency. The problem with this, however, is that it falls into formalism. The object of philosophy ought to be, rather, the dynamic ways in which human beings engage their reality, not the achievement of formal consistency. Adorno writes: "[Marburg neo-Kantianism] has preserved its self-contained form as a system, but has thereby renounced every right over reality and has withdrawn into a formal region in which every determination of content is condemned to virtually the farthest point of an unending process" (*AP* 326/25). Obviously enough Marburg neo-Kantianism, conceived in this way, represents philosophy at its most distant from the apparently objective reality of experience. It has no capacity to explain the reciprocity and transformation which Adorno sees as essential qualities of experience. By thinking of formal consistency as appropriate to the subject's engagement with the object, Marburg neo-Kantianism cannot explain engagement itself other than as a process of manipulation.

By rejecting formalism it might be imagined that Adorno is inclined toward some form of irrationalism.[6] (3) Irrationalism in its strict philosophical form claims that since categorial thought distances us from the content of experience we must abandon conceptual thought altogether. But this is very far from being Adorno's conception of philosophy. His insistence that we examine reality in "traces and ruins" in order to recover "correct and just reality" requires reflection, not an abandonment of our capacity to understand. By abandoning critical reflection irrationalism loses what is essential to philosophy. Instead "the given" is accepted without reflective understanding: "[Irrationalism] has lost all claims to make sense out of the empirical world which presses in upon it, and becomes resigned to 'the living' as a blind and unenlightened concept of nature . . ." (*AP* 326/25). Of crucial significance here is the claim that understanding is a key element of philosophy. Because Adorno believes that understanding—a conceptual activity—is a property of experience, the subject must thereby always be in a conceptual relation to the object. Subject and object do not melt into some kind of nonconceptual unity. Interestingly, the claim to such unity turns out (as we shall later see) to be an elevation of the subject: the thoughts, feelings, or whatever of the subject are simply elevated to pure truth.

Positivism (4), according to Adorno, assumes that its methodologies accurately capture the nature of things. It does not realize that its methodologies are historically developed, and hence are not pure ahistorical ways of apprehending objects. Adorno is alluding here in particular to logical positivism. It is obvious enough that Adorno, in common with most others, rejects logical positivism's restrictive principle of verification. But he also raises questions about logical positivism's lack of any ability to question the findings of the separate sciences and, more interestingly, the viability of a separation of the sciences. Thus in positivism experiential insights, Adorno argues, are subordinated to the unquestioned procedures and distinct departments of the sciences, whereas, Adorno hints, the separate sciences should be considered critically in light of the insights of experience. It is critical reflection, indeed, that marks the philosophical enterprise: "Philosophy will not be transformed into science, but under the pressure of the empiricist attack it will banish from itself all questioning which, as specifically scientific, belongs of right to the separate sciences and clouds philosophic questioning" (*AP* 333/30). The problems with positivism lead to deeper issues—if such questions remain unanswered it is possible that the prevailing intellectual climate will regard them as essentially unaskable: "Every philosophy which today does not depend on the security of current intellectual and social conditions, but instead upon truth, sees itself facing the problem of a liquidation of philosophy" (*AP* 331/29).[7]

That is, by thinking about questions which lie outside the scope of any scientific methodology, philosophy appears to stand outside the norms of rationality.[8]

2 Rationality and Philosophy: The Lukácsian Influence

But demonstrating the incoherence of philosophy today is not, Adorno knows, enough to change it. As I mentioned above, truth is not efficacious under the conditions of a distorted rationality. Adorno is committed to the Hegelian–Marxist view that the prevailing forms of rationality within any given society determine the self-limitations of that society. The significance of this view for the philosophy of experience lies in Adorno's contention that contemporary Western societies are shaped by a form of rationality that actually prevents the articulation of the idea of experience which Adorno believes is possible and exclusively compatible with a nonideological rationality. Society operates, he believes, by means of a rationality that reduces experience to processes of subject-object manipulation. To generate a fuller notion of experience therefore entails the implicit practical element of criticizing the form of rationality sanctioned by contemporary society in which, according to Adorno, reduced experience has come to seem natural. In this respect Adorno's philosophy is strongly marked by the influence of the Hegelian–Marxism of Georg Lukács. It is important to consider in some detail what Lukács argued since Adorno often takes the thesis of such a connection between the critique of society (and its rationality) and the critique of philosophy as a given thesis in need of little elaboration. In *History and Class Consciousness* (1923) Lukács, like Marx, reread Hegel's metaphysical dialectic of history from a materialist perspective, arguing that the proletarian class rather than *Geist* is the real subject-object of history (*HCC* 46–83); that is, that society, through the eventual agency of the proletariat, and not *Geist*, would become the realization of freedom. His distinctive contribution lay in claiming that reification—literally, making into a thing (*res, Ding*)—was the impediment to emancipation.

In the fourth essay of *History and Class Consciousness*—"Reification and the Consciousness of the Proletariat" ("Die Verdinglichung und das Bewußtsein des Proletariats")—Lukács argues that a society that operates through exchange economics transforms products from being the expression of the producer's "organic necessity" (*HCC* 88) into abstract entities—"things"—separated from the producer. Ideally, however, productive activity should be understood as the realization of a human expression, yet through the requirements of an exchange economy a *qualitative* character of human life (production) is reduced to a fragmentation of *quantitative* realities.[9] (This, indeed, becomes one of Adorno's concerns, for the ideal nonreified physical activity of labor is expressive of somatic experience, our whole engagement with objects.) This thought is perhaps recognizable from Marx's Paris Manuscripts of 1844, but Lukács gives it broader extension than Marx and identifies it as the key sociophilosophical concept: "What is at issue *here*, however, is the question: how far is commodity exchange together with its structural consequences able to influence the total inner and outer life of society?" (*HCC* 84). To elaborate on this, the crucial question here is that of how forms of social life can manifest themselves in forms of philosophy such that the critique of philosophy becomes, as an entailment, social critique—and implicitly, how such philosophical forms can aid the task of social transformation.

To see Lukács's answer to this question we need to look at some of the detail of what he sees as the effects of reification. He claims that reification has objective and subjective dimensions (*HCC* 87). *Objectively*, the world appears to be governed *naturally* by these reifying laws to the extent that they are apparently merely discovered by the individual and also unalterable. Thus the world is experienced as one composed of discrete and disconnected entities. Hence society in its current form comes to seem natural to discrete and disconnected individuals whose primary interaction is that of economic exchange. (Adorno echoes this thought: "[T]he hardening of bourgeois society into something impenetrably and inevitably natural is its immanent regression.")[10] *Subjectively*, the individual is deformed by reification to the extent that she now perceives her proper activities in terms of a society governed by quantitative laws. The subject as producer reflects in herself the fragmentation of the rationally produced object. She takes on the rules of rationalized production, and must therefore deny her idiosyncrasies in order to function consistently. The result, Lukács concludes, is that the subject no longer stands as "the authentic master of the process," but rather as its servant (*HCC* 89).

The effects of reification upon cognitive activity, in Lukács's view, are to reduce the active dialectical intercourse between subject and object in the act of knowledge. Once thought becomes calculation—as it does in its reified forms—it loses its critical capabilities. According to Lukács this mere concept manipulation enforces the semblance of the naturalism of rationalized social totality, for the subject is unable to think in terms of possibilities which would transcend this order: "[T]he essence of rational calculation is based ultimately upon the recognition and the inclusion in one's calculations of the inevitable chain of cause and effect in certain events—independently of individual 'caprice.' In consequence, man's activity does not go beyond the correct calculation of the possible outcome of the sequence of events (the 'laws' of which he finds 'ready-made'), and beyond the adroit evasion of the disruptive 'accidents' by means of protective devices and preventive measures (which are based in their turn on the recognition and application of similar laws)" (*HCC* 98). For Lukács this belies the claim that the bourgeois age is one of productive and enterprising creativity, in that, for him, all decisions are in reality taken according to the ever determining form of rationality (*HCC* 98). Reification, in short, now pervades every aspect of human life: "This rationalization of the world appears to be complete, it seems to penetrate the very depths of man's physical and psychic nature" (*HCC* 101).

In the "The Antinomies of Bourgeois Thought" section of "Reification and the Conciousness of the Proletariat" Lukács explains the way in which this reified thought penetrates into philosophical forms. The analysis opens up the influential idea that the critique of philosophy goes beyond philosophy in that it entails a critique of the forms of socially sanctioned rationality. It is a striking thesis—utterly central to Neo-Marxist philosophy—that noncritical philosophy in its presuppositions and difficulties is somehow to be characterized by the same rationality that is constitutive of social life. Lukács writes: "[T]he character of this [social] existence is revealed at least as clearly by what philosophy does *not* find problematic as by what it does" (*HCC* 112). Lukács sees it as especially revealing that philosophy has failed to accommodate a positive concept of matter within its systems. He believes that this problem is most clearly discovered in Kantian epistemology (*HCC* 114). Kant had regarded the thing-in-itself as representative of the limits of human knowledge, and concerned himself mainly with phenomena. But Lukács argues that Kant had to promote the duality between phenomena and noumenon in order to avoid the undermining factor of matter. Since phenomena are the ultimate contents of knowledge, as such, Kant transcended the real contribution of matter and thus could make claims for the creativity of the knowing subject with even greater force. The problem of matter arises simply because of philosophy's claims to totality (something that we have seen Adorno too criticize). Kant's philosophy, according to Lukács, is designed to prove the priority and centrality of the subject. But it cannot, however, claim that it creates the object entirely, for the matter of every object precedes any possible interpretation. There is therefore an irreducible givenness that stands over the claims of subjective idealism. Acknowledgement of this givenness, claims Lukács, tends to threaten idealism with its own collapse. For if "rationalism"—Lukács's term for the totalistic ambition of philosophy—cannot account for irrational matter then it must be a "register, an account, as well ordered as possible of facts which are no longer linked rationally and so can no longer be made systematic even though the forms of their components are themselves rational" (*HCC* 118). In other words, rationalism is merely a system of schematization in which again prejudicially atomized pieces of reality are ordered.

Lukács argues that the subjectivist aim of rationalist philosophy has its origins in modern society. Kant's creative epistemological subject resembles the ideal of the bourgeois individual: "[T]he man who now emerges must be the individual, egoistic bourgeois isolated artificially by capitalism and that his consciousness, the source of his activity and knowledge, is an individual isolated consciousness à la Robinson Crusoe" (*HCC* 135). In precisely the same way is the Kantian subject allegedly isolated and enclosed by the rational unity of consciousness. In neither case—social and philosophical—can the concept of community be comprehended, except as the collection of atomized individuals. And the absence of this idea of community also, it seems, leads to a different relation between subjects and what they perceive as other than themselves. That is, the subject simply cannot account for the presence of an object in any sense that would entail an ethical recognition of this object.

Not only, however, are there parallels between philosophy and certain supposedly foundational principles of bourgeois society, but the very problems found within the general project of modern philosophy are ultimately tied in some way to deeper failures in society itself. There are two specific failures within bourgeois society, according to Lukács. First, rationalist epistemology claims that we can know the object only insofar as we have created it; similarly, bourgeois society "acquires increasing control over the details of its social existence, subjecting them to its needs" (*HCC* 121). Bourgeois society defines social existence, the possible forms and structures of life, only in terms of its own requirements. Second, rationalist epistemology can account for the forms of thought, but not for the irrational givenness of matter, and thus it undermines its own claims to be paradigmatic from the point of view of reason; in modern society the limitation of bourgeois control derives from its narrow class interests, and, like rationalist philosophy, it "loses ... the possibility of gaining intellectual control of society as a whole and with that it loses its own qualifications for leadership" (*HCC* 121).

Adorno shares Lukács's concern about the crisis of rationality in modernity, but he nevertheless disagrees that this crisis is connected with the problems of class. It lies far from Adorno's social theory that "the history of all hitherto existing society is the history of class struggles."[11] Adorno's concern centers around the historical reduction of the individual of any class. He tells us that "to this day history lacks any collective subject, however constructible" (*ND* 299/304). Adorno therefore redirects the concept of reification with the question of how it prevents the possibilities of subjective experience, understood as the objective possibilities of the subject. Lukács with his more generalized interest in social transformation does not address the philosophy of experience.

The Lukácsian moment in Adorno, then, is precisely the view that forms of philosophy are manifestations of the forms of rationality that are constitutive of social life. The forms of social rationality are not neutral in the sense of being ahistorical laws of thought: rather they are rules of thinking and of organization that society itself sanctions. Rationality, then, has a normative basis in precisely this respect, and on that basis the critique of philosophy as the product of this rationality must entail the critique of rationality in the broader sense. This critique would be otiose were different philosophical systems and their determining rationalities nothing other than incommensurable normativities. But, as Adorno believes, "truth is objective" (*ND* 52/41) even it if is not persuasive. "Direct communication," he writes, "is not a criterion of truth" (*ND* 52/41). Adorno sets out to provide an account of experience that he sees as exclusively expressible by a nonreified rationality. What I want to do in this book is to consider that philosophy—a philosophy for modernity—as Adorno himself develops it.

1
The Role of German Idealism in the Negative Dialectic

I have claimed in my introduction that Adorno's philosophy has a commitment to the notion of a nonrelativist truth. Specifically, I say that Adorno holds that there is only one comprehensively rational account of experience, such that any alternative account can be shown to be incoherent. In this respect there is transcendental necessity to his concept of experience. This will come as a surprise to those who tend to see Adorno's philosophy somewhat like Nietzsche's, that is, as straining at all points to reject the traditional concepts and arguments of philosophy. Surprising or not, I think it ought to be clear, if we pay close attention to Adorno's arguments, that Adorno is a transcendental philosopher. The negative dialectic contains the following two elements, which together are constitutive of a transcendental philosophy: first, it identifies the conditions for the possibility of experience; and second, it holds, further, that philosophy cannot be coherent if it denies or excludes any of the conditions identified as the conditions for the possibility of experience. In other words, the conditions for the possibility of experience must necessarily be accepted, otherwise philosophical discussions of experience deprive themselves of the concepts that would allow a coherent position to be expressed. This transcendental aspect of Adorno's work is significant in that it indicates a belief in a strong notion of rationality: what transcendental arguments do—the way in which they refute—is to establish that there are certain objective principles that are rationally compelling.

Another aspect of Adorno's philosophy that I briefly noted is its development of a subject-object model of experience. The essential elements of this model are certain versions of (i) subjectivity, (ii) the object, and (iii) the interaction of (i) and (ii). (In the next two chapters I shall examine them—(i) and (ii)—in their distinguishable roles.) This interaction entails, in Adorno's exposition, the concepts of nonidentity and the priority of the object. Furthermore, Adorno insists that this interaction is not a mechanical causal relation, but one that involves rationality. In this chapter I want to outline the historical background of these issues. I think it is obvious to most who read Adorno that the concepts that support the negative dialectic have conspicuous Kantian and Hegelian colors. Adorno clearly appropriates and develops Kant and Hegel without, most challengingly for his readers, explaining in detail what it is in the arguments of these predecessors that really lends itself to the position—the new concept of philosophy—that he is attempting to develop. So looking at Kant and Hegel in some detail is not merely historical background: it is an absolutely indispensable preparation for making any progress at all in the task of understanding Adorno's philosophy.

Kantian and Hegelian concepts are used by Adorno, as I have said, to give substance to the basic philosophical outlook that we saw announced in "The Actuality of Philosophy." But how, it might be asked, are Kantian and Hegelian ideas to be put together given the extraordinary differences between the two philosophers (differences elaborated not least by Hegel himself in his various histories of modern philosophy)? To preempt the extensive analysis below, I want to suggest here the complementary relationship that Adorno finds between Kant and Hegel. For Adorno experience is a relationship of subject to object, but this relationship takes two directions. First, there is what we might call a *vertical dimension* in which a subject has directly physical yet significant experience of an object. Second, there is a *lateral dimension* in which a subject judges—applies a concept to—an object which is itself a conceptual whole. Kant's philosophy in particular respects helps Adorno to develop a model of the vertical dimension of experience, whereas Hegel's is used to develop a notion of the lateral dimension. What Adorno emphasizes in Kant's thought are the various theses to the effect that a subject is unrealizable without an object, and that there are features of the object that are in some sense both beyond the reach of subjectivity yet also capable of providing a key requirement for the realization of subjectivity. I want to explore the basis in Kant for these attributions. And in Hegel's philosophy I will examine the idea of conceptual adjustment, which Adorno emphasizes as a key rational component of experience. From Kant, then, we get the transcendental structures of experience, whereas Hegel can explain the nature of our experiential engagements, engagements by subjects in the conceptual activity of knowing particular objects. This latter claim may not sound purely Hegelian. In fact it is not. It is, however, part of the version of Hegel that Adorno develops in light of the epistemological materialism that he appears to accept from Kant. I shall explore Hegel's philosophy in order to find the basis of Adorno's version of Hegel's view of experience.

Clearly Adorno has a rather busy agenda to bring to the interpretation of Kant and Hegel. His reconstruction of their accounts of experience is motivated by his independent view that, as he puts it: "The matters of true philosophical interest at this point in history are those in which Hegel, agreeing with tradition, expressed his disinterest. They are nonconceptuality, individuality [*Einzelnen*], and particularity [*Besonderen*]—things which ever since Plato used to be dismissed as transitory and insignificant, and which Hegel labeled 'lazy Existenz' " [*ND* 19–20/8]. Remarkably, then, as we shall see, it is from the very tradition that Adorno criticizes in the above remark that resources are to be found for the revolution in philosophy. This chapter will examine the potential that Adorno finds in Kantian and Hegelian philosophies for the "new philosophy" which might express the reality of "full unreduced experience."

There is a preliminary terminological issue. In his appropriation of German Idealist philosophy Adorno makes frequent use of the terms *identity* and *mediation*. It is important to get a working sense of what these ideas involve. Confusingly, Adorno appears to offer two quite different explanations of the concept of identity. I should like to distinguish them under the headings *de facto identity* and *de jure identity*. First, *de facto identity* posits the exclusive meaningfulness of concepts. No claim is made with respect to the identity of object and concept, but since concepts alone are explained as the meaning element of the relationship it follows, de facto, that the object is what it is only as articulated through concepts. The object is thereby identical with its concepts, from the point of view of meaning. The object as such is merely an instance of some predicate. Adorno notes that "identity thinking says what something comes under, what it exemplifies or represents and what, accordingly, it is not itself" (*ND* 152/149). But what happens here is that concepts are hypostatized: "Like the thing, the material tool, which is held on to in different situations as the same thing, and hence divides the world as chaotic, many-sided, and disparate from the known, one, and identical, the concept is the ideal tool, fit to do service for everything, wherever it can be applied" (*DA* 56–57/39). *De jure identity* misconstrues the subject-object relation as one of exhaustive correspondence. In this case there is an alleged identity between concepts and the inherent determinations of the object. Meaning is a matter of an object strictly fitting a concept, characterized by Adorno as "wretched cover-concepts" (*armseliger Oberbegriffe*) (*ND* 155/152). This process of an object corresponding to a concept is, Adorno hyperbolically suggests, a form of identity.[1] He argues that predication is simply an assertion of identity: the "mere form of predicative judgment postulates identity" (*ND* 92/85). This is a highly controversial contention, and I shall examine its validity in the following chapter (section 6).

"Mediation," in the sense relevant here, is the form of interrelation of subject and object. It is, in effect, an interdetermining relation and is the structure of experience. Adorno's defense of this theory of mediation will have significant implications for the "concretion" claims of his philosophy. If it is impossible to justify the claim that experience has a structure which allows the dynamic interaction of subject and object then a key aim of critical theory, that of showing that the relation of subject to object—of individual to society—can be transformed into one of reciprocity, will be left without the philosophical foundation Adorno thinks it important to provide. For Adorno the mediation structure contains the interdetermination of both subject and object (though obviously in respectively different ways). In contrast to identity, in mediation both sides are understood as operating interdependently in the production of knowledge. The Hegelian origins of this concept may seem obvious. Michael Rosen argues convincingly, though, that mediation in Adorno never really operates in the rigorous way intended by Hegel. Hegel himself, Rosen claims, does not, in effect, use it as another word for "interaction."[2] This is a confusing issue, certainly, given that Adorno credits Hegel with the invention of the concept. Hegel, in fact, though not all that clear about what he himself means by mediation, never says anything that might suggest anything like Adorno's version of this concept.[3]

1 The Kantian Influence

The presence of Kant's philosophy in Adorno's mature work seems virtually inevitable when we consider his intellectual formation. It is reported that Adorno's earliest introduction to philosophy, whilst still a teenager—an introduction he experienced apparently without terror—was in the form of private tuition on the *Critique of Pure Reason* given by a family friend, Siegfried Kracauer. Then as a graduate student in his early twenties he wrote a doctoral dissertation and a *Habilitationsschrift* from the perspective of his Neo-Kantian mentor, Hans Cornelius.[4] Adorno's philosophical works, from his first book in 1933 (on Kierkegaard) to his posthumous masterpiece of 1970, *Aesthetic Theory*, are replete with Kantian allusions and references. But this is just the problem that confronts a comprehensive evaluation of his attitude towards Kant: so much is allusion and reference, and so little is substantive argument. It is as though Kant's philosophy had taken root so early in Adorno's development that it was more than an influence. It had utterly integrated itself with part of Adorno's philosophical consciousness. The task I have set myself in this section is to give shape to this presence and to elucidate what seem to me to be the key Kantian assumptions within Adorno's work.

Because of Adorno's unusual understanding of Kant's philosophy, his Kant will be unfamiliar to someone reading him with the expectations and perspectives of present-day philosophy. From Adorno's perspective, the valuable side of Kant's philosophy provides the ingredients which are necessary for overcoming subjective idealism;

that is, it contains arguments that support a form of critical materialism. This is quite a distance from the current version of Kant that sees the first *Critique* as an investigation of epistemic conditions alone.[5] The theory of critical materialism referred to here is one that holds *both* that the subject does not passively receive meanings from the object, *and* that the activity of the subject is circumscribed by the determinate independence of the object. To put this in broad terms (for the purposes of the present chapter), Adorno often appears to endorse Kant's conception of objects as things-in-themselves as a realist position "free from the subjective spell" (*SO* 752–753/147). From this starting point Adorno develops arguments that aim to show that without the idea that the thesis of the alleged ontological reality of the thing-in-itself tries to express—namely, that objects are not reducible to the concepts of a subject—epistemology would be unable to explain the self-evident facts of experience. As Adorno claimed in his lecture course on the first *Critique* in 1959: "[O]n the one hand, the *Critique of Pure Reason* is, if you like, an identity-thinking; that is to say, it actually wants to ascribe synthetic *a priori* judgments and finally every organized experience, every objectively valid experience, to the analysis of the consciousness of the subject.... On the other hand, however, this thinking would like equally to renounce the mythology that the human being absolutizes and regards as the whole truth whatever ideas that dwell inside him. In so far as it does so Kantian thinking is also a thinking that most emphatically wants to bring the moment of *nonidentity* to validity" (*KK* 104). In other words, Kant has conflicting tendencies. First, he wants to explain all experience through subjectivity, but second, he also argues against the reducibility of subject to object: he therefore seems to hold to what Adorno sees as a form of nonidentity.

Adorno's view of Kant is, I think, well founded. The idea that Kant can contribute to the nonidentity requirement is supported by evidence from the Refutation of Idealism section of the first *Critique*, which is why, in this chapter, I shall give it some attention. The Refutation of Idealism is the pivotal point of Kant's engagement with idealism. The Refutation aims to prove that idealism in its Cartesian and Berkeleian sense is incoherent since that form of idealism, with its prioritization of subjectivity, cannot explain the actual experiences of subjectivity, something that can be done only with reference to objective "external" conditions. As far as is possible, I shall attempt to present the Refutation of Idealism from the perspective of Adorno. To that end, I shall be analyzing this key Kantian source out of the context in which Kant intended it. This is appropriate, however, given Adorno's rejection of the official Kantian enterprise. It is my intention to reflect Adorno's selective endorsement of Kant's philosophy. In a later chapter we shall see Adorno's criticism of Kant's official doctrine; a doctrine that centers, in Adorno's view, on the *constitutive subject* which is beyond all knowable reality. And interestingly, we will see that the methodology employed by Adorno in his critique of Kant and other philosophers is in large part derived from certain parts of Kant's philosophy.[6]

Having considered the Refutation of Idealism I will then turn to the Antinomies section of the *Critique of Pure Reason*. My reading of the Doctrine of the Antinomies argues that this doctrine is highly relevant to Adorno in that it gives him the substance of the transcendental theory that becomes so evident in his work. For Kant, failure to work within strictly defined structures of experience leads to antinomy. Adorno adapts this theory to the needs of his theory of subject-object reciprocity.

1.1 The Refutation of Idealism

I want to outline, as briefly as I can, what is involved in the argument put forward by Kant in the Refutation of Idealism. The kind of philosophical position that his refutation seeks to undermine is what he calls "*material* idealism . . . the theory which declares the existence of objects in space outside us either to be merely doubtful and indemonstrable or to be false and impossible" (*CPR* B274). Kant claims that Descartes and Berkeley are proponents of this form of idealism. It is not, however, their idealism per se that concerns him, not at least according to conventional definitions of idealism. His aim is a refutation of the form of skepticism that arises from what he takes to be their indirect realism. Indirect realism attempts to conclude that only our ideas or representations are certain, and it is a matter of insecure inference as to whether there are independent objects that correspond to those ideas. Famously, Kant calls it a "scandal to philosophy and to human reason in general that the existence of things outside us ... must be accepted on faith" (*CPR* Bxxxix).[7]

The thesis of the Refutation is: "*[t]he mere, but empirically determined, consciousness of my own existence proves the existence of objects in space outside me*" (*CPR* B275). Kant's strategy is to show that outer experience—experience of objects—is somehow a condition of inner experience, and that is something which the "material idealist"-*cum*-skeptic must, of course, deny. What Kant hopes to show is that the certainty of inner experience is impossible without perception of external objects. For Kant our inner experience could not consist of a flow of imagination, containing illusory beliefs about objects (as the skeptic has to say). If this argument is correct, then the Cartesian and empiricist model of representation is undermined, for the assumptions of "indirectness" and "inference" that led to skepticism are seen to be untenable.

The argument takes as its focus the nature of inner experience. In speaking of inner experience Kant refers only to the most general characteristic of empirical self-consciousness, the awareness of the temporal sequence of one's experiences. He means to argue, here as in many other parts of the first *Critique*, against a conception of self-consciousness as the arcane alleged awareness of an essential ego. The most general characteristic of empirical self-consciousness is, as Kant himself puts it, "consciousness of my own existence as determined in time" (*CPR* B275). This, as I have said, seems to mean the awareness of temporal sequence in my thoughts or experience. The argument that follows is that this awareness "presupposes something permanent in perception" (*CPR* B275). Without something permanent which is distinct from the representations (thoughts or experiences) themselves there would be no way, it seems, of realizing the contrasting representations that I actually have. In the preface to the second edition Kant notes: "For all grounds of determination of my existence which are to be met with in me are representations [or ideas] and as representations themselves require a permanent distinct from them, in relation to which their change, and so my existence in the time wherein they change, may be determined" (*CPR* Bxl). For Kant, this distinct permanent element secures the

German Idealism in the Negative Dialectic

possibility of self-consciousness and must be something other than a representation or indeed an ordered sequence of representations. Kant argues that this must be an external object. Self-consciousness, it turns out, is unrealizable without experience of actual objects or "outer experience." The actuality of inner experience entails outer experience. Without reference to it empirical consciousness is nothing more than an inert possibility at best. Thus Kant, as Graham Bird neatly puts it, shows by a transcendental argument "that to doubt or deny outer experience the skeptics must also deny inner experience; and that in accepting inner experience they must also accept outer. What they cannot coherently do is to accept inner but reject outer experience."[8]

Against the indirect realist Kant claims that outer experience is "immediate," neither inferential nor indirect. To explain experience using a conventional model we have (i) the mind, (ii) a representation or idea, and (iii) the thing. The actuality of the thing is merely inferred from the immediate presence of the representation. Kant's ingenious strategy is to show that (i) mind itself is unintelligible without immediate outer experience. It is not on the nature of the representation that Kant focuses in the effort to repair the bridge between inner and outer experience. Rather, it is the nature of mind, or consciousness, understood under the limited aspect of time consciousness, on which his argument for the certainty of outer experience turns. The burden for Kant, as he himself sees, is to show that time determination cannot be achieved by any purely subjective source: that is, the relative permanent cannot be purely subjective. Hence he denies that the transcendental "I think" (the transcendental condition of the possibility of consciousness) or the modes of intuition can provide the relatively permanent element which is required for the possibility of time consciousness. The subject does not possess the resources to fulfill the criteria of permanence since the subject is, on the empirical level, a series of experiences.

At the conclusion of the proof Kant writes: "Now consciousness [of my existence] in time is necessarily bound up with consciousness of the [condition of the] possibility of this time-determination; and it is therefore necessarily bound up with the existence of things outside me, as the condition of this time-determination. In other words, the consciousness of my existence is at the same time an immediate consciousness of the existence of other things outside me" (*CPR* B276). What Kant is trying to establish is that the ultimate claim by the Cartesian that consciousness is more immediately known and is thus more certain than outer objects can be seen to rest upon a false assumption, for our temporal consciousness cannot be separated from these outer objects, and in knowing consciousness I must *first* be aware, at some level, of these outer objects.

At this point I note what seems to me to be a problem with the argument. Kant is relying heavily on the vague connecting term "bound up with" to characterize the relationship between self-consciousness and the experience of objects. In the preface [B], Kant specifies that it means "bound up in the way of identity." Kant thus wants it to denote some kind of direct connection between "consciousness of my existence" and "an immediate consciousness of other things outside me." But the argument seems to have missed a step. Kant, I think, has merely shown that the idea of time consciousness requires some objects "outside me." That, however, is some way away from our having an immediate experiential grasp of them. What Kant is doing thereby is conflating the conditions of inner experience—namely, that there are objects outside us—with inner experience itself, which is nothing more than consciousness of my existence in time. There is an interesting view of experience contained here. The certainty of the existence of external objects does not derive from their being experienced as actual but is based on the idea that they provide the conditions of inner experience. Hence, I think that Kant is drawing the wrong conclusion from his argument: he shows that we require external objects, but he does not show that there need be any correspondence between these objects and our representation of them. There is no reference to the content of our representations, merely the consciousness of their order, and this problem in the argument, I want to suggest, leads to conflicting accounts of what objects are: are they representations, or are they entirely other than representations, being things-in-themselves that underlie representations?[9] And this missing step, I think, has interesting implications for the version of Kant that Adorno wants to develop: Kant rightly points out the limitations of subjectivity—in terms

German Idealism in the Negative Dialectic

of what it needs in its engagement with outer objects—but he cannot give substance (quite literally) to the objects which mark these limits.

But it is important to see just what Kant's position seems to allow. The notion of experience always entails an immediate relation with an outer object: even the very possibility of inner experience relies on this condition. This relation is, in a sense, nonconceptual in that it is not a relation of subject to an object with particular conceptual determinations. However it is not a relation that lies outside the space of reasons in that its necessity can be shown by philosophical argument. Kant seems to think that it is shown by experience too. This arrangement of the nonconceptual within the space of reasons will be a telling element in Adorno's account of nonidentity.

1.2 Antinomy and Transcendental Argument

It may seem strange to put the ideas of antinomy and transcendental argument together. After all, Kant makes no connection between the two.[10] But there is an important reason for drawing the connection, and that is that Adorno's critique of idealism brings both ideas together. And the connection is found in what I have referred to as the epistemological norm of correctness, as we shall see. Obviously enough, as we saw in the Refutation of Idealism discussion, Kant draws a tight connection between the rationality of philosophical argument and the structures of experience. The Antinomies section argues similarly for this connection, proposing that philosophy itself can fall into a debilitating antinomy when it does not operate within what can be legitimately claimed for experience.

Kant argues in the Antinomies that questions whose answers require evidence beyond the limitations of what the structures of our experience can allow are the product of an antinomical rationality. The result is that two internally consistent, individually demonstrable but mutually exclusive answers to questions of this nature can be given. This, not dissimilarly to the equipollence method of argument used by ancient skepticism, undermines the exclusive truth claims of either position. What is required to escape from this, according to Kant, is that we recognize the necessary limitations of experience as identified by critical philosophy itself. The critical philosophy therefore shows us that we can know only what is experienced and what the conditions of that experience are. We cannot know any phenomenon outside those limitations. That is to say, in Kant's language, we cannot know anything *unconditionally* or *absolutely*.

Likewise, Adorno, as is particularly evident in his critique of phenomenology, argues that antinomical conclusions will arise from the philosophical effort to establish absolute foundations. There is, however, a key difference between how Adorno and Kant respectively see the presence of antinomy in various philosophical positions. We might term this difference *internal* and *external* antinomy. Kant identifies antinomy *externally* in the following way: he places one internally consistent position (say, determinism) alongside another internally consistent but opposing position (say, libertarianism). The antinomy here is external in that it becomes apparent only when one kind of position is contrasted with another. Adorno sees antinomy as *internal* to particular philosophical positions. What this means is that a position is internally antinomical in so far as it contains conflicting tendencies, tendencies that actually undermine the coherence of the position itself. Internal antinomy—unlike external antinomy—does not become apparent by way of contrast. In his critical application of transcendental argument Adorno reveals the *internal* problems of a given position and this, I contend, is the conceptual basis of Adorno's well-known idea of *immanent critique*. Adorno's view is that antinomies are immanent to certain given positions. Immanent critique involves, then, identifying the internally conflicting tendencies of a position. As Adorno dramatically puts it: immanent critique pushes with the force of a position's commitments to where that position "cannot afford to go" (*ME* 14/5). The conflicting tendencies that are latent in a position are articulated in immanent critique. For Adorno and for Kant antinomy arises in the production of extra-experiential doctrines. The form that the antinomy takes, however, differentiates Adorno and Kant on this issue.

It is this *internal* version of antinomy that suggests the connection with transcendental argument. Transcendental arguments, broadly speaking, claim that internal inconsistencies arise from arguments that fail to appreciate the fundamental conditions that make certain kinds of experience possible. It seems to me, at least, that Adorno means precisely this when he "uncovers" the antinomies of "absolutist" claims. This will be most clearly seen, I think, when we see Adorno's actual "immanent critique" of particular philosophical positions.

There is no doubt that Adorno has here also been at least partly influenced by Hegel's version of antinomy. For Hegel, antinomy signifies the incomplete, or not yet systematized, nature of our understanding of objects: "The main point that has to be made is that antinomy is found not only in the four particular objects taken from cosmology, but rather in *all* objects of all kinds, in *all* representations, concepts, and ideas" (*EL* §42). The fact that there are antinomies obliges us, in Hegel's view, to understand objects dialectically. That is to say, we are to accept that the fullest understanding of an object *ought* to contain contradictions. It lies in the nature of objects, according to Hegel, that we must proceed through contradictions in our philosophical account of the real (*EL* §92). However, the essential point in understanding Adorno's use of antinomy is its relation to transcendental argument. To relate antinomy to transcendental argument is to see contradiction as fatal to any philosophical discourse. Contradiction therefore cannot be, *contra* Hegel, merely a moment of speculative thought (*EL* §79). Again, for Hegel antinomy provokes deeper dialectical progression, whereas for Adorno antinomy concludes with the undermining of antimaterialist epistemology. The difference in intention is pretty clear. In any case, Adorno explicitly acknowledges the force of Kant's version:

> *Prima philosophia* came to awareness of this in the doctrine of the antinomies in the *Critique of Pure Reason*. The search for the utterly first, the absolute cause, results in infinite regress. Infinity cannot be posited as given with a conclusion, even though this positing seems unavoidable to total spirit. The concept of the given, the last refuge of the irreducible in idealism, collides with the concept of spirit as complete reducibility, viz. with idealism itself. Antinomy explodes the system, whose only idea is the attained identity, which as anticipated identity, as finitude of the infinite, is not at one with itself. (*ME* 37/29–30)

For Adorno Kant's criticism of idealist efforts to reach unconditioned knowledge is historically significant in that for the first time the attempt to reduce object to subject is shown to be inherently contradictory.

Why is it, though, that epistemological arguments which transgress the prescribed limits of knowledge conclude antinomically? For Kant and Adorno, even though they respectively deal with external and internal versions of antinomy, there is an undefined connection between philosophical rationality and the necessary conditions of experience. In this case philosophical rationality, I want to suggest, is guided by the norm of correctness. It seems that the coherence of rational experience is a precondition of our ability to reconstruct it rationally: rationality is in some respect embedded in experience. If this is the case, then there will be strict limitations within which our descriptive efforts must operate. If our efforts lead to conclusions that fail to explain features of experience—experience understood as containing the subject-object structure described by Adorno—then those descriptions are incoherent. This incoherence may manifest itself externally, as Kant succeeds in showing. The incoherence might also be understood internally, as Adorno argues, in that a theory that is at odds with rational experience—as Adorno describes it (subject-object reciprocity, and so on)—can never make sense, simply because it misuses a rationality which is embedded in experience albeit distorted in philosophy and socially sanctioned rationality.[11] Adorno's thought seems to be that all philosophical talk about experience operates within a more fundamental, but as yet unarticulated, relation with objects. Those philosophies that argue for unexperiential theses—for example, a transcendental ego—do so by assuming the possibility of experience yet they operate with concepts which have no basis in any intelligible notion of experience. The incoherence that arises here is that of the copresence of (a) the assumption that experience is possible (a correct assumption) with (b) concepts that articulate it in ways that fail to deliver what is assumed. In the critique of Kant, Husserl, and Heidegger we will see Adorno use the *implicit* against the *stated* in precisely this way. (Adorno's transcendental strategy is discussed in further detail in section 3 of the following chapter.)

German Idealism in the Negative Dialectic

2 The Hegelian Precedents

In this section I want to examine Hegel's contribution to the development of Adorno's position. The introduction to Hegel's *Phenomenology of Spirit* is particularly important in that it provides Adorno with a model of how consciousness is determined through the experience of objects. I want now to present Hegel—in the same manner as I have presented Kant—from the point of view of the issues which Adorno emphasizes in his subject-object theory. The issues of particular significance are: the idea that the subject-object relationship can be conceived as an ongoing interaction, not one of identity; that the nature of the interaction is rational in that the process is determined by the requirements of rational conceptualization; and that the subject has a particular and irreducibly positive role. I am suggesting that the operation of rationality in Hegel's theory of experience provides Adorno with an account of a subjective, spontaneous component in which thought operates in accordance with rationality. Indeed Adorno directly acknowledges Hegel's insight on this issue: Hegel's *Phenomenology* follows "the movement of the concept ... *actively* directing this movement, thus transforming the object" (*ME* 33/25, my italics). Without the element of spontaneity, epistemology is mere empiricism; based on it, however, it is complete idealism. Through his reconstruction of Hegel's philosophy Adorno acquires all the remaining pieces for his subject-object theory—his negative dialectic—that together with the Kantian elements give argumentative support to his solution to the problem of meeting the basic requirements of philosophy.

2.1 Hegel's Idea

The following reading of the *Phenomenology* extracts the introduction from the context in which Hegel wrote it. For Hegel the introduction to the *Phenomenology* aims to provide a kind of methodology that would allow thought to proceed in the systematic reconstruction of reality. It has no application, as far as Hegel is concerned, in the examination of particular experience, the sort of experience that concerns Adorno's negative dialectic. However, the introduction to the *Phenomenology* will be a rich source of ideas for Adorno when Hegel's insights are taken out of their original speculative context.

Hegel, as is well known, sets out to explain the process of absolute knowledge, that is, the process of *knowing absolutely*. To know absolutely, as contrasted with *knowing the absolute*, is to know without qualification. It is knowledge that cannot be characterized as provisional or partial. It is specific, too: knowing absolutely in Hegel's texts always pertains to knowledge of, for instances, the structure of being, the realization of freedom. To attain "absolute knowledge" we must necessarily go through a process of provisionality or partiality: we begin with knowledge that is hugely qualified, that is to say. This is a process in the sense too that absolute knowledge is an achievement gained after ongoing revisions of earlier efforts: successful knowledge is therefore never a spontaneous intuition. Eventually Hegel believes that knowledge can culminate in a system where all of the steps can be seen to be elements in a total body of knowledge. Of course Hegel intends by this metaphysical knowledge, knowledge that deals only with universals. Hegel's metaphysical impetus, needless to say, holds no appeal for Adorno. (Indeed it is for that reason that the Hegelian account of antinomy is less influential than Kant's, as I suggested in the previous section.) But the elements of the process by which knowledge is to be achieved and Hegel's views about the relation between subject and object that lie behind this process are crucially important to him.

It is in the introduction to the *Phenomenology* that Hegel attempts to explain the process in which we move away from partiality and towards conclusive knowledge. The term Hegel gives to this process is *experience*. In his own nomenclature he describes experience as the "*dialectical* movement which consciousness exercises on itself" (*PhS* 55). He argues that experience has a discernible rational structure. This means, in effect, that the process of moving from partial to conclusive knowledge is neither haphazard nor random. Each phase of experience is produced by a rational compulsion. Experience does not simply settle at any point which falls short of rationally acceptable knowledge. Rather, thought adjusts itself until it is satisfied that it has grasped the object it is attempting to understand. In essence, then, experience is the process that is driven by the rational requirement that we overcome incompleteness and, for reasons that we shall see below, incoherence. It is worth bearing in mind this quite singular sense of "experience." Insofar as it uniquely can explain the conceptual content and character of experience it will be of enormous significance to Adorno. It provides a model of the lateral relations of experience, the process of the subject's coming to understand its environment. It expresses too the notions of adjustment and transformation that Adorno—as we saw in his discussions in "The Actuality of Philosophy"—requires in a theory of experience.

As Hegel presents it, experience is a matter for consciousness. That is to say, no element of experience can be explained by realities which are allegedly independent of consciousness. The process through which the elements of experience are put together is judgment. Judgment typically involves placing elements of experience together under the categories of concept and object. Since it is Hegel's view that in experience concepts and objects are in a more or less satisfactory relationship at any given point, it follows that experience is a judicative process. In other words, concept and object will at any given point be united in a judgment that expresses either partial or conclusive knowledge. (Obviously enough, judgments stand or are revised according to their inherent rationality, that is, whether they are complete, incomplete, incoherent. So a judgment is not rational—contrasted with logical—if it is incomplete.)

There are further aspects of Hegel's theory of judgment. His theory attempts to account for what he regards as the *dynamic* and *historical* qualities of knowledge. Knowledge is *dynamic* in that it is achieved only after revisions that are compelled by the experience of an unsatisfactory judgment—that is, where concept and object do not agree. Knowledge is *historical* also in that the epistemic content of any judgment is the accumulated achievement of previous knowledge. And it is the historical qualities in the judgment that allow us to see knowledge as a result, as an accumulation. Judgment 2 is necessarily aware of the inadequacy of judgment 1, and so on. An alternative theory that sees judgments as atomically separated from other judgments could not explain the qualities of knowledge—that is, dynamism and historicality—identified by Hegel.

Hegel argues in the *Encyclopaedia of Philosophical Sciences* that to simply arrest our thinking at the complicated moment where dialectical thinking is evident—the moment in which the inadequacy of our judgment is experienced—is *mere* skepticism. Here we exploit "the mere negation that results from the dialectic" (*EL* §81) and take a skeptical position in that we see the problematization of an item of knowledge as the end of the process. In other words, we conclude from the complication of our knowledge—the complication which arises at the dialectical moment—that knowledge itself is unattainable. Instead, according to Hegel, we must understand what has brought about the complication or problematization (the "negation"), and that ought to give us a deeper understanding of the object. We reflect on what it is that has led to this complication. And when we understand the reason behind the complication—the problem in the way we have considered the issue that has now become complicated—we give ourselves the grounds of further thought in that we have arrived at a more sophisticated understanding of how the matter is to be understood if we are to avoid complication. The overriding motivation here is rationality itself. And we can see at work here the version of epistemological normativity that I earlier ascribed to Adorno, namely a normativity of correctness. Establishing the rationality of one's position in terms of its argumentative coherence, as opposed to attempting to justify a state of affairs or a desired state of affairs, is what pushes the dialectic to the ideal of rational transparency.

In the *Phenomenology* Hegel makes considerable efforts to distinguish his dynamic theory of judgment from skepticism. He does so because of a possible confusion that could be caused by a similar looking element in both positions, namely, negativity. Hegel claims that the basis of skepticism is the recognition of the moment in experience where concept fails to concord with object. Skepticism concludes from this, according to Hegel, that no object can thereby be known. In this sense skepticism leaves us with a purely negative knowledge by abstracting, as Hegel puts it, "from the fact that this nothingness is specifically the nothingness of that *from which it results*" (*PhS* 51). That is, it does not realize that negativity or nothingness is an element of the process of knowing, not its condition. By contrast

Hegel interprets negativity as a rational element of experience that compels us to seek a more satisfactory judgment. Importantly, this negativity is not merely the recognition of error: it is edifying too. It intimates something about the object that the concept could not specify. The rational implication of this negativity is a new truth and a refinement in our conceptualization of the object. We discover something about the object in that it is the object that ultimately refuses the identity with the concept. For that reason, Hegel calls the negativity of experience "a *determinate* nothingness, one which has a *content*" (*PhS* 51).[12] For Hegel, the only alternative to this movement is "unthinking inertia" (*PhS* 51). "Unthinking inertia" represents the nonoperation of rationality.[13] It is a refusal to examine one's version of objectivity, and it is, in effect, to ignore the contradictions that a particular criterion of objectivity—a consciousness—may allow.

An excellent example of this triple movement of thought is provided by Jon Elster. He notes that we can see belief formation "beginning with dogmatic belief, passing through doubt and arriving finally at a more reflective level."[14] This process can also be stated more formally, as Elster puts it: "Tentatively I suggest that the characteristic feature of this process is the presence of three successive stages—p, q and r—such that (i) they are pairwise incompatible with one another, (ii) the step from p directly to r is impossible and (iii) the step from q back to p is impossible."[15] In the *Phenomenology* Hegel expresses the result of these moments rather grandly. He tells us that through these moments consciousness transcends itself. Put another way, in revising its concept of an object, consciousness must revise its presuppositions about what the object is: it transcends or transforms itself. Consciousness does not simply settle at a fixed point: a "limited satisfaction." Rationality compels it forward: "[C]onsciousness suffers this violence at its own hands: it spoils its own limited satisfaction" (*PhS* 51). Unsatisfactory judgments are overcome until finally concept and object agree.

It is important to note that Adorno does not accept that dialectic has this ineluctable progressive characteristic. He agrees that dialectic represents a moment of complication in thought, one that may be informative. But we cannot conclude, he thinks, that each complication is necessarily productive. To be obliged, as Adorno sees it, to proceed forward—toward the absolute—is identity thinking: it is motivated by the belief that the nonidentity of subject and object—the point at which concept and object do not coincide—can eventually be overcome. However, what is important in Hegel's idea of dialectic, in Adorno's view, is that it names that critical moment of thought that deepens our experience of the object.

2.2 Experience and Conceptualism

At this point we have to specify more precisely the conceptualist implications of Hegel's position, as it is here that Adorno will differentiate his account of experience from Hegel's. It is important to be aware that judgment for Hegel cannot be understood as conceptuality adjusting to nonconceptuality, as empiricism might argue. Were it so then consciousness would be transformed in a relationship with something that is allegedly the other of consciousness—say, independent material reality. In that case the scope of rationality—"the space of reasons"—would be fatally circumscribed. Material objects would determine what concepts we must employ. But Hegel, by contrast, stipulates that "consciousness suffers this violence at its own hands," not at "the hands" of material reality. This point deserves some elaboration. The argument is implicitly aimed against the traditional materialist notion that consciousness is determined by something that is radically other than consciousness. If the materialist position is false then the alternative route, taken by Hegel, is to see experience as a fully ideal process in which none of its elements are ascribable to a nonconceptual reality. Hence objects, insofar as they are of interest to us, are conceptual.

But something seems to be forgotten by the rejection of materialism. Experience apparently shows thought confronted by a reality that is not identical with thoughts. It feels as though we are endeavoring in our epistemic efforts to reach something "out there," and "out there" looks like the opposite of whatever we tend to think of as the "in here" of thoughts. Since, in Hegel's idealism, all elements of experience are ideal, in the sense that the object is a conceptual totality that we attempt to understand in our conceptual activities, another way of explaining the experience of the distinctness of thought and reality must be found. Michael Oakeshott, in his masterful recasting of Hegel's idealism, provides a lucid answer to this problem: "The notion that thought requires raw material, a datum which is not itself judgment, and the consequent eagerness to discover its character, may be traced to the fact that in experience, so far as we can recollect, we find ourselves always manipulating some material independent of the actual process of manipulation. But it is false to infer from this that what is manipulated is not itself judgment."[16] So what is manipulated is not different in species from what manipulates. For that reason Hegel claims that unless concepts and objects are *for* consciousness they cannot apply to each other: "[The concept] would lie within ourselves, and that which was to be compared with it and about which a decision would be reached through this comparison would not have to recognize the validity of such a standard" (*PhS* 53). Concepts would be one thing, reality another. Experience is the constant adjustment of concept to other ideal material. And valid knowledge can be nothing other than a rationally compelling arrangement of these concepts. That is, valid knowledge is a coherent relationship of ideal material. So long as the relationship expressed by a judgment is coherent then there is no compulsion to revise that judgment.

It follows for Hegel from the rejection of a nonconceptual explanation of experience that experience must be explained purely within consciousness. In this regard he makes the further claim that consciousness has two elements. The idea that consciousness has two elements might seem extravagant. The idea is, however, straightforward enough. We have already seen that experience is a judgmental process. Since judgment is an activity of consciousness it follows that each element of the judgment must in some way be an element of consciousness. Hegel puts it in the following way: "Consciousness simultaneously *distinguishes* itself from something [the object], and at the same time relates *itself* to it [by concepts], or, as it is said, this something exists *for* consciousness" (*PhS* 52). Consciousness distinguishes itself from the reality of the object and it relates, at the same time, to this object through concepts. At this point Hegel multiplies his terminology: he sees concepts as *knowledge* and the object as the *True*.

The idea that consciousness determines objects may present an interesting difficulty. Hegel is claiming that objectivity is always *relative* to a consciousness in that consciousness provides the criterion of objectivity. But we have already seen the programmatic announcement that the task of the *Phenomenology* is to show "the untrue consciousness in its untruth." This appears to presuppose some form of *nonrelative* truth. However, Hegel is fully aware of this complexity. Indeed his philosophy provides a way of maintaining both this form of relativity and objectivity. It is the immanent method. In demonstrating "the untrue consciousness in its untruth," that is, revealing the limitations of a given consciousness, one needs to be able to point to inconsistencies within the judgments of that consciousness. That is, if the criterion of objectivity produces unsatisfactory knowledge then that criterion can be judged to be incompatible with the True. And this brings us back to the theory of judgment. If my concept consistently fails to agree with its object, and is an inadequate judgment, then the concept must be revised: "Consciousness must alter its knowledge to make it conform to the object" (*PhS* 54). Altering knowledge, as Hegel puts it, means adjusting the concepts by which we judge the object. Hegel sees concepts, actually, as the standard (*Maßstab*)—or "criterion" (*PhS* 55), as he also puts it—by which an object is judged.

So if, for instance, I take the lyric ballad as my standard of what constitutes a poem I will attempt to read the elements of a given poem as exemplifying the characteristics of a lyric ballad. Obviously enough this standard will come to be examined if there is a significant lack of agreement between the standard (the lyric ballad) and the object (the given poem). As Hegel puts it: "An examination consists in applying an accepted standard, and in determining whether something is right or wrong on the basis of the resulting agreement or disagreement of the thing examined" (*PhS* 52). An important idea here is that a standard is something "accepted." It is not given. It is not a piece of reality that is independent of consciousness. The phrase, that we have already seen, "would not have to recognize the validity of such a standard" is important here. What Hegel is getting at is that when we consider judgment in a *nonidealist* framework we lack the elements that enable us to understand why judgment should strike us as a matter of compulsion. A given, in a purely empiricist sense, has no conceptual qualities that can compel us to think anything and therefore provides us with no grounds for revising our standard.[17]

The standard of objectivity, then, is no tautology in which standard and objectivity are identical. What we take the object to be—the standard by which we judge the object—must in fact be coherent with our idea of the object. If, however, it is not, then we discover that what we took the object to be—how we articulated it for ourselves—is mistaken. We must then abandon our concept of that object and find one that is more adequate. If, for instance, a hypothesis cannot account for the specific activities of phenomena then that hypothesis plainly fails to cohere with the object. Of course, what would be more adequate is suggested by the way in which the hypothesis failed. We have already encountered that idea in Hegel's discussion of determinate negation. A determinate negation leads to a new articulation of the object, in effect to a new determination of the object. In this process the object is changed for us in that we now determine it, through different concepts, in a different way than before: "[I]n the alteration of the knowledge, the object alters for it too, for the knowledge that was present was essentially a knowledge of the object: as the concept changes, so too does the object, for it essentially belonged to this knowledge" (*PhS* 54).

In looking at Hegel's account of experience we have seen certain significant ideas. These are that thought operates in a conceptual reality, and all experience is a matter for consciousness. Experience is fully rational since it is the process of understanding, a process that, as we have seen, can be described as the activity of judgment. Furthermore, rationality allows dynamism in our judgments by pushing them to more satisfactory judgments. It is the moment of dialectic—or determinate negation—that demonstrates perhaps most clearly the capacities of thought to determine its environment in accordance with rationality. As we shall see, Adorno rereads these theses through a nonconceptualist framework. He takes from Hegel the theory of judgment and the logic of the dialectic, but denies that experience can be fully explicable through concepts.

2.3 Epistemology and Practice

It might seem that Hegel's use of language, in the phrase "[C]onsciousness suffers this violence [*leidet diese Gewalt*] at its own hands: it spoils its own limited satisfaction" (*PhS* 51) is simply an extravagant way of expressing the revisionistic component of the process of knowledge. However, something deeper is actually conveyed here, the significance of which becomes clear only in the later master–slave dialectic section of the *Phenomenology*. What emerges from that section is that the introduction has provided us with the formal structure of an account of the relation of any subject to any object, and that relation is ultimately one with a practical implication: the compulsion to achieve greater accuracy in our knowledge is not merely a matter of logic or formal reasoning: it is compelled by the ideal of reason that we do justice to the object. However, it is not that the object as such makes an "ethical call to us," as Levinas might put it, but rather the object has qualities that will not cohere with our presuppositions. And the lack of coherence demands a rational response. This entails, at least as Hegel works it out, the need to go beyond preconceptions of what an other (the object or another person) is. The dynamic that this compulsion generates is one in which self-subsistent positions (an allegedly final judgment, or a self "unencumbered" by sociality) are constantly forced to move beyond themselves. Crucially, in this dynamic, external reality comes to be seen as a key condition of inner states. The master–slave dialectic closely follows the structure of experience set out in the introduction to the *Phenomenology* in that it examines the processes and implications of overcoming the limited conception of "an other." But in the master–slave dialectic the suggestive normativity of the introduction—the suffering of violence—becomes thematic. The master–slave dialectic reveals to us that the normative processes of dialectical thinking have a practical dynamic, an idea that comes to be adopted by Adorno.[18]

The background to the master–slave dialectic is that of how the complex "self-conscious" individuals of modern civil society have emerged as entities with awareness both of their agency as free beings and as social entities constitutively tied to others through community. In a unique philosophical parable, the master–slave

German Idealism in the Negative Dialectic

dialectic examines a series of stages in which a simple consciousness develops into what Hegel sees as a complex self-consciousness by means of a growing sophistication in his or her awareness of how he or she needs another consciousness; that is, a growing sophistication in how he or she sees his or her completion by means of another. Part of what it means to be self-conscious, in Hegel's specific sense, entails that one is engaged with another self-consciousness who is aware of you as a self-consciousness. The mechanism of this mutuality is *recognition*: "Self-consciousness," he writes, "exists in itself and for itself when, and by the fact that, it so exists for another; that is, it exists only in being recognized" (*PhS* 111). The problem with the process of self-consciousness through recognition is this: if I am to receive the sort of recognition that affirms me I have to be able to respect that person who recognizes me, for otherwise their recognition is worthless. However, our ability to do so is historical, not natural. That is, outside the achievement of civic society individuals are not inclined to recognize other persons as persons in their own right. The master-slave dialectic section of the *Phenomenology* therefore examines the development of self-consciousness as a cumulative series of phases.

I want to look briefly at these phases to see how the metaethical principle of mutuality begins to emerge from the dynamic process of interaction. The phases—which begin with the most primitive—can be broken down into distinctive elements, or moments.

Phase 1.1 One consciousness sees another consciousness and takes it as a threat to its own independence: the "I" cannot allow its own absoluteness to be challenged or qualified by another "I."

Phase 1.2 In affirming one's own self—by making it independent of an other—the other thereby also becomes independent, since no relationship now exists between the two. The self is independent of an other and sees other selves merely as though they were objects. Hegel argues that this state of affairs in which there is no mutuality—simply independent selves who do not recognize each other as selves—does not provide the conditions for self-consciousness.

Phase 2 Because each consciousness can only recognize the other as an object—and not as a potential agent of its recognition—each comes to believe that it can affirm itself only through its own self-assertion, and that leads, it seems, to the need to destroy the other: each aims thereby to become the only self, unbounded by the very presence of an other. Needless to say, both consciousnesses—when they are at this phase—feel much the same about each other and a life and death struggle develops: "In so far as it is the action of the *other*, each seeks the death of the other. . . . Thus the relation of the two self-conscious individuals is such that they prove themselves and each other through a life-and-death struggle. They must engage in this struggle, for they must raise their certainty of being *for themselves* to truth, both in the case of the other and in their own case as well. And it is only through staking one's life that freedom is won . . ." (*PhS* 113–114). Hegel's rather strong point is that one is a fully constituted self-consciousness only if one has undergone (or even, it sometimes seems if one's society has historically undergone) *a struggle for freedom*. (But there are echoes too of the notion of progress in knowledge being a matter of a "suffering of violence.")

Phase 3 If one should die in this struggle the conditions of recognition are thereby denied. Far from achieving an affirmation of the self, the victor in the struggle deprives itself of that by which it affirms itself: "This trial by death, however, does away with the truth that was supposed to issue from it, and so, too, with the certainty of self generally . . . death is the *natural* negation of consciousness, negation without independence, which thus remains without the requisite significance of recognition" (*PhS* 114). Hegel characterizes this as "abstract negation" in the sense that it does not achieve a stage in which progress towards self-consciousness is possible. Indeed, what emerges is that regression to an earlier state of affairs is problematic for a consciousness that has already "transcended" its own earlier conception and that has now in some sense experienced "an other." Again the introduction to the *Phenomenology* has explained how knowledge involved a productive negation—a determinate negation—in which one's own presuppositions are tested, rather than the object negated.

Phase 4 However, the results of Phase 3 need not remain unproductive. The death of the other consciousness brings awareness of one crucial condition for self-consciousness: namely, other human life. What Hegel suggests here is that the violent struggle for self-affirmation can have an alternative outcome; namely, a consciousness affirms itself by enslaving another. In enslavement self-affirmation through domination is achieved. And from this arrangement two unequal consciousnesses—two unequal relations to the world—are generated: "... [O]ne is the independent consciousnesses whose nature is to be for itself; the other is the dependent consciousness whose essential nature is simply to live or be for another. The former is Master, the other is Slave" (*PhS* 115).

The subsequent phases of the master–slave dialectic deal with the effects of the differentiation of each consciousness's tasks (master tasks; lordship and slave tasks; labor). There is no phase in this section of the *Phenomenology* in which mutuality is achieved. The conclusion is developed in other ways in the book. We are left with two "unhappy consciousnesses"—the master who although master does not determine himself through labor; the slave who although self-determining through labor remains a slave. The conclusion must eventually be the achievement of mutual recognition that incorporates both the interdependence and freedom of self-consciousness through another self-consciousness. The master-slave dialectic, then, gives graphic practical content to the formal structure of knowledge. It demonstrates the unsustainability of a consciousness that philosophers imagine can be understood as constituted in isolation from the non-I. Just as the criterion of knowledge (the concept) is constantly adjusted though our engagement with objects, so too is a self that sees itself as complete in isolation from engagement with others. From the process of the development of self-consciousness an ethics emerges in which the dynamic of selfhood realizes the need for an acknowledgement of something outside itself.

In the *Phenomenology of Spirit*, then, epistemological normativity evolves a distinctly practical dimension. The structure of knowledge turns out to be also about the structure of relation to an other. Adorno is overtly committed at times to this integration. As we saw earlier, "The Actuality of Philosophy" discusses epistemological problems within the major philosophical positions of Adorno's time, and even the epistemological analysis employs the curiously normative idea that reason must seek to express "correct and just reality" (*richtige und gerechte Wirklichkeit*) (*AP* 325/24). This thought indicates that what Adorno is engaged in is no conventional epistemology that takes as its ultimate task the description of the conditions of valid cognition. Rather, Adorno maintains that epistemology is, or at least ought to be, the effort to do justice to reality; that is, to find the appropriate structures that will allow us to articulate what has been suppressed or neglected by traditional epistemological models. This motivation can be one of rationality of the kind we have just seen in Hegel.

Strikingly, Adorno sometimes employs the language of moral psychology in what might otherwise have seemed to be epistemological questions within a philosophy of experience. He speaks about a phenomenology of "guilt" that drives us toward the need for a mode of thought—one not offered by the contemporary philosophical models—in which our experience can be understood as the open engagement of a subject with an object. This mode of thought will be called "dialectics" in that it alone, according to Adorno (as we shall see in the following two chapters), can account for particularity—the nonidentical, that which is irreducible to universals and categories. Adorno writes: "Dialectics is the consistent sense of non-identity. It does not begin by taking a stand-point. My thought is driven to it by its own inevitable insufficiency, by my guilt of what I am thinking" (*ND* 17/5). The term guilt here plays on the potential ambiguity of the German word, *Schuld*, which refers both to guilt and to debt: it is as though thought has a debt to the nonidentical, as that which in some way determines its content. Further passages link this normative notion with the sheer activity of thought. In the *Metacritique*, for instance, Adorno argues that the "metacritique of epistemology requires reflection upon its structure as one of guilt and punishment, necessary error and futile correction" (*ME* 32/25). In other words, the metacritique of epistemology—the effort to reconstitute epistemology itself—will have to account for experience as ideally the compelling attempt to describe the object as it is through a constant process of correction ("punishment") in which preconceptions about what the object is are overthrown. For that reason the task of the philosopher effectively entails the normative requirement of, as Adorno puts it (in a line from *Negative Dialectics* which reminds us of the thought from "The Actuality of Philosophy"), doing "justice to reality" (*Realitätsgerechtigkeit*) (*ND* 51/41). The commitment to rationality is identical with the commitment to "doing justice." Indeed, in this very sense, Adorno's project might be seen as a project of *recognition*, one in which our potential for rationality brings us to the reality that is otherwise distorted in our false forms of consciousness.

The examination of Kantian and Hegelian philosophy has provided us with the background to a number of Adorno's key ideas. These ideas are (in no particular order) (a) that experience is a subject-object process, (b) the nonidentity of subject-object, (c) the independence and priority of the object, (d) the possible rationality of experience, (e) transcendental necessity, (f) epistemological normativity. All of these ideas will be developed by Adorno in a kind of debate with his predecessors. There is a constant process of appropriation, adjustment, and revision. In the remaining chapters I will examine how Adorno uses these concepts to form a synthetic philosophical position, his negative dialectic.

2

The Structure of Adorno's Epistemology: The Priority of the Object

"The Actuality of Philosophy" shows us clearly Adorno's dissatisfaction with the contemporary models of philosophy available to him. In essence the failure of these philosophies, as Adorno sees it, is their commitment to various forms of subjectivism that exclude the possibility of a model of experience in which subject–object reciprocity can be accommodated. However, subjectivism contains a further difficulty: it cannot explain the particularity of objects. Subjectivism—in Adorno's broad definition—assumes the priority of concepts or categories that are supplied by the subject for any given experience. That is, it stipulates meanings in advance, and since, according to Adorno, concepts—the meanings—are essentially universals they cannot encapsulate particularity when employed as the sole meaning-bearing element of our experience. Given that *the object* is a particular—it is essentially individuable—a subjectivist philosophy (which gives priority to concepts, as the allegedly exclusive epistemic part of experience) is simply structurally unable to withstand the relevance of particularity.

Adorno sees the retrieval of particularity as involving, in effect, no less than a reversal of the priority of subject to object that has characterized the subjectivist tendency of modern philosophy. This means constructing a philosophy built around, what Adorno polemically calls "the priority of the object." The thesis of the priority of the object holds that objects are irreducible to concepts, that they cannot be made *identical* with concepts. So what is required, to put it within these terms, is an account of the subject-object relation—of experience, in effect—that can establish the *nonidentity* of concept and object. For Adorno, this entails that experience has a nonidentical moment in which the irreducible particularity of the object (and not just our concept of it) is a significant or meaningful element of the experience.

Adorno does not present his thoughts on particularity and nonidentity as a systematic position. However, his various claims might all be considered as contributions to a theory of mediation. Close analysis of what Adorno has to say on the matter reveals that mediation is no vague cover term for relations between subject and object (although it might seem that way at times thanks to Adorno's allusive way of presenting it). Rather, mediation can be specified as the structure of meaningful experience. Now given that Adorno thinks of experience in contemporary life as "withered," he means by mediation the structure of possible experience, that is, the structure of nonreified experience. Current experience cannot be characterized as mediation in this sense.

Adorno's thoughts on the basic elements of meaningful experience very discernibly share a distinctive characteristic of the Kantian and Hegelian views of experience (a characteristic that has been examined in the previous chapter): namely, that experience takes place only where judgment occurs. Experience is not mere awareness: it is understanding. To appreciate fully what Adorno's account of the possibility of experience is attempting to establish, then, it is crucial that we follow his account of judgment. Indeed we can already infer from "The Actuality of Philosophy" that Adorno was effectively pointing to the deficiency of contemporary philosophy's understanding of judgments. For instance, irrationalism abandons concepts and employs only the object component of judgment in its leap into experience, whereas Neo-Kantianism and logical positivism conversely are accused of emphasizing conceptual frameworks at the expense of particularity or objects, and hence of misconstruing the meaning-bearing relation of concept and object in judgment. But what make for Adorno's distinctive account of judgment are his views on what meaning that structure can produce. A judgment—as the structure of nonreified experience—must be able to express our experience of particularity, and the nonidentity of our concepts with the object. It must encapsulate the reciprocatory character of unreduced experience.

However, Adorno's task is not simply an epistemological one. His aim is not that of providing an account of how individuals—through the criteria of a reified consciousness—actually understand experience. After all, if the conditions of modernity prevail as Adorno and Lukács believe, then philosophy must offer a model of *how experience might be*, a model in which experience is not distorted by reification. To experience fully—that is, to recognize one's experience as a process of subject-object reciprocity—would involve the subject relating to a particular without reducing it, or reifying it, by means of a preconceived concept of what the particular must be. Hence to undermine the reifying consciousness that reduces experience is actually to release subjects to the experience of particularity.

In this chapter I will begin with a general account of the role that Adorno believes objects play in experience. Next I will discuss Adorno's justifications for the view that objects rather than subjects have priority in experience. After that I want to point out a significant part of Adorno's position which has not generally been noticed; namely, that his view of the priority of the object is defended by means of transcendental argument. The two following sections deal with two different, but easily confusable, lines of thought on the properties of the object: these are Adorno's discussions of objects as conceptual wholes—as realities of the human realm (lateral relations)—and as physical entities—irreducible particulars (vertical relations). The final section will bring together the preceding sections under a consideration of Adorno's account of judgment. Then we will be able to see how it is that a particular theory of judgment can supply the justification for the view that experience might be full, unreduced, and in the medium of conceptual reflection. Such a theory unifies Adorno's thoughts on the conceptuality and nonconceptuality of our experience of objects. The intellectual background discussed in the previous chapter will be seen to crystallize in Adorno's developed position.

Chapter 2

1 Objects and the Structure of Experience

It is significant that Adorno argues for a subject-object model, even though others in his century have attributed many of the ills of philosophy precisely to subject–object thinking. (Indeed the four main positions considered in "The Actuality of Philosophy" would certainly all reject the subject–object mediation model of experience.) But for Adorno the subject–object structure, appropriately modified, offers the only way out of the subjectivist tendencies in philosophy. As he notes: "The duality of subject and object must be *critically maintained* against the *thought's* inherent claim to be total" (*ND* 177/175, my italics). Obviously enough, however, he sees this idea of mediation as an *evolution* within subject–object epistemology in that in its nonreductive account of the subject–object relation it achieves greater comprehensiveness than earlier models. As we shall see, this comprehensiveness lies in its ability to express the claims that the subject is not merely passive in relation to the object and the object is not exhausted by the categories of the subject.

"Mediation" is the term Adorno uses to capture the meaning-producing qualities of the reciprocatory and nonidentical dimensions of the subject–object relationship. As Adorno puts it, in mediation subject and object "constitute [*konstituieren*] one another as much as— by virtue of such constitution—they depart from one another" (*ND* 176/174); subject and object "reciprocally permeate each other" (*ND* 142/139). Mediation is not a matter of connecting two separate independently meaningful moments—subject and object—but is constitutive of subject and object: subject and object each "necessarily requires the other in order to be thought at all" (*PT* 220). An implication of this is that mediation, as a meaning-explaining theory, must be able to account for particularity and for Adorno that means a philosophy capable of expressing nonidentity, or the particularity of the object that is not subjected to universalizing concepts or categorization. The thesis of mediation, then, is quite central to Adorno's account of experience in that it sets out to accommodate the following: (1) that meaningful experience is the product of subject-object reciprocity; (2) that the object is more than the conceptual determinations of a particular subject (nonidentity); (3) that the object is in

The Priority of the Object

part determined by a subject in that it is apprehended through consciousness. This latter idea will be developed in the following chapter.

Adorno appears at times to argue rather obscurely for his ideas of nonidentity, the particularity and priority of the object, adopting, as Anke Thyen points out, a myriad of expressions for the very idea of nonidentity: "[T]he nonconceptual, the conceptless, the heterogeneous, nonconceptuality as the content of concepts, the irreducible, the qualitative, the mediated, the other, the different, the alien, the open, the uncovered, the undistorted, what has come to be, the unidentical."[1] I want to suggest that this obscurity is merely apparent, however, disappearing when we recognize that Adorno's account of objects comprises two different claims; namely, first, the idea that objects are meaningful in the sense that they are significant within language because they can be conceptualized (section 4 below), yet, second, objects are individuals because they are nonconceptual (section 5 below). These claims correspond respectively with Adorno's understanding of Hegelian and Kantian theories of judgment (lateral and vertical relations within judgment) and must be distinguished.

The question for this section however, is, what does Adorno mean by objects? This question is, in Adorno's view, less straightforward than it might seem. For him the critique of reification actually raises awareness that epistemology itself may be committed to reifying assumptions. For that reason there are, Adorno points out, two difficulties in describing either subject or object in isolation from each other. The first is that if the basic structure of mediation is accurate then an epistemology that begins with either the subject or the object alone will produce a distorted picture: any such one-dimensional epistemology would fail to appreciate the positive epistemological contribution of *both* poles. Adorno writes: "The reified nature [*Dinghaftigkeit*] of the method, its inherent tendency to nail down the facts of the case, is transferred to its objects ... as if they were things-in-themselves and not hypostatized entities" (*SeF* 200–201/72). Hence to describe either subject or object in isolation risks establishing one or the other of them as the foundational principle of experience.

Chapter 2

The second problem is that the terms "subject" and "object" describe dynamic aspects of experience:

[T]he concepts of subject and object—or rather, the things they intend—have priority before all definition. Defining [*Definieren*] means that something objective, no matter what it may be in itself, is subjectively captured by means of a fixed concept. Hence the resistance offered to defining by subject and object. To determine their meanings takes reflection on the very thing which definition cuts off for the sake of conceptual flexibility. (*SO* 741–742/139)

[N]o matter how hard we try for linguistic expression of such a history congealed in things, the words we use will remain concepts. Their precision substitutes for the thing itself, quite without bringing its selfhood to mind; there is a gap between words and the things they conjure. Hence the residue of arbitrariness and relativity in the choice of words as well as in the presentation as a whole. (*ND* 62/52–53)

Objects, then, are linguistic or conceptual and also nonconceptual: we cannot capture objects exclusively through their conceptual properties, and yet their nonconceptual properties—what is "captured" or "conjured"—cannot be positively articulated through concepts. The object then is articulated through concepts, but not reducible to them.

When Adorno suggests that the object is irreducible to concepts or categories he may seem to be committed to a rather conventional view, a view sometimes called naive realism. However, Adorno is anxious to distinguish himself from that view. Naive realism holds that the object is independent of subjectivity and is apprehended as it is in-itself. It presents the order of knowing as a fully given object being passively received by a subject. Hence it might seem to hold something like Adorno's own priority of the object thesis. But Adorno rejects the very idea that subject and object can be entirely independent of each other, or, as he puts it, the "naive ... view that a knowing subject, whatever its kind, was confronting a known object, whatever its kind" (*SO* 742/139). The independence here excludes the active role of consciousness. It simply fails to consider that the object is given to a subject, a subject which, for Adorno, is characterized as engaged in processes of rational reflection in its attempts to achieve coherent knowledge of the object. As Adorno puts his differences with the naive view: the priority of the object "is the corrective of the subjective reduction, not the denial of a subjective share" (*SO* 747/143).

Adorno's contrasting claim is that the subject in full experience is essentially critical (a claim that will receive extensive analysis in the following chapter). A theory that characterizes the subject as essentially passive, however, will fail to recognize the contribution the subject actually does make—that it must make if experience is to be possible—and this contribution will be confused for a purely neutral and objective receptivity. The end result here is that the object is "unreflectively" manipulated by a subject that is unaware of its activity. The lack of reflection on the contribution of the subject actually produces a distortion of its relation to the object: "The mind will then usurp the place of something absolutely independent—which it is not; its claim of independence heralds the claim of dominance. Once radically parted from the object, the subject reduces it to its own measure; the subject swallows the object . . ." (*SO* 742/139–140). The significant argument being put forward by Adorno here is that passivity in experience is a fallacious thesis which unintentionally conceals the subject's active engagement in experience. (In the previous chapter I described this as a form of identity—de facto identity.)[2]

From the point of view of the "critical theory" question naive realism presents quite a serious issue. After all, naive realism entails the assumption that there is necessarily in experience a noncritical subject whose role is that of passively receiving objects. Critical theory, however, requires a theory of experience that can support the idea that the subject is capable of engaging its environment in a process of reciprocal transformation. Through that theory, grounds are given to the idea that the reification of the individual in society and the static relations that have developed between the individual and society are not necessary states of affairs. Naive realism, by contrast, gives epistemological validation to the reified world.

2 The Priority of the Object

Adorno, though maintaining, as we have seen, that subject and object cannot be adequately expressed in isolation from each other, holds also that the object has a certain kind of priority (*Vorrang*).

This priority cannot be analogous to the role objects play in naive realism: objects are not simply some self-constituted authority for the content of experience. Rather, the priority of the object must be established within the mediated structure—the structure of reciprocity—which the naive view simply does not recognize. For that reason Adorno argues for this priority without, as he sees it, hypostatizing the object. To hypostatize the object would obviously be incompatible with the idea of mediated objects and would also plainly exclude the possibility of a critical subject.

The notion of a priority of the object arises as a polemical rejection of subject philosophy—*the priority of the subject*. It holds that experience cannot be generated through subjectivity alone in that objects are the irreducible data of conscious acts and of knowledge. In that sense the object is "prior" to the subject as that part of experience which can be pointed to as "given," that is, as there for consciousness, as something to be responded to: "[T]he given [*Gegebene*], the irremovable skandalon of idealism, will demonstrate time and again the failure of the hypostasis [of the subject]" (*SO* 746/142); "Subjectivity changes its quality in a context which it is unable to evolve on its own. Due to the inequality inherent in the concept of mediation, the subject enters into the object altogether differently from the way the object enters into the subject. An object can be *conceived* [*gedacht*] *only by a subject* but always remains *something other than the subject* . . ." (*ND* 184/183, my italics). Its reality as what we might call "something to be known" constitutes its independence and, for Adorno, its priority in the epistemic process: "The object, too, is mediated; but according to its own concept, it is not so thoroughly dependent on the subject as the subject is on objectivity" (*SO* 747/143). Adorno in this regard sees the subject as the "how" and the object as the "what" of the mediational process (*SO* 746/142).[3] It is as the "what" that the object has, according to Adorno, its priority.

It is in this context that Adorno's rejection of subject philosophy has to be understood. His argument is not opposed to the view that the subject has determinative capacities (and we shall see the positive role of subjectivity in the following chapter), but is aimed, rather, at theories that understand experience to be entirely explicable by reference to the capacities of the subject. To put this another way: certain

The Priority of the Object

positions confuse the subjective quality of experience—that experience is impossible without consciousness—with the idea that experience is produced by consciousness. These investigations remain, ultimately, locked into subjectivity and thereby fail to explain the reality of the external sources of experience. As Adorno puts it: "Traditional philosophy believes that it knows the unlike by likening it to itself, while in doing so it really knows itself only" (*ND* 153/150). As a consequence, the object in traditional philosophy, according to Adorno, is never known, since it is reduced to the categories of the subject. But without the concept of the independence of the object the subject's thinking becomes mere "tautology" (*ND* 185/184), a matter of the subject observing the products of its own activities. This tautological model arises when the philosophical scrutiny of experience turns only to the structures of thought, rather than to the external sources of experience. We might well see in Adorno here a philosophical vice—one that arguably extends back to Aristotle[4]—of characterizing the history of philosophy in a slightly caricatured manner: after all, is traditional philosophy always synonymous with subject philosophy, or even philosophy that is implicitly subjectivist? Hardly. Adorno's unjustifiable use of such a broad brush stroke, however, should not distract us from (what we shall see as) the significance of his criticisms of those philosophies which can be validly characterized as subjectivist.

Adorno recognizes the need for rational substantiation of the principle of the object's priority, given that this principle is intended to be taken as an important extension to—if not completion of—our understanding of subject-object epistemology. So what arguments does he provide? One of them is the ability of the object to surprise our expectations and to be unpredictable. Were all experience directly attributable to the determinative capacities or interests or concepts of a subject then that would suggest that nothing outside these activities could contribute to what we experience. But that directly denies the common experiences of surprise. Nowhere is this more dramatic than in science where theories are overthrown by evidence that could not be reduced to the theory (Kant's alleged subjectivism is criticized by means of that observation): "One argument for the priority of the object is indeed incompatible with Kant's doctrine of constitution: that in modern natural science, the ratio peers over the very wall it has built, that it grabs a snippet of what differs with its well-honed categories. Such broadening of the ratio shatters subjectivism" (*SO* 748/144). Interestingly, though, this argument is not the strongest one taken by Adorno. His most forceful strategy is a form of transcendental argument.

3 Adorno's Transcendental Strategy

I have referred several times to Adorno's obvious intention to provide compelling arguments in support of his view that experience has a mediated subject–object structure. When looking at Kant's account of the Antinomies of Reason in the previous chapter I noted that for Adorno a theory that is at odds with the structure of full unreduced experience can never make sense, simply because through its very stated commitment to a different version of experience it will have to suppress one of the key elements identified by Adorno as necessary elements of a concept of experience. However, if the position offered is to be recognizable to us as one about experience it must implicitly relate back or refer to the elements Adorno regards as constitutive of the only rational account of experience. That is to say, the philosopher who discusses experience must be using the term in a sense that is familiar to us. However, by offering an account of experience that does not allow for the key elements of the concept of experience discussed by Adorno, the philosopher in question is committed to a distorted version of experience, employing the term "experience," in effect, against its own meaning. Adorno argues that the distortion of the idea of experience can produce only antinomy: internal incoherence discernible by conflicting commitments. The task of philosophical analysis is to reveal the nature and implications of the distortion.

Although Adorno never refers to the idea of transcendental argument or transcendental critique as a component of his philosophy, it becomes clear, with a certain amount of clarifying of the lines of his strategy, that he is committed to a critique of philosophy that uses such an approach. I argued earlier that Adorno's form of philosophical critique draws together the two components of antinomy

The Priority of the Object

and transcendental argument. (In chapter 1, section 1.2, the Kantian background of this idea was discussed.) I want to continue now with that idea and show that arguments for the mediated priority of the object—equivalent to his arguments against those who posit the priority of the subject—are transcendental in structure. Adorno concentrates on *the priority of the object* as a necessary feature of experience, as a feature that must be assumed in any intelligible discussion of experience. That is, he wants to show that experience, in which there is the reciprocity of subject and object, can be explained only when the priority of the object is a feature of the account.

As with transcendental arguments used by other philosophers, Adorno's sets out to show structural features that necessarily follow from moderate, intuitively plausible principles.[5] For Adorno there are certain conditions necessary for experience, the denial or exclusion of which can produce nothing but philosophical incoherence.[6] Adorno specifically aims his arguments at positions that both commit themselves to the idea of independent objects, yet rely on other theses incompatible with the notion of independent objects. To put this in Adorno's terminology, these positions do not understand the full significance of the "priority of the object." A position may grant that there are independent objects. However, given that these objects may be "reified," under other principles or theories operational within that position, they actually do not genuinely fulfill the criterion of independence. And, by operating with an inadequate version of independence, they cannot escape from a form of subjectivism that effectively runs counter to their objectivist pretensions.

Adorno argues that the irrationalism of contemporary society, which penetrates (as Lukács put it) into philosophy, has failed to carry through on the implications of what experience can entail. Reified philosophy—reified intellectual life, for that matter—deprives us of the capacity to articulate the complex dynamics of experience. Developing a line of thought from Hegel's dialectic Adorno suggests that the contemporary understanding of experience is in an arrested condition, a condition in which it cannot realize the implications of the idea of experience. This arrested condition is a state of irrationality in that it consists of incompatible tendencies: in essence, we cannot argue that the object must have independence in experience yet also proffer methodologies that ultimately rest on some form of subjectivism or reification.

Adorno's strategy is to make us consider what we could be committed to in the claim that there is *experience,* understood as the collective name we give to our epistemic activities and our physical and temporal engagement with objects. What Adorno aims to show are two correlative claims: (i) that *experience* cannot be realized without external realities (objects that are irreducible to the subject's agency, objects that are nonidentical), and (ii) that external realities have a determinative role in the context of *experience.* Conceived from a particular point of view, the first claim entails strictly no more than that there is matter. It does not force us to go any further than to accept the tentative Kantian conclusions of the existence of an unknowable thing-in-itself.[7] Thus it might offer some kind of objection to idealism, but only to idealism of an antimaterialist variety, something like an unrestricted Berkelianism. It must be shown, however, that external realities are not simply indeterminate matter, and that they can be coherently understood as determining the *actual content* of *experience*—otherwise, a subjectivist account might seem viable. The possibility of such determination will allow the conclusion that there is not just matter as a limiting idea, but that there are objects "in the weighty sense," to borrow Strawson's phrase. I take this conclusion to be equivalent to showing that objects have meaning-bearing properties. The ultimate aim of the argument is to show the essential role of mediation in experience.

Adorno's argument may be formalized as follows:

(i) *It is agreed that there is experience.*

(ii) *There must be something to which the subject relates.* If this something were the subject itself, its own concepts, it would not be explained how it is that experience has an apparent externally directed relation, unless an extravagant intrasubjective explanation of this structure were to be proposed: "If this moment were extinguished altogether," Adorno writes, "it would be flatly incomprehensible that a subject can know an object; the unleashed rationality would be irrational" (*ND* 55/45).

(iii) *The notion of an external relation entails that experience is the relation of the subject to something that is not purely subjective.* Thus experience is a relation of subjects to nonconceptual objects. (To understood objects as being purely conceptual would be to reduce the nonconceptual dimension of their otherness.)

(iv) *The commitment to the notion of experience therefore entails a belief that there are objects to which the subject must necessarily relate in order to experience: these objects are not reducible to concepts.* This conclusion is what Adorno means by the mediated priority of the object.

The claims to explain experience by those philosophies that do not understand their implicit commitment to a reduced form of object—positions with assumptions of nonconceptual immediacy between subject and object, or those with the thesis that objects conform to our categories—are compromised in that they are deprived of the relational dimension essential to the very idea of experience. It may seem that this set of claims is uncontroversial, but the background in which they are made is that of alleged reified consciousness that ultimately cannot conceive of objects that are irreducible to concepts.

The strategy Adorno adopts should demonstrate two things: (i) experience entails the relation of subjects to irreducible objects; and (ii) experience involves the influence of objects. Requirement (ii) can in fact be seen as an entailment of (i). To recognize the nonconceptual dimension of objects as we experience them is to recognize their influence on our epistemic activities. The relational quality of experience is the attempt of conceptuality to map out the nonconceptual, an attempt that involves the assumption that our conceptuality is limited by the experience of the nonconceptual. The subject is related to something that is not purely subjective, and this becomes evident from the contribution made by objects to the regularity of our experience: "[I]n the extreme into which subjectivity contracts, from the point of view of that extreme's synthetic unity, what is combined is always only what goes together anyway. Otherwise, synthesis would be nothing but arbitrary classification" (*SO* 755/149). That is, our knowledge-producing activities are inseparable from the determinations of things—"the determinations that make the object concrete" (*ND* 188/187). And for that reason our knowledge is an engagement of an object by a subject.

Adorno's actual employment of this style of critique is largely negative in that he tries to reveal the incoherence of systems that step outside this account of experience, systems that in their arrested condition fail to consider the contribution of the object. (This will be shown more concretely in the chapters that deal with Adorno's critiques of Kant, Husserl, and Heidegger.) Adorno claims that the notion of a nonsubjective element is implicit in all epistemic activity. Even logic requires, however minimally, material content. That is, it requires a nonsubjective referent:

"Something"—as a cogitatively indispensable substrate of any concept, including the concept of Being—is the utmost abstraction of the subject-matter that is not identical with thinking, an abstraction not to be abolished by any further thought process. Without "something" there is no thinkable formal logic, and there is no way to cleanse this logic of its metalogical rudiment. The supposition of an absolute form, of "something at large" that might enable our thinking to shake off that subject-matter, is illusionary. Constitutive for the form of "subject-matter at large" is the substantive experience of subject-matter. (*ND* 139/135)

This is important as it tackles the claim that logic is purely analytic and self-referential. It might be objected that logical knowledge is nothing like *experience* in Adorno's sense and that his objection therefore misses the target. Adorno's point, however, is that since logic is the most formal expression of experience, and the means by which its coherence is measured, it must ultimately refer to the fundamental elements of experience. (This is, no doubt, a rather quaint view of the business of logic.)

The object's priority means, then, that the object is independent of the subject in the sense that it has properties that are independent of the individual subject who is attempting to understand the object: it is an irreducible particular. Subjectivity by itself cannot account for the different possibilities of experience. To deny the priority of the object—that is, to deny the mediated subject–object structure of experience—is to deprive oneself of the condition that makes any knowledge claim possible. The very notion of experience requires it.

The Priority of the Object

However, the reification of experience suppresses this idea. By means of this transcendental strategy Adorno attempts to demonstrate the irrationality of the reified version of experience.

4 The Conceptuality of the Object

In this and the following section I want to consider the varying ways in which Adorno claims the object enters experience or, more specifically, the role it plays in nonreified experience. Earlier I noted that Adorno discusses two aspects of the experience of objects: conceptual and physical, or nonconceptual aspects. The latter aspect names that part of experience that is irreducible to the activities of the subject. In this section, however, I want to consider Adorno's thoughts on the conceptual aspect of experience—that is, how objects come to be experienced as conceptual.

Adorno claims that the object gains conceptual qualities through a process of *historical sedimentation*: "[A]n immanent generality of something is objective as sedimented history. This history is in the individual thing and outside it; it is something encompassing in which the individual has its place.... The history locked in the object can only be delivered by a knowledge mindful of the historic positional value of the object in its relation to other objects..." (*ND* 165/163). The object, then, must be mediated by subjectivity at various points, mediations which eventually lead to its historically sedimented character: an accumulation of uses and meanings. The picture of objects that emerges from this idea of "sedimented history" is that of objects as a complex of concepts. These concepts are acquired and accumulated in the history of the object's position in what Adorno terms the social totality; a neo-Marxist version of the phenomenological life-world.

Adorno argues that the social totality has a determinative influence on objects. Objects, he holds, do not have inherent conceptuality. However, their conceptuality confronts the individual as being independent of him or her. The invention of an object or of an idea clearly requires the activity of a subject. Indeed it is in this respect that Adorno can be understood as a materialist in that he is committed to the view that the articulable constituents of experience—concepts—arise through human activities: "[E]pistemological analysis of the immediate cannot explain away the fact that the immediate is also mediated" (*ME* 134/129). (The social totality is, in a way, the theater in which these activities take place.) However, these meanings are sustained independently of any given subject—even the inventor of the meaning—in the social totality. To take an example of a purely conceptual object discussed by Adorno (*ND* 153–154/150–151), the concept of freedom is a human invention and it has various connotations. Clearly these connotations have arisen from the efforts of people—not least of philosophers—to articulate a theory of freedom: yet the notion of freedom, which comprises the complex of its various connotations, cannot be reduced to the intention of any individual. Ideas of freedom have arisen through the activities of subjects and they are sustained in the social totality as experientially independent of subjects. In this way the concept of freedom comes to have an objectivity that resists arbitrary subjective determinations. (I quite simply cannot say that freedom is serfdom or capriciousness.)[8] By virtue of the significance of the object in the social totality its meanings necessarily transcend the individual subject. As the individual subject confronts the object, the latter contains an irreducible independence that, in the orders of experience and explanation, grants it, so Adorno's argument concludes, the status of priority.[9]

We articulate objects, obviously enough, through concepts. Indeed in this respect Adorno endorses the central idea of idealism: he notes "[idealism] was the first to make clear that the reality in which men live is not unvarying and independent of them. Its shape is human and even absolutely extra-human nature is mediated through consciousness" (*ME* 35/28). And our apprehension of the object, as something significant, is also possible because of our conceptual engagement with it. As Adorno puts it: "Because entity [*Seiende*] is not immediate, because it is only through the concept, we should begin with the concept, not with the mere given [*bloßen Gegebenheit*]" (*ND* 156/153).[10] Thus our efforts at understanding take the form of our concepts attempting to determine objects that have a significance within the social totality. This can be seen as a kind of Hegelianism in which experience involves a lateral relation of concepts to other, as it were, conceptual material.

5 Nonidentity, Nonconceptuality, and the Material Moment

However, Adorno does not ultimately offer an idealist or conceptualist epistemology, because, as noted earlier, he sees the problem for epistemology as that of how we can account for the particularity of physical objects in our experience. The model of nonidentity as the moment of negativity within conceptuality (the Hegelian model) cannot capture this because Adorno sees this moment of experience as nonconceptual. This is what I referred to as the vertical element of experience. On this specific issue Adorno turns from the quasi-Hegelian idea of mediation (lateral relations) to Kant's notion of a relation between concepts and nonconceptuality. Kant, in fact, provides Adorno with the model of mediation specific to the vertical component of the subject-object relationship. Adorno adverts to the important distinction in Kant—a distinction that is central to this section—between the *thing-in-itself*, as that aspect of the object which is "non-identical, free from the subjective spell," and the *object*, as that which "has been posited by the subject" (*das vom Subjekt "Gesetzte"*) (*SO* 752–753/147). Adorno refers approvingly to these ideas:

> By the retreat to formalism, for which Hegel and then the phenomenologists reproached Kant, he did honor to the non-identical. He did not deign to involve it in the identity of the subject without residue. (*ME* 38/30)
>
> Kant still refused to be talked out of the moment of objective priority [*Vorrang*]. He used an objective intention to direct the objective analysis of the cognitive faculty in his *Critique of Pure Reason*, and he stubbornly defended the transcendent thing-in-itself. To him it was evident that being in itself did not run directly counter to the concept of an object, that *the subjective mediation of that concept is to be laid less to the object's idea than to the subject's insufficiency*. The object cannot get beyond itself for Kant either, but he does not sacrifice the idea of otherness. (*ND* 185/184, my italics)

According to Adorno there are in Kant two distinct senses of what an object is. Both senses are epistemological in that they do not designate two different ways in which the object exists, but rather two ways in which the object can be thought of as relating to the subject; that is, as representation and as thing-in-itself. The representation of an object can be understood as a relation of *immediacy* to the subject. It is the alleged point at which the subject determines the object through concepts. However, a representation for Kant—no matter how comprehensive the resources of subjectivity allegedly are—is always a *representing of something*, and Adorno thinks that this something represented is, as Kant himself called it, noumenal. This something, in itself, is only partially captured in the representation. (Ralph Walker points out that the representation of an object is not entirely a matter for spontaneity, even in Kant, since were there no "topological isomorphism" between representations and the thing-in-itself there could be no regularity in the things that we experience.[11]) That entails that the representation is also an *indirect* relation to an object. For that reason Adorno writes: "The non-identical is not to be attained immediately as something positive ..." (*ND* 161/158). Kant himself had approached the problem in this way: "[T]hough we cannot know these objects as things-in-themselves, we must yet be in a position at least to think them as things-in-themselves, otherwise we should be landed in the absurd conclusion that there can be appearance without anything that appears" (*CPR* Bxxvi). This claim relies on a debatable connotation of the word "appearance" in that it avails of a distinction between appearance and reality, a distinction that in this case is semantically derived. However, another way in which Kant sets this up is through the argument that something underlies the data we receive through sensibility and, as such, it is logically the opposite in qualities to what we can know: it is nonrepresentational and, a fortiori, nonconceptual. It is therefore beyond the reach of concepts: "The true correlate of sensibility, the thing-in-itself, is not known, and cannot be known, through these representations; and in experience no question is ever asked in regard to it" (*CPR* A30/B45).

There are, however, limits to how far Adorno can take the Kantian idea of the thing-in-itself as a model for the vertical relation in experience. The problem is that the thing-in-itself, being a noumenal object, falls outside the compass of mediation and is actually therefore not accessible to experience. Adorno is not unaware of this and, rather inconsistently, also criticizes the very notion of the thing-in-itself. At one point he accuses Kant of "degrading ... the thing [in-itself] to a chaotic abstraction" (*ND* 142/139) and, similarly, of attributing dynamics to the categories but not to things as they are in-themselves (*ND* 98/91). In opposition to a thing-in-itself lacking all characteristics, Adorno wants to establish that the object determines, in some way, the kind of predicates we ascribe to it: "Essence can no longer be hypostatized as the pure, spiritual being-in-itself. Rather, essence passes into that which lies beneath the façade of immediacy, of the supposed facts, which *makes the facts what they are*" (*ND* 169/167, my italics). Furthermore, Adorno stipulates, at one point, that if we are going to establish the priority of the object then the object cannot be understood as the thing-in-itself: "Priority of the object can be discussed legitimately only when that priority—over the subject in the broadest sense of the term—is somehow determinable [*bestimmbar*], when it is more than the Kantian thing-in-itself as the unknown cause of the phenomenon" (*SO* 478/143). So despite Adorno's occasional endorsement of the thing-in-itself as a model for the vertical component of experience his position simply cannot go with it. The problem with the theory of the thing-in-itself is that in the Kantian exposition it is a purely philosophical notion, not a feature of experience, whereas Adorno wants to establish that there is a nonidentical/nonconceptual quality in experience.

Looking at Adorno's own remarks on the vertical relations we can see his requirement that what we name as the nonidentical element of experience must actually be a referent within experience; that is, more than the Kantian idea that "in experience no question is ever asked in regard to it":

In truth, all concepts, even the philosophical ones, *refer to non-conceptualities*. . . . (*ND* 23/11, my italics)

That a concept is a concept even when dealing with things in being does not change the fact that on its part it is *entwined with a non-conceptual whole*. Its only insulation from the whole is its reification—that which establishes it as a concept. (*ND* 24/12, my italics)

The concept is an element in dialectical logic, like any other. What survives in it is the fact that *non-conceptuality has mediated it by way of its meaning*, which in turn establishes its conceptuality. To refer to non-conceptualities . . . is characteristic of the concept, and so is the contrary: that as the abstract unit of the noumena subsumed thereunder it will depart from the noumenal. To change this direction of conceptuality, to give it a turn toward non-identity, is the hinge of negative dialectics. Insight into the non-conceptual in the concept would end the compulsive identification which the concept brings unless halted by such reflection. (*ND* 24/12, my italics)

Adorno may share Kant's motivation, that of marking the limits of agency, but he has the further ambition of validating the experience of nonidentity—what it is about the object that undermines its identity with the "subjective" concept.[12]

It is difficult not to think that what Adorno should really avail of in Kant for a model of nonidentity is the latter's theory of intuition. Intuition occurs whenever, as Kant puts it, "an object is given to us" (*CPR* A19/B33): "Intuition is that through which [a mode of knowledge] is in immediate relation to [objects]." For Kant intuition arises—familiarly enough from empiricism—through sensibility. As we would expect from sensibility it is a receptive and passive capacity: "The capacity [receptivity] for receiving representations through the mode in which we are affected by objects, is entitled *sensibility*" (*CPR* A19/B33). This is the essential first step of knowledge: "But all thought must, directly, or indirectly, by way of certain characters, relate ultimately to intuitions, and therefore, with us, to sensibility, because in no other way can an object be given to us" (*CPR* A19/B33). However, there is more to experience than just sensation; there is a rational element. That is to say, in experience objects are understood, to use Kant's term. And we understand an object when we can apply a concept to it. Our concepts arise from, what Kant terms, the faculty of understanding: "Objects are *given* to us by means of sensibility, and it alone yields us *intuitions*; they are *thought* through the understanding, and from the understanding arise *concepts*" (*CPR* A19/B33). Together concept and intuition go to make up the basic elements of an experience, and furthermore neither element can be epistemic outside their connection in experience. As he famously puts it: "Without sensibility no object would be given to us, and without understanding none would be thought. Thoughts without content are empty, intuitions without concepts are blind" (*CPR* A51/B75). In this account of experience it does seem indeed that Kant has provided an explanation of the vertical component of experience which unlike the thing-in-itself is very close to what Adorno means by nonconceptuality. It can be referred to through concepts, and it is nevertheless other than concepts. Yet, as we shall see in chapter 4, Adorno argues that Kant's notion of intuition—being explained by Kant as a transcendental faculty—idealizes experience

The Priority of the Object

and actually fails to grasp nonconceptuality. The basic idea is that as intuition is announced in Kant's Transcendental Aesthetic as a mode of subjectivity—as "in us"—it is not capable of reaching the nonidentical element of the subject's relation to objects.

6 Adorno's Critique of Judgment

In the previous two sections I have discussed respectively Adorno's view of the conceptual and nonconceptual qualities of experience. These qualities do not operate independently of each other: they are unified in experience. This unity can be explained by Adorno's thesis that experience has a structure of judgment in which concept and object are brought together, in the right theory at least. In this section I want to consider this idea, as it will enable us to see Adorno's thoughts on the synthetic relation of conceptuality and nonconceptuality in experience.

Adorno shares the Kantian and Hegelian idea that experience is a matter of understanding. This means that experience is the activity of conceptualization of the objects which are given. The form in which the elements of *conceptualization* and *object* operate together is that of judgment. Adorno wants to radicalize the theory of judgment by encouraging us to think that judgments bring together subject and object, or more properly concepts and objects without a loss of the particularity of the object. So what Adorno has to show is that judgment is not—as much of modern philosophy in his view construes it—a matter "reducing" an object to a concept, but rather the vehicle for meaning that is produced through the coexistence in experience of conceptuality and nonidentity.

The best place to begin an examination of Adorno's thoughts on judgment, perhaps, is with one of his programmatic announcements: "[Negative dialectics] says no more to begin with than that objects do not go into their concepts without leaving a remainder, that they come to contradict the traditional norm of adequation" (*ND* 16–17/5). The idea, then, is that there is a difference between objects and concepts. (It is clear, we should note, that Adorno means "predicate" by "concept," since concepts, in his analysis, have no other role than to predicate. "Concept" and "predicate" are thus interchangeable terms.) The analysis of concepts as a way of establishing this idea, Adorno argues, should investigate the concept's inherent limitation, or, as he puts it, "what it fails to cover, what its abstractionist mechanism eliminates, what is not already a case of the concept" (*ND* 20/8). And this investigation involves a close examination of the definition and precise logical function of a concept, "logical" in the sense that it is concerned solely with the *definition* of concepts as essentially distinct from objects.

Adorno's case is that a radical reevaluation of the function of concepts has become necessary in order to correct a misconception by representationalism regarding the kind of knowledge expressed through judgment. He contends that the object–concept relation has been misconstrued as one of identity; that is, that the distinction between objects and concepts has not been fully appreciated with the result that the object in its particularity is understood as primarily a case of what Adorno polemically terms the "subjective concept" (*ND* 92/85). Indeed he even claims that predication is identity and that assertoric propositions also express identity. Nobody explicitly claims that predication is identity, but Adorno argues that object–concept propositions are used *as though* they were expressions of identity. And the reason they are so used is because the very function of a judgment has not been understood. Indeed at one point he observes that the "copula"—the connective in an assertoric judgment—is misused as the vehicle of identity: "The copula says: It is so, not otherwise. The act of synthesis, for which the copula stands, indicates that it shall not be otherwise—or else the act would not be performed. The will to identify works in each synthesis" (*ND* 151/147–148). Such expressions of identity mean, as we might expect, that the uniqueness of objects— their particularity—is missed. Adorno's target often appears to be Hegel, as Hegel notoriously dismisses the significance of particulars. Adorno, we recall, notes: "The matters of true philosophical interest at this point in history are those in which Hegel, agreeing with tradition, expressed his disinterest. They are non-conceptuality, individuality, and particularity ..." (*ND* 20/8). Though it is Hegel who is referred to here, Adorno is prepared, at times, to indict the entire philosophical tradition for its failure to offer a model of conceptuality that can

The Priority of the Object

include nonuniversals. Indeed, we have already seen just that criticism of contemporary philosophy in "The Actuality of Philosophy." Clearly there is something hyperbolic about this. Nevertheless, Adorno insists that the object–concept judgment has mutated, in modern epistemology, to a relationship of identity. The root of this mutation is a misunderstanding of the logical function of the concept.

It is Adorno's view that conceptualization cannot be understood as a logically primitive activity. To assume that concepts are logically primitive, Adorno argues, is to make the mistake of not understanding their essentially constitutive relation with objects. Concepts, in other words, become meaningful only in reference to an object. (Again we are reminded of Kant's remark that "[t]houghts without content are empty, intuitions without concepts are blind.") To think otherwise involves taking concepts to be independently meaningful. And if concepts are falsely held to be independently meaningful objects will then, Adorno argues, become subordinate to them. That is to say, once concepts are construed as independently meaningful then the conventional assumption of the meaningfulness of any object to which concepts are applied, or that falls under concepts, becomes groundless (this is what we saw earlier as *de facto identity*). It is obvious from this that Adorno is trying to analyze concepts as they have been understood by the forms of idealism derived from representationalism. The historical mistake of this position has been to imagine that the indispensability of concepts accords them semantic priority: "Necessity compels philosophy to operate with concepts, but this necessity must not be turned into the virtue of their priority" (*ND* 23/11).[13]

In this regard Adorno notes: "Intentionally or not, every judgment ... carries with it the claim to predicate something that is not simply identical with the mere concept of the subject" (*ND* 78/71). The idea here is not unobvious. Adorno wants to claim that meaningful judgments, by their very nature, express both the identity and nonidentity of object and concept. The nonidentity is a product of meaning itself, not a mystical alternative to predication. Adorno holds that the nonidentical element of an object–concept judgment has semantic force in that it is "the more," as he puts it, implied by the inherent limitation of concepts. That is, the very employment of a concept implies something which is to be conceptualized—"the more"—and that element is part of the meaning structure of judgment: "With this anti-positivistic insight we do justice to the concept's surplus over factuality. No concept would be thinkable, indeed none would be possible without the 'more' that makes a language of language" (*ND* 112/106) (the object being "the more" in that it is not merely a case of the concept); "What is, is more than it is. This 'more' is not imposed upon it but remains immanent to it, as that which has been pushed out of it" (*ND* 164/161).[14]

However, Adorno has a complex idea of the role that concepts play in judgment: to predicate and thus to identify, to predicate and thereby to express difference. For that reason Adorno describes concepts as "an element in dialectical logic" (*ND* 24/12) (the tag "dialectical" expressing what Adorno takes to be two functions of concepts). In the latter sense of expressing difference, predication is nonreductive and concepts, in that respect, are nonidentical with the object: "For what we mean in the judgment is always the entity due to be judged *beyond* the particular that is included in the judgment—otherwise, according to its own intention, the judgment would be superfluous" (*ND* 155/152). Conventional formal presentation of a prediative proposition obscures this double aspect—dialectical possibility—of concepts: *S is p* simply denotes a relation. What Adorno is getting at can only be gained through what German Idealism calls reflection: "Reflection upon its own meaning is the way out of the concept's seeming being-in-itself as a unit of meaning" (*ND* 24/12). Predication identifies the particular as a case of a universal (*S* is *p* entails that *S* belongs to class *p*). But the form of the predication effectively states that *S* is an instance of *p* and thereby irreducible to *p*: "The non-identical element in an identifying judgment is clearly intelligible insofar as every single object subsumed under a class has definitions not contained in the definition of the class" (*ND* 153/150). Adorno claims therefore that an object-concept judgment is inherently and ineluctably *ambivalent* in that it is the vehicle of identity and nonidentity: "What survives in [the concept] is the fact that nonconceptuality has conveyed it by way of its meaning, which in turn establishes its conceptuality" (*ND* 24/12).[15] In this way Adorno tries to combine the two ideas discussed separately above as

The Priority of the Object

the conceptuality and nonconceptuality of the object. Through judgment the object is conceptualized, but as something to be conceptualized its very sense implies something other than its total conceptualization; that is, the particularity of the object is also implied.

In this chapter we have seen that Adorno remains committed to an epistemological treatment of experience despite his view that epistemology, hitherto, has not been able to account for the various components of experience that we have just examined; namely, the priority of the object, the nonidentity of experience, and the irreducible particular. It cannot be forgotten, however, that although these issues are treated epistemologically they are not, in fact, primarily motivated by epistemology. Adorno believes that the nonidentical moment of experience is a product of our physical engagement with the world, an engagement that takes the form of feeling, emotion, suffering, and the like. This element—which Adorno terms alternatively our somatic or sensory experience (the next chapter)—brings us, in fact, to an engagement with the sheer particularity of things, which no complex of concepts can. Although our epistemic activities can be expressed as the labor of conceptualization, our experience goes further in that conceptualization by itself cannot account for particularity simply because concepts are, for Adorno at least, expressive of universalizable properties of an individual. And for Adorno the ultimate concern in all of this is the possibility that unreduced experience—unreified rational relations between individuals—might be possible.

3

The Structure of Adorno's Epistemology: The Role of Subjectivity

It is striking that Adorno's priority of the object thesis does not eliminate the notion developed in classical German philosophy that subjectivity plays a role in the shaping of experience. Adorno's idea that experience has conceptual qualities clearly leaves room for subjective agency. Indeed, it is no exaggeration to say that this is the point at which the philosophical foundations for the possibility of a critical theory need most firmly to be established. Adorno must make good a basic thesis of critical theory that subjects are involved in the mediation of meaning and that the social totality, therefore, is a dynamic entity in which consciousness can be understood as having a critical and transformative function. That the object is mediated through consciousness is not equivalent, therefore, to the claim that consciousness is some kind of receptacle. Rather more strongly, consciousness provides the *criterion* of knowing by which the object is judged. Furthermore, consciousness is capable of change: the *criterion* can be adjusted if it seems no longer to be compatible with the object. It is malleable if engaged in what Adorno sees as objective experience. In this chapter I want to look at this matter in some detail.

But there is a further aspect of his view of the role of subjectivity suggested in the previous chapter, namely, that in experience there is an irreducible nonidentical moment that intimates the particularity of the object. This moment is physical and nonconceptual. What this moment of experience reveals is that the subject is not simply a

Chapter 3

concept manipulator, but is also a physical entity with direct engagement with material reality. In nonreified experience this engagement is one in which the very particularity of the object could be acknowledged. This moment necessarily leads to a greater appreciation of what the object contributes. The object must be an explanation for features of experience that subjectivity, by itself, could not possibly generate. The qualities or determinations that we consistently attribute to the object cannot be explained purely as the categorial activity of the subject; there is a physical moment in which the subject experiences something other than its own conceptuality. (In the following chapter I shall deal with Adorno's critical application of this principle to Kant's theory of knowledge.)

As something which is to be distinguishable from the object the subject must have specifiable characteristics. Adorno identifies these characteristics with particular caution. He is determined to avoid the idealist position in which subjects are construed as the *absolute* opposite of objects, that is, the position that subjects cannot be determined by causality. This will turn out to be a complex issue for Adorno in that he holds that the subject is both distinguishable from objects, yet also like objects in key respects (otherwise the idealist principle would be conceded). In the first and second sections of this chapter I shall consider Adorno's conceptions of the critical subject and the naturalistic subject. The appendix section turns to ways in which Adorno's thoughts on subjectivity may have a place in certain recent debates.

1   The Agency of the Subject

Adorno argues that *there is an irreducibly active role for the subject in experience*, but that role does not extend to constitution in either the German Idealist or phenomenological senses. Adorno considers this idea in two ways. First, the object is mediated by the subject in that it is subjectivity that articulates our reality (i.e., nature is not inherently conceptual, as his commitment to Marxist materialism entails). The second is that the individual experiencing subject is engaged in a process of understanding the object. The subject's concepts are applied, but validated against the object. This is the activity of

The Role of Subjectivity

understanding itself. This will be a good point at which to discuss the differences between Adorno and Hegel because Hegel, in Adorno's view, although offering the promising model of experience that we saw in chapter 1, fails to follow through his insight into the dynamic nature of the subject-object relationship. What Hegel is accused of, in essence, is the reduction of subjectivity to the role of affirmation, as opposed to the possibility of negation which, in Adorno's view, marks all of our critical or rational engagements with objects.

1.1 The Truth in Idealism

A subject that actively applies its concepts to the object is in no way inconsistent with the thesis of the priority of the object. The subject as the "how"—to use Adorno's schema—is the active agency of the object: it judges, conceives, and so on, the object. Its concepts have significance for the *human* representation of the world: they are attempts to describe objects. But in this descriptive activity the subject is restricted by the determinations of the object—the object's particularity. Yet the subject must decide in accordance with rationality what seems to be the most accurate description of an object. This idea is important in that it suggests that Adorno has found a way of utilizing the valuable insight of idealism yet at the same time constraining it. Put another way, Adorno has replaced the generative forms of idealist subjectivity, in which the object is nothing other than the way it is constituted, with a restricted theory in which the subject has a positive epistemological role in the mediation of the object. Mediation allows the reconstruction of idealism, which is the basis of Adorno's *critical* version of materialism. The priority of the object means that the object is determinative, but its determinations are articulated by the subject. This idea accommodates Adorno's conception of a critical subject. It is interesting to note that Adorno sees significant implications here for a more radical, politically oriented philosophy. The idea that the mind is not just a passive piece of the world is central to the idea of liberation, as it was for the followers of German Idealism. As Adorno writes: "The subject is the object's agent, not its constituent; this fact has consequences for the relation of theory and practice" (*SO* 752/146).

In retrieving the valuable contribution of idealism Adorno achieves what he calls the sublation of subjectivity "in a higher form" (*SO* 743/144): the subject is neither just passive as in the alleged case of empiricism, nor just constitutive as in the case of German Idealism. The subject, in fact, is both, but in synthesizing both empiricist and idealist subjectivity Adorno modifies the claims of both models in their original forms. The priority of the object means that the possibilities of what the subject can experience are restricted by the object. That restriction, however, does not amount to naive realism (for reasons that should be clear from above). In essence, then, Adorno's theory of mediation allows him to include the idea of a subject that is active without, at the same time, falling into another version of subjective idealism.

1.2   Negative Experience

The second aspect of subject mediation is that of a subject achieving understanding through its active engagement with the object. Adorno's position, as we saw in the previous chapter, is that objects are part of the social totality—they are constituted through their sedimented history. To understand an object is implicitly to understand its place in the social totality and, in a way, also to grasp the role of the social totality in the object. For Adorno, then, the object must be seen in the context of concrete social existence; not just concrete social existence in general, but the historically specific experience of contemporary Western capitalist societies.[1] In this context the capacity for reflection, it is argued, is diminished. The idea here is that the prevalence of a certain rationality has, in fact, taken hold of the criterion by which we conceptualize. To put this another way, consciousness is in the grip of a particular model of rationality, one that accepts appearances as truth.[2] Thus it is limited to accepting society as it is given—its appearances—as the *whole* of society and does not examine the structures that lie behind those appearances. Hence it cannot achieve the sort of understanding that grasps the contextual position of objects. The role of the subject in this environment—if it operates under this rationality—is simply to affirm reality since this rationality gives the subject no motivation to reflect more deeply. For Adorno this is the

The Role of Subjectivity

neutralization of critical consciousness, critical consciousness being the ability to reject a prevailing paradigm of interpretation when it becomes clear that this paradigm falls short of an adequate grasp of an object (in this case, failing to contextualize the object). So to understand what Adorno means by subjectivity in this respect we have to see it as implying the possibility of criticism—the ability to negate or not accept what is allegedly given.

For Adorno, as we have seen, true experience is transformative: it is not passivity in relation to the given. In that respect then a subject can actually fail to explain an object if the rationality with which it operates gives it no motivation for transformation. This is a rationality that offers the subject no motivation to go beneath the surface of things. Against this inert rationality Adorno writes: "[S]uch a rigid and invariant basis contradicts that which experience tells us about itself, about the change that occurs constantly in the forms of experience, the more open it is, and the more it is actualized. To be incapable of this change is to be incapable of experience" (*ND* 380/388). In line with this Adorno attempts to locate the negative moment in experience—the dialectical moment—at which consciousness is compelled by its own rationality to revise itself, and to do so by reference to the object. In this regard dialectic must therefore be understood as a moment of rationally motivated experience, not as a method or argumentative strategy—the latter being what Adorno terms *"prima dialectica"* (*ND* 157/154), that is, dialectic prior to experience. (This claim marks an important distinction between Adorno's and Hegel's uses of dialectic, as we shall see in the next section.) Hauke Brunkhorst puts this issue well: "Dialectic is the reflexive, conceptual penetration of experience. . . . It is the continuous liquefaction of objectivistic self-misunderstanding, the demonstration of the mediation of all objectivity through cognitive work."[3]

In proposing his particular concept of experience Adorno argues against those theories which place the subject in a passive relation to its environment. The notion of passivity needs some elaboration. One version of passivity sees the subject as the inactive receiver of data. Some versions of this see the theory of determinism as the logical implication of the concept of empirical passivity. The subject is thereby just one event in a causal sequence that transcends it. Purely as a reaction to the determinist model, gratuitous and incoherent philosophies of freedom have been proposed. What needs to be considered, however, is a model of experience in which the subject might be seen to engage with the object without either being reduced to the object or radically choosing its own mode of experience in a Sartrean manner. Adorno believes that without a theory of experience that makes the mediation of subject and object crucial we end up with one of two equally one-sided accounts of experience: *either* one in which the subject accepts its immersion in its environment as wholly constitutive of itself, and thus (*uncritically*) takes its experience to be natural, *or* one that offers the illusion of a subject not engaged in its environment. In neither case is there an analysis that articulates a critical relationship to the world, an analysis of the forms of consciousness that shape and threaten to limit experience itself. The determinist model leads, ultimately, to our incapacity to distinguish the subject from the world in any way. The subject is, for determinism, just a peculiarly observable part of a causal chain. The freedom model detaches the subject from this situation and hubristically elevates it beyond its environment. But, as Adorno argues, this is not, strictly speaking, experience at all: "[E]xperience lives by consuming the [detached] stand-point; not until the stand-point is submerged in it would there be philosophy" (*ND* 41/30). What Adorno suggests, through his revamping of Hegel's model of experience, is that the very structure of experience contains a critical logic and that this process—which is the basis of rationality—has to be retrieved in order to enable us to confront the modes of consciousness through which we engage our environment. Otherwise we lapse into the "unthinking inertia" described by Hegel.

1.3 Positive Experience? Disagreements with Hegel

It is for this reason that experience needs to be understood in a further sense as negative—as critical rather than as integrative. The integrative model proposed by Hegel's speculative philosophy—in which through the "completed series" of thought subject and object achieve identity—ends up, in Adorno's view, by underpinning a positive model of experience in that the integrative compulsion of Hegel's dialectic overrides the moment of critical engagement. Experience refers to the point at which the subject is changed by its confrontation with the object. In a sociohistorical context in which, as Adorno alleges, consciousness is constrained by ideology, the only possible alternative is to uncover a negative logic within experience to provide us with a moment of resistance: "Thought as such, before all particular contents, is an act of negation, of resistance to that which is forced upon it ..." (*ND* 30/19).[4] Experience, as such, not the conventional practices of positivist rationality, contains the negative aspect of this operation: "Experience forbids the resolution in the unity of consciousness of whatever appears contradictory.... [C]ontradiction cannot be brought under any unity without manipulation, without the insertion of some wretched cover concepts that will make the crucial differences vanish" (*ND* 155/152).[5] Experience is only possible in as much as the subject adjusts to the object. It does so reflexively, in judgment: "It is up to dialectical cognition to pursue the inadequacy of thought and thing, to experience it in the thing" (*ND* 156/153).[6]

We have seen points of agreement between Adorno and Hegel on what a theory of experience should contain. Clearly Adorno believes that Hegel's theory possesses some of the essential elements, but that the system within which the elements are located—with its idealist teleology—actually threatens to undermine their ability to explain experience, contrary to what seemed to have been promised in the introduction to the *Phenomenology*. As he sees it, Hegel oscillates "between the most profound insight and the collapse of that insight" (*ND* 161/160). What that really means, for Adorno, is that Hegel may indeed have a potent arsenal of philosophical concepts and insights. However, the reality of Hegel's texts is that these concepts and insights are ultimately subordinated to the needs of Hegel's architectonic. Hegel strives to assemble the encyclopaedia of concepts in a logical and quasi-deductive system. But by so doing, Adorno argues, he actually undermines the negativity—the insight into the moment of nonidentity—in his philosophy.

Perhaps the most important of Adorno's statements on the problem of Hegelian philosophy relates to the idea of negation. For

Adorno, Hegel's concept of negation *almost* captures a central part of the thesis of subject-object mediation: namely, that the priority of the object means that in mediation there is both *identity* and *nonidentity* (or "negativity") between subject and object. However, Adorno argues that Hegel's version of negation ultimately fails to capture the ambiguous nature of the subject's relation to objects as a consequence of an assumption that even nonidentity or negation is ultimately to be considered positive. It is positive, Hegel allegedly believes, since it can be interpreted as a mode of the subject's identity with the object. Adorno argues, however, that "[t]he nonidentical is not to be obtained directly, as something positive on its part, nor is it obtainable by a negation of the negative. The negation is not an affirmation itself as it is to Hegel" (*ND* 161/158). The basic thesis of absolute idealism is that there can be no ultimate nonidentity between thought and object. For post-Kantian German idealism, as a rule, the idea of the thing-in-itself is irrational, and on that basis—it is argued—there is nothing with which thought is not ultimately identical. For that reason Hegel's apparently critical moment of thought, dialectic—in which the inadequacy of the concept is evinced by its own self-contradiction (*EL* §81)—is prejudiced by the assumption that the object *must in the end* be fundamentally identical with some concept (again this being the problem, as Adorno sees it, of Hegel's architectonic).

Adorno argues that, by assuming that all possible descriptions of the subject-object relation can be reduced to identity, Hegel vitiates the realist character of the dialectic: "At each new dialectical step, Hegel goes against the intermittent insight of his own logic, forgets the rights of the preceding step, and thus prepares to copy what he chided as abstract negation: an abstract—to wit, a subjectively and arbitrarily confirmed—positivity" (*ND* 162/159); "The thesis that the negation of the negation is something positive can only be upheld by one who presupposes positivity—as all-conceptuality—from the beginning" (*ND* 162/160). Hegel's logic, according to Adorno, attempts to "dispute away the distinction between idea and reality" (*ND* 329/335) and this means that the concept of dialectic in Hegel cannot be reconciled with the account of experience Adorno wants to defend. One might argue that these are unfair criticisms given that they are

The Role of Subjectivity

based on a presupposition about Hegel's philosophy which Hegel himself would hardly accept. Hegel is not trying to overcome idealism; rather, he seems to assume programmatically the identity of the absolute from the beginning. Thus it is inaccurate to suggest—as Adorno sometimes does—that Hegel *almost* understands the implications of his dialectical moment. But what Adorno is saying is that Hegel's philosophy does, at least in places, lend itself to—if not amount to—a materialist theory of experience. Yet, for Adorno, Hegel dogmatically pursues a metaphysical agenda, one that is most strongly undermined by his own materialist theses. In the following passage, for example, Adorno cites Hegel and then provides a gloss outlining how Hegel has missed the point of his own philosophy:

> "Truth is also positive, as knowledge coinciding with the object, but it is this self-sameness only if knowledge has reacted negatively to the Other, if it has penetrated the object and has voided the negation which it is."
>
> The qualification of truth as a negative reaction on the part of the knowledge that penetrates the object—in other words: extinguishes the appearance of the object being directly as it is—sounds like a program of negative dialectics as knowledge "coinciding with the object." But the establishment of this knowledge as positivity abjures that program. (*ND* 162–163/160)

Several clarifications need to be made of this passage. First, what have positivity or negativity got to do with anything? The context of Hegel's idealism helps make sense of this. Adorno takes Hegel's system to be aimed at completeness, and interprets the latter as positivity inasmuch as, as the passage goes, "it has penetrated the object and has voided the negation which it is." If experience can be, as Adorno has stipulated, "full unreduced experience in the medium of conceptual reflection" then Hegel seems to have prejudiced the outcome of an examination of the nature of experience by pinning it to a presupposed order of conceptual positivity. Hence Hegel's system has not fully absorbed the logic of experience. Adorno is claiming that Hegel is right in so far as he argues—to put it in Adorno's epistemological terms—that knowledge is determined by the object: knowledge coincides with the object in that sense. But Hegel is more fundamentally committed to the idea of absolute identity, and that commitment "abjures" his implicit materialism.

Chapter 3

In essence, then, Hegel's view of experience produces a distorted picture of subjectivity in that it deprives subjectivity of the ability to discriminate—to criticize—and replaces it with the ineluctable goal of identity. The effect of this, Adorno argues, is that the experience of particularity, which is achieved in the successful dialectical thesis of the introduction to the *Phenomenology*, is subordinated to the needs of the system: particularity itself is lost, and instead is transformed into a philosophical version of particularity. Adorno writes: "Hegel is constantly forced to shadow-box because he shrinks from his own conception: from the dialectics of the particular, which destroyed the primacy of identity and thus, consistently, idealism itself. For the particular he substitutes the general concept of particularization pure and simple—of 'Existenz,' for instance, in which the particular is not any more" (*ND* 175/173). Indeed there is a passage in Hegel that certainly seems to say exactly what Adorno is here attributing to him. In one part of the *Encyclopaedia* Hegel argues that particular sensible objects are unintelligible apart from their concept, which he sees as their essence. And that cognizance of essence appears to be an activity quite other than that of the experience of particulars described in the *Phenomenology*:

> With regard to the equally immediate consciousness of the existence of *external* things, this is nothing else than *sensible* consciousness; that we have a consciousness of this kind is the least of all cognitions. All that is of interest here is to know that this immediate knowing of the *being* of external things is deception and error, and that there is no truth in the sensible as such, but that the *being* of these external things is rather something contingent, something that passes away, or a *semblance*; they are essentially this: to have only an existence that is separable from their concept, or their essence. (*EL* §76)

A grand conclusion that Adorno attempts to draw from what he sees as the problem of Hegel's treatment of particulars is that subjectivity, too, is thereby eroded in some way. A subject which achieves identity willy-nilly is, then, an inadequate subject. This conclusion is as ironic as it is radical. Far from empowering the subject, the achievement of identity reduces the subject by depriving it of the structures that could explain its critical, negative dimension. The *Phenomenology* had sketched out a compelling account of the way in which the

The Role of Subjectivity

subject's engagement with objectivity is critical. And that critical dimension is, as we have seen Adorno argue, incompatible with a system that, in essence, has the metaphysical motivation of validating the nonexperiential notion of identity.

2 The Materialist Subject

In addition to its conceptual activity the subject must, Adorno believes, also be characterized as a physical entity, one that is in direct engagement with nonconceptual reality. In a striking passage Adorno explains why it is that this aspect of the subject must be considered by philosophy: the privileging of the purely mental aspects of experience has somehow eroded the epistemic significance of physical pain. Sheer physical experience simply lies outside the sphere of what philosophy has been prepared to consider. And without the consideration of the physical the mental, Adorno seems to think, gives itself no epistemic constraints. He writes:

> The course of history forces materialism upon metaphysics, traditionally the direct antithesis of materialism. What the mind once boasted of defining or constructing as its like moves in the direction of what is unlike the mind, in the direction of that which eludes the rule of the mind and yet manifests that rule as absolute evil. The somatic, unmeaningful stratum of life is the stage of suffering, of the suffering which in the camps, without any consolation, burned every soothing feature out of the mind, and out of culture, the mind's objectification. (*ND* 358/365)

Adorno makes three different claims with regard to the physicality of the subject. (1) The first is that *the priority of the object entails that in experience the subject reacts to a physical environment*. The transcendental argument that we saw in the previous chapter captures this relation to some extent, although it emphasizes the idea that the object anchors our systems of knowledge, rather than that the subject is conditioned in some way by the object. (2) The second claim is that *the subject cannot be characterized as spirit if it is to have any reality*—it is part of nature. Adorno's point here is that the subject does not exist in a private space in which it is unaffected by a material environment. (3) A third claim, related to the second, is that *the subject has somatic experience* that is irreducible to conceptuality. These three closely related claims are not distinguished by Adorno, although they are supported by very different kinds of arguments. Since these arguments are clearly distinguishable however, I shall, after a little disentangling, examine them separately, and this section is subdivided accordingly.

2.1 The Priority of the Object and Subject Determinacy

What this aspect of the subject-object relation emphasizes is not the necessity of the object's priority in the structure of the subject-object relation, but the effects of that relation on the subject. Adorno, as we have seen, makes a correspondence between the subject as the "how" and the object as the "what" of the mediational process (*SO* 746/142). This idea is by no means identical with the argument for the priority of the object. The claim that the subject is determined by the object is, however, an important corollary of that argument. This corollary gives emphasis to the idea of the *determinative dependence* of the subject on the object (or subject determinacy), and not the determinate independence of the object (the latter being the *real* priority of the object). Adorno gives various formulations of what is involved in subject determinacy. In general, these formulations express the dependency of the subject on something other than itself as the very source of its activity: "It is the mind's definition as an activity which immanently compels philosophy to pass from the mind to its otherness. From Kant on, no idealism could escape this definition, not even Hegel's" (*ND* 201/200); "Only if the I on its part is also not I does it react to the not-I. Only then does it 'do' something. Only then would the doing itself be thinking" (*ND* 201/201). In essence, Adorno argues that the subject would have no activity—it would not think or exist *qua* consciousness—if it did not relate to some object. Understanding this idea will make sense of Adorno's claim (which we saw earlier) that the object has an independence that the subject does not: "The object, too, is mediated; but according to its own concept, it is not so thoroughly dependent on the subject as the subject is on objectivity" (*SO* 747/143). That is, the object has priority in that its determinations give motion, so to speak,

The Role of Subjectivity

to the activities of understanding, the effort of the subject to achieve veridical judgments.

Adorno's argument for the relationship between the object's priority and subject determinacy, though not systematic, parallels the argument advanced by Kant for the objective necessity of outer objects in the constitution of self-consciousness. The following remarks suggest that same idea: "Subjectivity changes its quality in a context which it is unable to evolve on its own" (*ND* 184/183). Subjective acts must, as Adorno puts it, "adjust to a moment which they themselves are not" (*ND* 142/138). The subject is determined by the object. In this respect the subject is "thoroughly dependent" on the object (*SO* 747/143). To put this another way: the sources of subjective determination—the quality of consciousness—do not all lie purely within subjectivity. It is a condition of subjectivity to be determined by what Kant called "outer objects."

As this argument is a direct corollary of the argument for the priority of the object it largely depends on the validity of that latter argument. The basic argument for the priority of the object is, in my view, defensible as a cohesive argument. But its corollary—what we are here considering—seems to miss something. It does not seem to have all of the resources that would allow for a comprehensive explanation of the activities of consciousness. As it stands, Adorno's account of subject determinacy is quite narrow in that it explains only a certain kind of consciousness: namely, object consciousness ("objects" in the sense discussed in the previous chapter). It cannot explain the actualization of consciousness—in the case, for instance, of certain emotions—that is not directed toward objects (the "not-I"). Indeed, if the concept of subject determinacy were carried to its logical conclusion then that mode of consciousness would have to be denied altogether. Whereas this concept might be able to confront and undermine idealist (self-constituted) accounts of consciousness it is itself limited in that it is restricted to what seems to me to be a distinctly epistemological subject. I will only suggest for now that the commitment to the transcendental structure—though powerful in refuting other positions—leaves little room for the sort of detail that might provide a more concrete picture of consciousness.

2.2 The Naturalistic Subject

One of the most persistent ideas in Adorno's theory of subjectivity is that the subject *qua* consciousness does not have extramaterialist reality. (We have already introduced Adorno's distinctive understanding of materialism: namely, that matter should be taken to include all the processes of our experienceable reality in which meaning emerges for human beings.) Adorno argues that if we allow the dualism in which we have a nonmaterial subject interacting with a material object, we will simply place the subject in a position of preeminence. As Adorno puts it: "The mind will then usurp the place of something absolutely independent—which it is not; its claim of independence heralds the claim of dominance. Once radically parted from the object, the subject reduces it to its own measure; the subject swallows the object, forgetting how much it is an object itself" (*SO* 742/139). Adorno offers an argument against the substance dualism of spirit-matter. (The argument here seems to be distinctly Kantian, its source being perhaps the Paralogisms section of the *Critique of Pure Reason*.) Because there can be no grounds for a separation of the reality of the subject from some of the conditions that govern objects Adorno contends that the subject cannot be characterized as spirit. Subjectivity shares with objects the feature of determinability. That is to say, the subject is not a fixed essence: like material objects it changes. This contrasts sharply with idealist versions of subjectivity in which the subject is described as purely determin*ing*. There is, Adorno suggests, a further important similarity between subject and object: the fact that they can both be known through experience as part of the material world. This common availability—which enables both to be objectively known—further denies the characterization of the subject as immaterial. By arguing against any such characterization of the subject Adorno does not conclude that the subject is merely a physical object. As shall be seen in detail in the appendix to this chapter, he is far from arguing for a reductive materialist ontology in which the mind is thing-ly merely by virtue of the fact that its function is potentially explicable through certain physical processes (brain functions).

To understand the context in which Adorno arrives at this characterization of the subject we need to consider his reading of the

The Role of Subjectivity

problems of idealist subjectivity. Adorno argues that the supposed reality of the idealist subject cannot be coherently explained. This is because the idealist subject lies beyond any possible conditions in which it could be known, described, or justified. In "Subject and Object" Adorno employs this argument to reject the idealist version of apperception. In subjective idealism (Fichte, early Schelling, Reinhold, for example) the concept of apperception is used to explain the reflective act of an essentially nonempirical transcendental subject or self on the contents of consciousness. This concept attempts to justify the starting point of idealism. In general, modern idealism has been an introspective method in that the essential condition of knowledge—supposedly the subject—is revealed by an inward look. The classic problem with the form of philosophical introspection that is at the center of subjective idealism is that an infinite regress is suggested in the claim that the self knows itself: is the self that knows thereafter known by another self? In order to avoid this regress it is necessary to claim that idealist self-consciousness, or apperception, is radically unlike the way in which we know objects. Apperceivable reality is quite unlike anything we ordinarily perceive. It is in no way equivalent to an empirical consciousness that is determined by objects. To use Novalis's elegant phrase: "Consciousness is a being in being outside of being."[7] The concept of apperception thereby tries to explain the peculiarly prior nature of the subject.

Fichte describes apperception as follows:

This intuiting of himself that is required of the philosopher, in performing the act whereby the self arises for him, I refer to as *intellectual intuition*. It is the immediate consciousness that I act, and what I enact: it is that whereby I know something because I do it. We cannot prove from concepts that this power of intellectual intuition exists, nor evolve from them what it may be. Everybody must discover it immediately in himself, or he will never make its acquaintance.[8]

In this act of intellectual intuition—Fichte's version of apperception—the self can be differentiated from all other features of existence. If this is accepted, not only does it avoid the infinite regress—in that it identifies a self-evidently prior self that is not subject to empirical intuition—but also it neatly sets up the subject in a position of efficient causality: the apparent priority of the self means that the self constitutes the world. The subjective idealist's thesis of apperception is therefore a particularly suitable target for Adorno's criticism since it can only account for the reality of apperceptive acts by claiming a different nonmaterial, indeed unique, form of existence: "The subject itself is an object insofar as existence is implied by the idealist doctrine of constitution—there must be a subject so that it can constitute anything at all—insofar as this had been borrowed in turn, from the sphere of facticity. The concept of what 'is there' means nothing but what exists, and the subject as existent comes promptly under the heading of 'object.' As pure apperception, however, the subject claims to be the downright Other of all existents" (*SO* 754/148). When Adorno writes, then, that the doctrine of apperception attempts to make the subject "the downright Other of all existents" the issue is that the subject elevates itself beyond all the intelligible conditions of possible experience. It shares none of the characteristics of existence, for if it did it would then be subject to an infinite regress since its empirical status would not give it the authority of priority. The subjective idealist makes the arcane subject in-itself the starting point of the analysis.

The idea of apperception, then, is the device that is used in the attempts to claim that this subject in-itself can be known. In opposition to the strategy of apperception Adorno argues that our knowledge of subjectivity must be based on the actuality of subjectivity: consciousness. By basing the analysis on consciousness Adorno restricts it to a phenomenon with materialist features. These features of determinability and epistemic objectivity make it possible for us to know our own subjective life. Significantly, these features are also what allow us to know objects: "The difference between subject and object cuts through both the subject and the object. It can no more be absolutized than it can be put out of mind. Actually everything in the subject is chargeable to the object; whatever part of it is not will semantically burst the 'is.' According to its own concept, the pure subjective form of traditional epistemology always exists only as a form of something objective, never without such objectivity; without that it is not even thinkable" (*SO* 754/148); "No matter how we define the subject, some entity cannot be juggled out of it. If it is not something—and 'something' indicates an irreducible objective

The Role of Subjectivity

moment—the subject is nothing at all; even as *actus purus*, it still needs to refer to something active" (*SO* 747/143). The critical implications of this conclusion are that both dualism (which defines the mind in opposition to the physical) and idealism (which relies on the extraexperiential activities of apperception) lose the vital element of their respective justifications: they can no longer claim that the mind is distinct in the senses required by their theories.[9]

2.3 The Somatic Subject

Further to the idea that the subject cannot be reduced to the pure subjectivity of idealism Adorno goes on to argue that its "somatic," bodily experience is a key feature that lies outside the reach of concepts while nevertheless intimating meaning. In order to defend his idea of somatic experience Adorno distinguishes it from the empiricist view, which also, of course, has something to say about the role through sensation of the body in experience.

Adorno finds a unifying thread to philosophy of the modern period in the concept of sensation. That the idealism of Descartes produced empiricism is a truism in the historiography of modern philosophy. But Adorno reveals this link—most critically for empiricism—in terms of its structural predisposition toward a mentalistic account of experience. Because he too adheres to this basic structure, Kant, when operating in his representational realist mode, is, from Adorno's perspective, one of the villains of the history of philosophy. In the first *Critique* Kant writes, for instance, that a "perception which relates solely to the subject as the modification of its state is sensation . . ." (*CPR* A320/B376). Sensation can be given a systematic place within idealism. The role played by sensation can be characterized as that of *indicating a state of the subject*. In this vital respect sensation performs the same function in both empiricism and idealism. Construed in this way, it is, as Adorno refers to it, "abstract sensation" (*ME* 161/156) since it pertains merely to a subjective state: it is not explained within the mediational structure of subject-object. In effect, then, the traditional understanding of sensation has an idealist tendency that transmits itself to empiricism. This subjectivist explanation of experience contrasts significantly with

Adorno's externalist arguments for the priority of the object. Through the idea of sensation Adorno develops a critical argument against empiricism.

Adorno begins the argument as follows:

> Sensation [*Empfindung*], the crux of all epistemology, needs epistemology to reinterpret it into a fact of consciousness, in contradiction to its own full character—which, after all, is to serve as authority for its cognition.
>
> There is no sensation without a somatic moment. To this extent the concept of sensation, in comparison with that which it allegedly subsumes, is twisted so as to satisfy the demand for an autarkic connection of all cognitive steps. (*ND* 193/193)

Adorno is thus far from denying that there is an element of physical contact between subject and object. His point is that this element is misconstrued by empiricist epistemology and consequently treated merely subjectivistically. The *autarkic* strategy that results is an attempt to explain all experience by reference solely to the conditions of subjectivity. Sensation, which is a basic feature of our material condition, is thereby reduced to a state of subjectivity. Furthermore, sensation is seen as something merely immediate since it does not point to an object beyond subjectivity.

Against Adorno's criticism it could be argued that empiricism does generally offer a distinction between the level of acquaintance and that of description. Thus empiricism does not reduce all outer experience to subjective states. In that respect classical empiricism might actually accommodate Adorno's principle that the object is *both* mediate and immediate since the level of acquaintance—unlike the level of description—is not subjectively categorized or "described." In other words, this distinction makes it plain that our *descriptive* knowledge of the object—that which is cognitively relevant—is *not immediate* (not *acquaintance*), and hence knowledge itself is no subjective reduction of the object. But this, from Adorno's perspective, would not do enough to extricate empiricism from a subjectivist position. In practice, empiricism turns the primitive level of acquaintance into rational knowledge through a categorial process. That is to say, what comes to us through acquaintance (through sensation) is supposed to be objective, and therefore entirely unqualified or undetermined by the concepts of subjectivity. However, if for the empiricist the level of acquaintance is to have any epistemic status it cannot remain at the primitive level; it must be "described." The primitive level of pure givenness is sometimes supposed to be a matter of "raw feels" and the like. But this predescriptive level is not available to concepts, and knowledge of its existence is therefore more than empiricism, *using empirical criteria*, would have a right to claim; the predescriptive level would be as mysterious as the noumenal object. It could only be inferred, and its rational defensibility would thus be problematic. For that reason the separation of raw feel and conceptualization can have no justification. And given this, the separation of acquaintance and description has no justification either. As a result, empiricism is, after all, fundamentally incompatible with Adorno's ideas of the mediacy and immediacy of objects.

Exposure of the unjustifiability of separating acquaintance and description leaves empiricism with two options: that there is (1) only conceptualization or that (2) there is a more synthetic account of the relationship between sensation and conceptualization. Either option, however, entails serious complications for empiricism. Here again we can see the application of transcendental argument: we cannot step outside the structure of mediation without incoherence. With the first option, empiricism would have to be understood as idealist, and with the second option the central idea of pure givenness—pure in the sense that it is received entirely without conceptualization—would have to be abandoned. In the light of the implications of these antinomical options it seems that sensation is, in a way, something of an addition to thought: it is reducible to mental activities or processes. As Adorno puts it: "Only thought which ceases to identify cognition with its subject could get by as the canon of cognition without the completeness of subjective forms of consciousness and would no longer need to add together experience out of the parts of the process of cognition" (*ME* 162/158). This is the point at which empiricism becomes pure immediacy: it cannot include the objective side of sensation, since it internalizes the source of objectivity.[10]

What then is the epistemological status of sensation? Since it is not pure immediacy (givenness), in the manner assumed by empiricism and manufactured by idealism, what is it? The difficulty in giving an account of sensation is, as we have seen, that it has to be distinguished from its subjectivist misconstructions. Adorno tries to establish the principle that "sensation is not to be dissipated [*verflüchtigen*] into 'spirit'" (*ME* 161/156). Clearly, an understanding of sensation which produces an alternative outcome requires some quite radical argument. It will be important to watch closely how Adorno avoids claiming the existence of a private sensory world.

The procedure offered by Adorno is familiar. He tries to understand sensation as a feature *within* the structure of the subject–object relation. Sensation has to be reinterpreted in this way if its epistemic function—that is, its emergence in the mediation of subject and object—is to be recovered. As he writes: "If one were to think away from a sensation of color that it is in space and time, i.e., that it is real [*wirklich*], then the sensation would become the concept of a sensed color. But in that case the simplest thing is misunderstood. The sheer idea of this one τόδε τι remains left over and its species is never attained" (*ME* 107/101). In other words, the basis of sensation is the subject's relation to real objects. Sensation is thereby part of the product of subject-object mediation. Any interpretation of sensation that fails to appreciate its mediational character inevitably reduces it to a purely subjective mode.

Adorno elaborates on this by attempting to identify the real basis of what has been distorted into pure sensation. This basis, he claims, lies in *somatic* experience. Empiricism, Adorno holds, has made it a principle that all experience can be reduced to processes causally acting upon the senses. Thus something like somatic experience, precisely as bodily experience, might seem to be translatable into sensory perception. In short, states of the mind—*sensations* as simple ideas in Locke for example—are produced by external stimuli and the body is the apparatus of external perception. But this translation reveals an aporia. It is constituted by an invalid move from the *somatic* to the *mental*. A typical view expressed in a philosophy of mind textbook shows this problem quite clearly. Its authors write: "It seems equally obvious that physical events can cause mental ones. For example, light stimulates the retina to have a visual experience. The dentist's probe hits a nerve and you feel pain. The sugar level in your blood drops and you start to want food. . . . We can sum up all these apparent truisms by saying that the mind and body causally interact."[11] It is strange, from an Adornian perspective, that pain and hunger should be described as mental, and all the more strange as this passage is a contribution toward a critique of mind-body dualism. In essence, it holds that all experience is ultimately mental states. This, surprisingly, makes empiricism somehow equivalent to subjective idealism. That, however, is the result of a subjective starting point, as Adorno argues.

Since Adorno believes that his account of subject-object mediation is true, it is no longer tenable, in his view, to assume subjectivity as the starting point for sensation. In fact, in *Negative Dialectics* Adorno consistently uses the term "somatic" rather than "sensation" in order to suggest the wider understanding of sensation in its mediational context: "The somatic moment as the not purely cognitive part of cognition is *irreducible*, and thus the subjective claim collapses at the very point where radical empiricism had conserved it. The fact that the subject's cognitive achievements are somatic in accordance with their own meaning affects not only the basic relation of subject and object but the dignity of corporeality [*Körperlichen*]" (*ND* 194/193, my italics); "The material element simply cannot be rooted out of [sensation]. Bordering on physical pain and organic desire, it is a bit of nature which cannot be *reduced* to subjectivity" (*ME* 160/155, my italics). Adorno—in contrast to neurophysiological accounts of sensation—does not give any explanation of the somatic nature of pain. There is a sense in which he feels he does not need to. The focus of his position, and the grounding of his epistemology in general, is the perspective of living experience [*lebendige Erfahrung*], a perspective which takes physical experience to be self-evident. A successful epistemology would be one that concluded that experience is externalist, that it does not take place purely in the mind, and that it is bodily. And this bodily experience is one that is nonconceptual yet meaningful. Adorno may seem to hold that there is an irreducible authority to this experience, one that denies the sensation construction placed on it by empiricism. But he is not dogmatic in that the route to a justification of somatic experience is via a critique of sensation as construed in modern philosophy. This critique once again confirms a characteristic of Adorno's approach: to demonstrate the experience concealed beneath the irrationality of modern philosophy and its subjectivist rationality.

Adorno's position is perhaps easier to understand in the light of these criticisms of the empiricist account of experience. It is informed by the view that such theories fail to develop a concept of experience that is more than subjectivist. By these standards the empiricist tradition is reductionist since it understands experience in terms of mental states:[12] "If it were true that material reality extends into so-called 'consciousness' only as sensation and 'sense-certainty,' then all the more would objectivity be turned into a categorial performance of the subject ..." (*ME* 161/156). It is clear from this that Adorno's position can be sharply distinguished from empiricism. The ultimate success of the position offered by Adorno, however, will be assessed in a later section.

From what we have seen we cannot say that Adorno offers a rigorously synthetic theory of subjectivity, but he certainly has a number of important views that together add up to an interesting position. His central principle is the principle of mediation. The nature of both subject and object can be understood only in relation to it, for they follow from it. I believe that the various commitments that follow from that principle have all been discussed in this and the previous chapter.

In Adorno's texts the concept of mediation is encountered most often in the context of criticism of specific alternative philosophical positions. In the following chapters I want to examine Adorno's philosophical critiques. The framework we have examined in the chapters so far is implicit in Adorno's reading of the idealist philosophical tradition (in which he includes phenomenology). However, insofar as these criticisms are applications of Adorno's general philosophical position to particular philosophical claims, significant implications of Adorno's position emerge. In the remaining chapters I shall therefore examine Adorno's critiques of Kant, Husserl and Heidegger.

Appendix: Subjectivity and Its Irreducibility—An Adornian Alternative

I want to highlight some further implications of Adorno's idea of subjectivity by reading it in the context of a central question in contemporary philosophy of mind. Even though the realization of

The Role of Subjectivity

mediation is an ideal, it nevertheless contains elements which are contributions to the philosophy of experience. I suggest that Adorno's account of experience can make a distinctive and interesting contribution to the issue of how we can justifiably claim that there is a subjective aspect to reality that cannot be reduced to the terms of "objective" physical reality. The issue in question arises from a debate between those who argue for a physicalist explanation of mind and those who are committed to some form of dualism. The former argue that there is nothing about subjectivity that could allow us to maintain its distinctiveness from the physical world, whereas the latter argue for its distinctness, and thereby feel (in some cases) compelled to offer a subject–object dualism. I shall contend that, from the point of view of Adorno's subject–object mediation theory, physicalism and dualism are not exhaustive options. They are both false. Like the position criticized by the classical Kantian Paralogisms, they both share a mistaken presupposition: they both ask what kind of *thing* subjectivity is. Adorno's approach seems to offer a way out of the antinomy of physicalism and dualism in that it asks—as we saw in the previous section—what distinctive *activity* is performed by the subject: can this activity be explained by certain central positions in philosophy of mind? This will be seen by contrasting Adorno's position with that of two philosophers who argue against physical reductionism: Thomas Nagel and John Searle.[13]

Of course an Adornian critique of this contemporary debate might be simply to dismiss it as the internal workings out of reified philosophy: the physical reduction of "mind" seems, indeed, to suggest that. However, Adorno, as we have seen, wants to explain the mechanisms of a new concept of experience, and that explanation brings him into epistemology. I am suggesting here that this epistemology identifies elements of experience that are problematically denied by recent influential accounts of consciousness.

Adorno holds that subjectivity is a feature of experience that cannot be adequately analyzed by the methodologies of empirical science. Subjectivity is not a physical object, but nor, as its structural role in epistemology indicates, is it "outside" or "beyond" the physical world. His approach contrasts with an investigation of subjectivity by empirical science. In Adorno's view empirical methodology attempts to establish the essence of any object in terms of categories. But when this methodology is applied to the subject it is presupposing that the subject can be understood essentially in the same way as physical reality. From an Adornian perspective this would be a failure to address the epistemological question of *what the subject does* that would distinguish it from objects. The empirical method can ultimately deliver only what its methodology allows. The result is that the subject comes to be understood as a quasi-physical object, operating under the causal rules that govern objects. For Adorno, subjectivity is part of the structure of mediation, a structure of interdetermination, and therefore has the ability to act with rationality; that is, without external necessitation. For this to be the case the subject of experience must have certain characteristics. The subject as an agent of experience must be more than an arbitrary bundle:

> Though empiricism as an epistemology tracks down the conditions of all knowledge in factical-psychological consciousness which it regards as an underlying physical principle, this consciousness and what is given in it could always be different according to empirical ground rules. Such consciousness contradicts the idea of the first which is nevertheless the only motivation for analysis of consciousness, even the empiricist analysis of the "human understanding," as philosophical method. The isolated subjective antipode within consciousness, however, or "spirit" [*Geist*], which withdraws from the isolated objective encounterability of the entity or the "given," thus withdraws from determination just as much as its opposite. Both spirit and its actions defy analysis. It does not let itself be established in the way that epistemology as scientific method should demand, while what can be established itself is already formed according to the model of that facticity to which spirit should present the antipode. (*ME* 32/24)

This passage indicates Adorno's identification of the empiricist method with an exclusively "bundle theory" of consciousness (that consciousness "could always be different"). From that it follows, he argues, that empiricism is insufficient for an understanding of the critical subject. Significantly, this argument shows that Adorno's position does not follow idealism in proposing subjectivity as the first principle of experience. Instead he is arguing against the misapplication of a method, one that reifies the subjective element.

In its consequences this approach is interestingly similar to objections that have been made by various contemporary philosophers against the reduction of subject-consciousness to physical reality.

The Role of Subjectivity

Thomas Nagel provides a clear account of what is entailed by this reduction. Nagel, on grounds that are close to Adorno, defends "the first-person perspective" against its diminution by "objective methods" of description. Unlike Adorno, who offers a transcendental account of experience, Nagel bases his position on something he takes to be experientially self-evident, first-person experience. He writes:

> [F]undamentally an organism has conscious mental states if and only if there is something that it is like to *be* that organism—something it is like *for* the organism.
> We may call this the subjective character of experience. It is not captured by any of the familiar, recently devised reductive analyses of the mental, for all of them are logically compatible with its absence.[14]

The emphasis here on the experience of subjectivity is important in that it marks out the key feature of the subject that cannot be translated into purely physical terms. In essence, Nagel rejects the reduction of first person experience to third person explanation on the basis that the latter does not and cannot include the idea of "what it's like to be," the *qualia* of mental life. No matter how comprehensive our description of the subjective perspective is, that description is not identical with the experience of that perspective. It is from this experience that Nagel's version of the distinction between subjective and objective arises: the subjective perspective versus the objective method that excludes perspectives.

Nagel goes further with this principle and concludes that mind and body cannot be essentially the same: the former is characterized by the subjective perspective whilst the latter is intelligible in the terms provided by the "objective" sciences. Nagel's difficulty is that he cannot set up this distinction between subjective and objective without committing himself to some form of epistemological dualism. In contrast, Adorno's version of the first-person question seems to avoid the two following and closely related problems, which Nagel identifies as inevitable perils: dualism and the construction of an independent *Cogito*. As Nagel puts it: "The irreducible subjectivity of the mental can make it seem radically independent of everything else, so that if one rejects psychophysical reductionism one is committed to the denial of any necessary connection between the mental and the physical";[15]

"The concept of the self seems suspiciously pure—too pure—when we look at it from inside. The self is the ultimate private object, apparently lacking logical connections to anything else, mental or physical. When I consider my own individual life from inside, it seems that my existence in the future or the past—the existence of the same 'I' as this one—depends on nothing but itself."[16] Adorno's principle of mediation can here be used as an epistemological alternative to physicalism and dualism. What this involves is that a hard physicalism that eliminated all distinctions between subject and object would be incapable of explaining experience. Without some distinctive characterization of subjectivity, however, we could never accurately explain the nature of experience since the qualitative distinction between subject and object, which Adorno delicately defines in order to accommodate the physical and mentalistic aspects of experience, is simply not acknowledged in any sense. The dualist concept of a radically independent subject is similarly incapable of explaining experience. According to the principle of mediation the idea of a radically independent subject is an aporetic hypostatization: it stands outside the conditions of mediation and is therefore epistemologically incoherent. Adorno, for these reasons, does not see the replacement of physicalism with idealism as the solution to the problem (unlike some other critics of physicalism)[17] since idealism is a foundationalist, subject-based approach to the question. As he notes: "The controversy about the priority of mind and body is a pre-dialectical proceeding. It carries on the question of a 'first.' All but hylozoistically aiming at an $\dot{\alpha}\rho\chi\acute{\eta}$, it is ontological in form although the answer may sound materialist in substance. Both body and mind are abstractions of their experience" (*ND* 202/202). It is on these grounds that Adorno rejects the antinomical options of physicalism and dualism. This is what I term Adorno's *epistemological solution*, in that it questions the ability of either traditional option to explain the structure of experience. We can see that Adorno's position is not established simply by finding a new way of accommodating subject consciousness within a nondualist account of epistemology. Rather, he offers a radical approach that (unlike Nagel) questions the legitimacy of the antinomical terms provided by the tradition.

Nagel's difficulties arise as a result of his reluctant belief in the dualism of subject consciousness and physical objectivity. In short, there are, according to Nagel, two distinct realities in the world, neither of which can be understood in terms of the other. Adorno is able to bypass this question by focusing on the epistemological efficaciousness of the subject. In this respect he is quite Kantian. He does not pursue the question, which was undermined in the Paralogisms, of *what kind of thing* the subject is, but, rather, the critical question of *what it does*, and what it does is distinguishable from the activity of material objects. Yet no dualism can be derived from this distinction because experience is the interdetermination of the subject and the object: "But spirit [*Geist*] can as little be separated from the given as the given from spirit. Neither is a first" (*ME* 32/24).

It seems to me in this respect that John Searle has an antireductionist argument that is quite close to Adorno's. Like Adorno, and unlike Nagel, Searle is interested in undermining structures that have given rise to reductionism, rather than the allegedly authoritative experiences that cannot be reduced. His approach may be characterized as "critical" for that reason. Searle holds the view that subject consciousness is irreducible, and also wants to show that this does not give rise to dualism. He argues against the physicalist reductive model and method, without at any time suggesting some privileged status for the subject.[18] His critical suggestion is that it is our "definitional practices"[19] which force us to make the distinction that introduces the reduction. That is, the ways in which our definitional practices divide up reality give rise to difficulties between what we call objective and what remains as subjective. Our definitional practices have given rise to a problematic distinction between "objective physical reality" and "subjective appearance"; a world that is real and verifiable and a realm that cannot be proven in like manner. Searle argues that the dichotomy contained in this distinction is false because both subject and object are appearance: they are both aspects of the world. Neither is more fundamental.

I would suggest that Adorno's position can give an interesting and alternative formulation of this claim. His account of the epistemological relation between subject and object justifies the terms "subject" and "object" themselves since they emerge as the elements of epistemological analysis. That is, without an epistemology it is not clear how the differentiation of subjectivity and objectivity can make much sense. For that reason there are thoroughgoing epistemological implications in Adorno's account of "irreducibility" that do not arise for someone like Searle. For Adorno the subject is not merely that which *cannot* be entirely explained in physical terms. By virtue of the thesis of mediation, the subject is a constitutive element of objectivity. Searle, it might be suggested, is also committed to the idea that the subject is an essential part of the world. But that is not precisely Adorno's point. Adorno's view about the contribution of subjectivity entails epistemological claims that, as I have argued above, are cashed out in terms of a substantial, nondualist distinction between subject and object. This is where Adorno's position really parts company with Searle's. Adorno focuses on the subject from the point of view of a reconstituted epistemology. In this light subjectivity has to be understood as mediational. What this involves is that truth and knowledge are ineluctably (*though not exclusively*) related to subjectivity. Adorno argues that subjectivity cannot be subtracted from the epistemic acts. Knowledge, as the principle of mediation is supposed to explain, is a complex of internal and external conditions.

The principle of mediation, then, provides a useful alternative to some of the contemporary efforts that have been made to affirm the necessity of subjectivity. Adorno understands subjectivity as a product of mediation and it follows from this that the idea of reducibility is based on the mistaken assumption that subjectivity is the same as physical objectivity. Such an assumption excludes any consideration of the epistemological role of the subject. If dualism is correct, on the other hand, then it is easy to see that its proponents have to make quite unattractive claims about the nature of subjectivity in order to make the reducibility of the subject impossible. I have tried to show that Adorno's epistemology provides a framework which avoids a problematic dualism, yet also offers a structural explanation of the basis of the very distinction between subject and object.

4
The Critique of Kant

In chapter 1 I examined those elements of Kant's and Hegel's philosophies that would provide argumentative support for certain principles that Adorno wants to establish. In the previous chapter I looked at, among other things, Adorno's disagreements with Hegel, disagreements that mark the limitations of Adorno's appropriation of Hegel and highlight, I think, some of his more significant philosophical commitments. In this chapter I want to undertake a similar analysis of Adorno's relation to Kant.

Adorno trenchantly criticizes some of the major principles of transcendental idealism, principles that, according to him, carry idealist implications. He is not alone in seeing transcendental idealism as containing residual elements of subjective idealism (nor is he perhaps accurate in so doing, as we shall see). In spite of Adorno's objection to Kant's alleged idealism he is at the same time, as we have seen, drawn to what we might call an unofficial Kant, the Kant whose philosophy is characterized exclusively as a critique of subjective idealism. What I want to do here is to reconstruct Adorno's critique of those parts of Kant's philosophy which for Adorno remain problematically within the sphere of subjective idealism, those parts that are inseparable from the idea of what Adorno criticizes as "constitutive subjectivity."

The basis of Adorno's unease with transcendental idealism is his view that Kant overplays the notion of a spontaneous subject. Because Kant's account of experience emphasizes the positive contribution of the "faculty of knowledge" or cognition it leaves itself with an insufficient account of what it is in the object that can delimit the activity of subjectivity. The result, Adorno believes, is a version of experience that valorizes a spontaneous mastering subject, one unconstrained by the qualities of objects. What is required, however—as Adorno's subject–object mediation theory proposes—is an account of a subject that can critically engage its environment from within its environment, as opposed to a subject that is allegedly explained as its apparent author: "[The subject's] absolute in-itself," Adorno remarks, "is merely absolute delusion about its own subjective mediacy" (*ME* 29/22).

Adorno criticizes transcendental idealism from the perspective of the materialist position he has developed (as set out in the two previous chapters).[1] Since that position has been established by his critical appropriation of certain parts of Kant—Kant the materialist anti-idealist—it is not too fanciful to suggest that his critique of transcendental idealism may be considered by Adorno himself in part as a reading of *Kant against Kant*. We can say, to put it broadly, that Adorno criticizes Kant by implicating Kant in theories that Kant himself had sought to deny. He tries to expose what he sees as the inherent ambivalences of Kant's philosophy. In this regard he notes that Kant's philosophy operates in a *Zwischenreich* (an in-between realm) (*KK* 40) in which it labors to avoid the problems of idealism and empiricism. However, the *Zwischenreich*, Adorno argues, is an illusion that collapses as soon as the commitments of transcendental philosophy are actually applied to experience.

Kant is not, of course, the only philosopher with whom Adorno expresses serious theoretical differences. His texts are littered with criticisms of Hegel (as we have seen), Husserl, Heidegger, and the catchall version of empiricist-analytic philosophy that he calls "positivism" (not to mention Adorno's early book on Kierkegaard). What we must understand is that these criticisms are intended as "occasions" (*ME* 9/1), to use Adorno's phrase, for the exploration of the commitments of his own position. But his critique of Kant together with the critique of Hegel are of greatest significance since they give sharper definition to the elements of the philosophy that he has appropriated. Thus they enable us to ask questions that, I suspect, were important to Adorno himself: what kind of Kantian or Hegelian is he? A further reason for looking at Kant in particular is that Adorno contends that his philosophy is guided by a fundamental concern with the problem of constitutive subjectivity. In the subjective idealism with which Adorno takes issue constitutive subjectivity is supposed to be the basis of all possible knowledge. That is, the world is unintelligible without reference back to a subject understood as the constituting agent at least of the experience of the world, if not of the world itself. It was Kant, in Adorno's view, who gave the principle its most important expression. In the preface to *Negative Dialectics* Adorno proclaims the central motivation of his own philosophy: "To use the strength of the subject to break through the fallacy of constitutive subjectivity—this is what the author felt to be his task since he came to trust his own mental impulses . . ." (*ND* 10/xx), and it is clear that the notion of constitutive subjectivity applies to a whole range of philosophers from Kant to Husserl. At which point in his career that self-confidence emerged is not clear. Whether it goes back as far as those famous private tutorials with Kracauer is a matter for speculation. What we can be sure of, however, is that Adorno saw his "task" as conducted largely through a critique of Kant.

The idea that the work of another philosopher is an "occasion" for the development of Adorno's position is not perhaps fully satisfying in that it seems to exploit rather than to understand the philosopher who provides the "occasion." It can seem that the need for scholarly accuracy is eschewed, and a defense against pedantic criticism of the critiques offered by Adorno thereby avoided. After all if the philosophers whom Adorno criticizes are merely occasions then they are archetypes (of Adorno's own constructing) and not the philosophers necessarily to be found in the complex texts in which they endeavor to set out and defend their positions. That is indeed a danger, and none of Adorno's readings of the history of philosophy is entirely devoid of this characteristic. (I will note the problems of accuracy in those readings as they arise.) However, it would also be unproductive to parody Adorno's criticisms: what makes his criticisms worth reading in addition to their ability to refine his own commitments is that Adorno actually has some significant observations to share about the inherent limitations of the positions he criticizes.

Adorno's criticisms of Kant's epistemology fall into two parts; first, an analysis of the very idea of constitutive subjectivity, and second, an analysis of epistemological self-consciousness, that is, of Kant's theory of the "I think."

1 Adorno's Early Criticisms of Kant

Before turning to an analysis of Adorno's critique of Kant I should like to explore, briefly, the Kantian prehistory of Adorno's mature philosophy. I call it prehistory because all of the academic work that Adorno completed prior to 1931 was heavily marked by the neo-Kantianism of his supervisor, Hans Cornelius. Nevertheless, this prehistory to some extent provides corroborating evidence for my claim that Adorno was deeply concerned with and aware of certain *internal incoherencies* in transcendental idealism (concerned, that is, with a reading of Kant against Kant). Even in his early work, Adorno identified inconsistencies in transcendental idealism—covered over as a *Zwischenreich*, to use the later metaphor—between constitutive and empirical subjectivity, as is apparent in his turning the argument of the Paralogisms section against the general strategy of the first *Critique*.

In order to deal fully with the relevance of the early Adorno's Kantianism to this study it would be necessary to examine the following range of issues: the form of Kantianism developed by Adorno's first important mentor, Cornelius; the influence of Cornelius on Adorno's doctoral dissertation, *The Transcendence of the Real and Noematic in Husserl's Phenomenology* (1924) and his first (though never submitted) *Habilitationsschrift*, *The Concept of the Unconscious in Transcendental Psychology* (1927);[2] and the possible continuities between this early period and Adorno's mature publications. Clearly, such a comprehensive undertaking is impossible here. I want to suggest briefly, though, that a study along these lines would reveal some important answers. It would show, first, that Adorno's early immersion in the problems of transcendental philosophy amounted, as already mentioned, to an *internal* debate within the Kantian tradition regarding the correct structure of transcendental philosophy and, second, that certain critical principles that Adorno was later to employ as part of his mature philosophical vocabulary are already discernible. By the first claim I mean that

The Critique of Kant

Adorno generally employed, in *The Concept of the Unconscious*, a Kantian critique of Kant.

However, the form of transcendental philosophy that he adopted in that work was the neo-Kantianism of Hans Cornelius. Cornelius proposed a thoroughgoing version of transcendental idealism that would attempt to widen the scope of the original version, and Adorno seems to have followed Cornelius quite closely in this respect. Indeed so strong is the influence of Cornelius that we must conclude that Adorno had not yet developed philosophical autonomy. His editor, Rolf Tiedemann, puts it as follows: "*The Concept of the Unconscious* and the early work on Husserl are school philosophy: works by a student of Hans Cornelius . . ."[3] Both the dissertation and the *Habilitationsschrift* "place themselves unreservedly within the standpoint of Cornelius' version of transcendental idealism."[4] This is apparently corroborated by Adorno's acknowledgement of his debt to Cornelius. Yet there are moments of originality—or at least of distinctive arguments—in the *Habilitationsschrift* that are noteworthy.

In the foreword to the *Habilitationsschrift* Adorno makes the following claim: "The epistemological standpoint presupposed here is that of Hans Cornelius, as presented in his book, *Transcendental Systematics*. We presuppose this standpoint everywhere and thus refrain from expressly citing it everywhere" (*BU* 81).[5] Despite this admission of his dependency on Cornelius there is at least one aspect of the work that Adorno wants to identify as his own product. He proudly announces that "the section on Kant's Paralogisms was already completed before the publication of Cornelius' commentary on Kant" (*BU* 81).[6] In fact in the section in question, entitled "Kant's Doctrine of the Psychological Paralogisms and the Idea of Transcendental Psychology," Adorno displays the philosophical ambivalence toward Kant that he was to demonstrate in all of his major subsequent works.

The prevailing theme of *The Concept of the Unconscious* is Adorno's effort to trace the philosophical significance of the idea of the unconscious. At this stage of his career he took the Freudian model of the unconscious quite seriously. Consequently he used it as a means of criticizing transcendental philosophy. His critical question was: could transcendental philosophy accommodate the idea of the unconscious? In his later work Adorno entirely abandoned this question. Ultimately, he held no doctrinaire or dogmatic views about the unconscious. In the early period, however, it was a critical issue, and Kant's failure to treat of it forced Adorno to conclude the Paralogisms section negatively: "We leave now Kant's doctrine of the psychological Paralogisms. The doctrine has clearly shown us that the Kantian critique of rational psychology allows no room for the concept of the unconscious within the framework of transcendental knowledge" (*BU* 174). This claim when taken together with Adorno's abandonment of a philosophy of the unconscious might seem to suggest that this early work has curiosity value at best: it contains a set of views that did not last into Adorno's later career.

The body of Adorno's arguments, however, is more important. He holds two views of the Paralogisms, though in a sporadic and unsystematic way: first, that Kant's critique of dogmatic idealism is broadly correct, and second, that the synthetic unity of apperception is possible only because of the experiential content of thought. This second principle means that if the reason the synthetic unity of apperception is possible is its experiential context then the *pure* independence of the "I think" is undermined. This second important claim is made in the following way: "The Kantian claim to derive transcendental psychology from the 'I think' would be correct if the 'I think' were actually understood as the unity of consciousness. Then, certainly, this 'I' would no longer be bare logical unity, but would take hold of 'the collected manifoldness of its experience in itself' [Cornelius]. The unity of my consciousness, then, is nothing other than the unity of my experiences, and has no validity whatsoever in independence from the connection of my experience. Kant, however, certainly does not want to grant this . . ." (*BU* 162). What Adorno is arguing here is that the Paralogisms assume that rational psychology is working with some equivalent, though misconstrued, notion of the "I think." This is not the case, according to Adorno. In fact, the form of consciousness assumed by rational psychology does contain actual thoughts and is not and cannot be the merely formal "I think." If the "I think" is conceived as a principle that has something to do with the unity of consciousness then it soon becomes apparent that it will have to forego the "purity" that is initially claimed for it. Adorno criticizes the very idea of pure apperception along

The Critique of Kant

these lines: "The 'I think' does not alone mean the formal unity of a represented subject of thinking (= *x*), but, as already said, the actual unity of my experiences in the empirical life of consciousness [*Bewußtseinsverlauf*]" (*BU* 163). This principle can be seen in effective employment throughout Adorno's career-long engagement with Kantian philosophy. Below we can see, in fact, that this principle is eventually developed by Adorno into one side of what he identifies as the antinomy of transcendental idealism.

But, as mentioned, Adorno's *Habilitationsschrift* is not entirely critical of Kant's Paralogisms. Adorno's criticisms are applicable to the extent that Kant relies upon the concept of the "I think" as the source of rational psychology. What remains is that the Paralogisms, in Adorno's view, correctly identify the proper experiential conditions within which consciousness is possible. This has obvious implications for the ego entities of idealist psychology. In relation to the first Paralogism (on the substantiality of the soul), Adorno writes: "Kant determined with unquestionable justification that from this substantial concept of the 'I'—which in the sense of the system of principles can only be applied to the objects [*Gegenstände*] of experience, not persistence [*Fortdauer*] etc.—the soul could not be inferred; because through those positings [*Setzungen*] the limits of the possibility of experience would be exceeded" (*BU* 165–166). What is important here is that Adorno gives credit to Kant for a principle that we will see him use against Kant: namely, that the conditions of consciousness are empirical, and that for that reason the "I think" cannot be allowed to be merely formal. In other words, if the "I think" is to be a condition of consciousness then it too must be empirical. Thus the insights of the Paralogisms are used to check the central principle of transcendental subjectivity: the transcendental unity of apperception.

Having said that, it would be a mistake to claim that Adorno had defined the essential core of his attitude to Kant at this early stage. Despite the two principles that I have picked out—that the synthetic unity of apperception is incoherent and that the Paralogisms are correct with regard to the rejection of a self-sufficient subject—Adorno's differences with Kant are at this time, in general, the result of his view that Kant's transcendental idealism is not sufficiently thoroughgoing: that is, it is not capable of including certain phenomena within the required explanation. Adorno, under Cornelius's influence, hoped to improve upon Kant in precisely that respect. This can be seen most vividly in his disagreement with Kant's attempt to distinguish between subject and object within transcendental idealism. Adorno, in line with his then Cornelius-inspired conception of an extended transcendental idealism, proposes his own radically immanentist solution: "Here, subject and object, however, are not ontologically separated, but rather 'subjective' and 'objective' signify different ways of the structure of the given: that is, 'subjective,' in *our* sense, is only the abstractive, separated out, immediate given as such, the 'objective' existing through the transcendental conditions of constituted connection" (*BU* 174). These views, with their idealist (indeed phenomenological sounding) reduction to the subject, are entirely at odds with Adorno's later subject-object theory. But the differences should not obscure some less obvious but historically important continuities. What the *Habilitationsschrift* shows is Adorno's early immersion in the technical if not scholastic problems of transcendental idealism, and that even then Adorno was prepared to correct the idea of a transcendental subject by means of some of Kant's antidualist arguments.

2 Constitutive Subjectivity

A key element of any conception of constitutive subjectivity is some notion of what Kant termed "spontaneity." To assert the "priority of subjectivity" we need to establish a notion of agency in some sense not determined by material reality. This idea also holds, in some way, for Kant's transcendental idealism. It is essential to his version of idealism that he sustains a working notion of spontaneity, as otherwise, obviously enough, he would be unable to gain significant advantage over empiricism. The precise meaning of spontaneity is complex, however, owing to Kant's contrastive way of defining it. It is, in effect, contrasted with the more easily intelligible idea of receptivity in empiricism. (And in the practical philosophy spontaneity contrasts with action that is causally determined.) According to Kant, we have a transcendental capacity for the application of rules or of judgments, and this capacity is exercised spontaneously. These rules reflect human modes of understanding, rather than information of some kind that is given to us by the object. The notion of spontaneity is a key element of Kant's response to Humean skepticism, a skepticism that was the logical implication of a purely receptive epistemology.

Modest though the Kantian account of spontaneity is—in that it explains the subjective aspect of experience as the application of certain circumscribed rules—Adorno nevertheless sees it leading directly to subjective idealism. His contention is that in Kant's account of the "I think" our judgments are not constrained by any causal or determinative features of the object. At most, the thing-in-itself underlies these judgments, but cannot, by definition, influence them: our judgments, then, do not necessarily reflect the nature of the object as it is in-itself. This extravagant interpretation of Kant is by no means unique. In a way Adorno here rather simply adopts the reading of Kant made popular by Hegel's history of philosophy and pays little attention to the details of Kant's actual argument. This is a serious limitation, which at times undermines the force of Adorno's criticisms. In this context it is important that we be clear about the applicability of Adorno's claims about "constitution." For that reason I will now delay the presentation of Adorno's position with an account of Kant's Transcendental Deduction.

Experience, Kant tells us, gives us objects that are "combined"; that is, not just scattered bits of information stuck together, not even objects that we see as bundles of qualities (Hume). Rather, they are experienced as combined wholes. The source of the "combination," Kant argues, cannot be the senses, since the senses provide us only with sensory aspects of things, not the things as "combinations." "Combination" is therefore spontaneous, Kant believes: it is a concept supplied by the so-called faculty of representation. That is, it is a quality of experience that can be traced back to our modes of representing objects, rather than the way that things are given to us. He writes: "But the combination [*conjunctio*] of a manifold in general can never come to us through the senses, and cannot, therefore, be already contained in the pure form of sensible intuition. For it is an act of spontaneity of the faculty of representation . . ." (*CPR* B129). The "subjective" quality of this activity is emphasized by Kant's further clarification: "To this act the general title 'synthesis' may be assigned, as indicating that we cannot represent to ourselves anything as combined in the object which we have not ourselves previously combined, and that of all representations *combination* is the only one which cannot be given through objects" (*CPR* B129). There must be a persistent "subjective" element, in effect, that supplies the quality of combination; there must be, that is, some aspect of experience that is not reducible to empirical passivity. For Kant, then, the possibility of experience must assume a self with some quality of identity. Kant calls this identical quality the "I think." And it is necessary for the possibility of knowledge for the following reason: "It must be possible for the 'I think' to accompany all my representations; for otherwise something would be represented in me which could not be thought at all, and that is equivalent to saying that the representation would be impossible, or at least would be nothing to me ..." (*CPR* B131–132). It is, then, a logical property of experience that there is an "I" quality. However Kant makes the further substantial claim that this "I" quality must have identity over time, otherwise, as he puts it, "I should have as many-coloured and diverse a self as I have representations of which I am conscious to myself" (*CPR* B134). The accompanying "I think," then, is the condition under which our empirical experience exhibits coherence (insofar as it is combined). The temptation to which the early German Idealists responded was to see in this the possibility of a spontaneous agent, rather than a mere logical condition.

The "I think" is characterized as spontaneous in that it is not given through experience—rather it must be presupposed if experience is to happen at all. (It is a priori.) As a representation bearing the quality of identity it cannot simply emerge from experience since identity is never a feature of purely sensory knowledge: "But this representation, 'I think,' is an act of *spontaneity*; that is to say, it cannot be regarded as belonging to mere sensibility" (*CPR* B132).

One of the most striking claims that Kant makes here, almost *en passant*, is that all knowing is implicitly self-conscious knowing in that it is the conscious possession of a thinker, the "I think": "I call it *pure apperception*, to distinguish it from empirical apperception, or, again, *original apperception*, because it is that self-consciousness which, while

The Critique of Kant

generating the representation '*I think*' ... cannot itself be accompanied by any further representation" (*CPR* B132). And it is transcendental in that it is a condition of knowledge; that is, it must be present if knowledge is to arise at all: "The unity of this apperception I likewise entitle the *transcendental* unity of self-consciousness, in order to indicate the possibility of *a priori* knowledge arising from it" (*CPR* B132). The *synthetic unity of apperception/self-consciousness* brings together/synthesizes the manifold of intuition—what we get/receive through the senses—under the categories and gives it the coherence that we experience in objects: "For the manifold representations, which are given in an intuition, would not be one and all *my* representations, if they did not all belong to one self-consciousness. As *my* representations (even if I am not conscious of them as such) they must conform to the condition under which alone they *can* stand together in one universal self-consciousness, because otherwise they would not all without exception belong to me" (*CPR* B132–133). Kant's discussion endeavors, as we see, to restrict the analysis of experience to the purely logical conditions of any epistemic claims.[7] I have noted that Adorno is unwilling to see this. Nevertheless he at times skillfully identifies problematic aspects of Kant's claim to have avoided subjective idealism: that is, the evidence of the first *Critique* does not always support a purely formal idealism. In the next section I want to examine Adorno's problematization of Kant's transcendental idealism through the concepts he has developed in his theory of experience.

3 Constitution in Kant's Notion of Intuition: The Transcendental Aesthetic

It is usually through a reading of the Transcendental Deduction that the case against Kant is made that his philosophy does not successfully avoid subjective idealism. Adorno, as mentioned, will argue that too, albeit with arguments drawn from his particular philosophical tradition. But he also contends, and this is a controversial matter, that the Transcendental Aesthetic section of the *Critique of Pure Reason*—a section which contains no reference to a thinking self—presupposes an idealistic account of experience. I will examine

Adorno's controversial position in this section. To an extent we will be already partly aware of Adorno's view of the Transcendental Aesthetic from an earlier discussion (in chapter 2) of Adorno's account of nonidentity. I noted then that the idea of intuition—a central element of the Transcendental Aesthetic—in Kant might serve Adorno's purposes very well, but that Adorno finds in this idea little but idealism. In this section we shall see why.

The Transcendental Aesthetic is an attempt to prove that space and time belong to the "subjective constitution [*Beschaffenheit*] of our mind" (*CPR* A23/B38). It concludes, after certain arguments, with the view that, "If our subjective constitution be removed, the represented object, which sensible intuition bestows upon it, is nowhere to be found, and cannot possibly be found. For it is this subjective constitution which determines its form as appearance" (*CPR* A44/B62). The point here is that the mind is the apparatus with which we intuit. And, as it so happens, space and time belong to the subjective constitution [*Beschaffenheit*] we have as human beings: space and time are our human modes of intuition. These modes of intuition take the form of inner and outer sense respectively. Thus we intuit the temporality of all objects through the mode of inner sense and the spatiality of objects through outer sense. This is a claim made on the basis of an implicit assumption of the existence of a constituting subject: the acts of intuition through which sensibility is constituted in space and time are subjective. But if subjective intuition is constitutive—all objects must conform to our modes of intuition—then we must, as Adorno will, conclude that constitution is an activity that is not limited to the understanding, the level of judgment.[8]

Kant attempts to demarcate the issues of the Transcendental Aesthetic from the issue of constitution. The Transcendental Aesthetic deals with intuition—the form in which the manifold is delivered to sensibility—whereas constitution is supposedly connected with the activity of understanding—the point at which "understandability" is introduced to experience. But since Kant considers space and time to be attributable to the subject, not to the world as it is independently of us, it seems like a mere terminological device to deny that the activity described in the Transcendental Aesthetic is not fundamentally constitutive. For Adorno, the fact that it does not have any explicit theoretical reference to subjectivity is not really important enough to avoid the fundamental similarity between intuition and constitution. He argues that the Transcendental Aesthetic is in fact dependent on the notion of constitution as later specified in the Transcendental Analytic: "the Transcendental Aesthetic is actually a function of the Transcendental Logic ..." (*KK* 338).

When we consider Kant's notion of positing in the Transcendental Aesthetic we can see that Adorno's suspicions about the commitments behind the notion of intuition are at least interesting. Kant holds that since representations must always appear in a fixed temporal order, all empirical appearances as representations are, essentially, the mind affecting itself. In other words, my empirical experience is temporal, but that temporality is the product of the "constitutive" faculty of inner sense. Whatever is known to me as existing independently in space and time is *posited* as other than me. Whatever way Kant may like to divide experience, positing—Kant's technical term for the activity of intuiting—is ultimately an activity that is the product of constitutive subjectivity. In the Transcendental Aesthetic Kant writes: "Since form does not represent anything save in so far as it is posited in the mind [*im Gemüte gesetzt wird*], it can be nothing but the mode in which the mind is affected through its own activity (namely through this positing [*Setzen*] of its representations), and so is affected by itself; in other words, it is nothing but an inner sense in respect of the form of that sense" (*CPR* B67–68). This account of positing certainly seems to emphasize the subjective structure of experience. It thereby attempts to account for the apparently independent cause of experience, givenness, in purely mental terms. (I shall return later to this point.) The very "appearing" of objects is explicable within the categories of constitutive subjectivity: "That which, while inseparable from the representation of the object, is not to be met with in the object in itself, but always in its relation to the subject, is appearance" (*CPR* B70n). The outcome of the Transcendental Aesthetic is, according to Adorno's interpretation, a claim for the ideality of experience. Hence experience is explained by some spontaneous action of the subject.

Adorno questions whether we can neatly divide the actions of the subject so as to produce experiential and constitutive explanations of the same features of experience. That is, how can experience be the product of both empirical and constitutive modes of the subject? Adorno argues that attempts to have it both ways are possible only because Kant operates with a fundamentally ambiguous notion of intuition. When this ambiguity is identified, Kant's concept of intuition can be seen to contain an impossibility; namely, that space and time are "on the one hand intuitions and, on the other, 'forms'" (*ME* 152/147). Kant's doctrine of intuition, according to Adorno, is committed to an "irresolvable contradiction" (*ME* 151/146): "The contradiction is linguistically indicated by the nomenclature 'pure intuition' for space and time. Intuition as immediate sense-certainty, as givenness in the figure of the subject, names a type of experience, which precisely as such cannot be 'pure' and independent of experience. Pure intuition is a square circle, experience without experience"[9] (*ME* 151/146). Kant, according to Adorno, then, is engaged in a contradictory task when he tries to explain intuition as a pure form. Since intuition is a mode of experience it cannot be separated from experience. Kant, however, tries to make it preexperiential (transcendental). This arcane element of experience—intuition—lacks the capacity to explain experience intelligibly since it is beyond the conditions in which alone experience is operative, material reality. (And by material reality Adorno means that realm that is the complex result of subject–object mediation.)

In Adorno's view Kant's contradictory notion of intuition arises from his effort to retain a role for receptivity. The idea of intuition attempts to explain the subject's original point of receptivity. But it turns out that intuition is an ideal capacity of the subject in that Kant argues that objects are *posited* as spatial and temporal through intuition. It therefore seems that intuition is both receptive *and* ideal. The result, as Adorno remarks, is that givenness is mysteriously transformed into "something mediated" (*ME* 152/147): what we receive as immediate we have supplied to ourselves through our own experiential apparatus (hence it is mediated). It would seem to be important for Kant to maintain this distinction between immediacy and mediation for the following reason: since he wants to establish

The Critique of Kant

a form of idealism compatible with empirical realism he obviously needs to establish the difference between what is given nonconceptually (sensibility) and what is established by concepts, this distinction being absolutely central to empirical realism. But, in Adorno's view, the idealization of receptivity means that this distinction cannot be realized. The very notion of what it is that is given to the categories is already caught up in a determinately idealistic framework. Adorno concludes that Kant's strategy contains the correlative principle that objects are empty. The emptier the object the more that must be explained through subjectivity. Kant introduces the ideas of intuition and categories to give just these explanations: "[T]he very exposition of the *Critique of Pure Reason* itself proves that what is absolutely subject independent, independent of that which is assigned to the subject, remains as something entirely empty and null" (*KK* 194).

The attempt to argue for a form of idealism in which spontaneity operates by means of formative or constitutive acts, but, at the same time, maintaining some ideal form of receptivity is, according to Adorno, the central tension within the concept of intuition, as found in the Transcendental Aesthetic.[10] The difficulty in such concepts as "ideal experience" and "ideal receptivity" is that "experience" and "receptivity" originally describe real, nonideal activities. If they are transposed to the allegedly ideal activities of the intellect then they seem to be fundamentally groundless.

4 Constitution and the Kantian Categories: The Transcendental Deduction

Determination (as discussed by Kant in the Transcendental Analytic), in contrast to positing, refers to the conceptual forms of the object that we encounter in experience.[11] Determination is, in Kant's schema, logically secondary to intuition. Kant's argument, in essence, is that the categories are spontaneously applied to the manifold—provided to us by intuition—and the manifold is determined accordingly: "All the manifold, therefore, so far as it is given in a single empirical intuition, is *determined* [*bestimmt*] in respect of one of the logical functions of judgment. . . . Now the categories are just these functions of judgment, in so far as they are employed in determination of the manifold of a given intuition. Consequently, the manifold in a given intuition is necessarily subject to the categories" (*CPR* B143). In a useful footnote Kant makes it clear that determination is to be seen as equivalent to spontaneity (the context of this definition is not important here): "... I cannot determine [*bestimmen*] my existence as that of a self-active being; all that I can do is to represent to myself the spontaneity of my thought, that is, of the determination" (*CPR* B158n). However, Kant's manner of making this connection between spontaneity and determination is immensely complex. Indeed it has given rise, one might argue, to the two traditions of philosophy: those who see Kant as the proponent of spontaneous subjectivity and those who understand him as explaining the conditions of our epistemic experience. For the latter the connection between "determination" and "spontaneity" is explained within the Transcendental Deduction as the rule-bearing structure of experience. For the former, however, it generates a myriad of temptations and criticisms.

The Refutation of Idealism and Paralogisms sections of the first *Critique* argue vigorously against the idea of an independent (self-founding) consciousness. Against this there is in Kant the concept of spontaneity, which, it seems to Adorno, requires a subjectivity that is in some respect independent of the conditions of the material world. Adorno exploits what he sees as this central tension within the Transcendental Analytic. As with the Transcendental Aesthetic the intended outcome of the Analytic is affected by the methodological contrast between spontaneous and receptive components of experience. We have already seen Adorno argue that both the act of intuition and that of understanding collapse into one another (since both are ideal acts). What then can be made of the distinction as it appears in the Transcendental Analytic?[12] And is Adorno wrong in thinking that the distinction between receptivity and spontaneity, as worked out by Kant, cannot be maintained? The spontaneity of understanding is logically dependent on the existence of an active agency that "constitutes" in accordance with its particular rules. This, however, is similar—similar enough for Adorno—to the subjective activity that is found in the Transcendental Aesthetic (even though the latter is not rule based in the way that the categories are). In the Aesthetic, the forms of intuition appear to be constitutive in that all objects are posited in space and time. The Transcendental Deduction and the Aesthetic, then, present the subject as both spontaneous and constitutive. (To add to the complexity: it is often assumed that the spontaneity of the "I think" in the Transcendental Deduction is analogous to the spontaneity that Kant requires for the possibility of moral freedom. The thought is that the epistemological and moral theory accounts of the spontaneity of the "I" similarly argue that the "I" acts spontaneously under laws, not passively on receipt of empirical information. But in the second *Critique* Kant makes a strong connection between the metaphysics of the Transcendental Aesthetic and the metaphysics of moral freedom: "[I]f the ideality of space and time is not assumed, only Spinozism [i.e. determinism] remains."[13] This introduces, then, yet further evidence in support of Adorno's contention that the doctrine of intuition—the central point of the Transcendental Aesthetic—has complicating idealistic implications.)

Kant certainly works hard to firm up the distinction between the respective activities of the Aesthetic and Deduction. He writes: "The categories of understanding ... do not represent the conditions under which objects are given in intuition. Objects may, therefore, appear to us without their being under the necessity of being related to the functions of understanding" (*CPR* A89/B122). It is important for Kant to demonstrate here why the categories are "spontaneously" applied. The Deduction set out to complete a transcendental idealist account of knowledge by showing that objects are necessarily known through the functions of the understanding: "[R]eceptivity can make knowledge possible only when combined with spontaneity" (*CPR* A97). But what must be noted is that the move from proving, as he believes he does, the objective validity of the categories to proving that they are spontaneously applied does not follow; that is, Kant has not shown that the categories are not purely responses to, say, inherently significant data supplied by sensibility. The fact that Kant insists upon transcendental spontaneity commits him, Adorno argues, to the idea of constitutive subjectivity. For Adorno, this argument, again, reveals a fatal tension in Kant's philosophy: as Adorno's effective restatement of the conclusion of the Refutation of Idealism puts it, "[s]ubjectivity changes its quality in a context which it is unable to evolve on its own" (*ND* 184/183). What Kant recognizes in the Refutation of Idealism is incompatible with the idea of constitutive subjectivity. Adorno's argument is that the conditions of subjectivity extend beyond the functions of the subject: subjectivity, in other words, cannot be accounted for without reference to conditions that are outside subjectivity, namely permanent objects in space and time. Adorno writes: "To Kant, every definition of the object is an investment of subjectivity in unqualitative diversity—regardless of the fact that the defining acts, which he takes for the spontaneous achievement of transcendental logic, will adjust to a moment which they themselves are not; regardless of the fact that we can synthesize only what will allow and require a synthesis on its own. The active definition is not something purely subjective; hence the triumph of the sovereign subject which dictates its laws to nature is a hollow triumph" (*ND* 142/138–139).

Following Adorno's reading of the first *Critique* we might regard the Transcendental Aesthetic and the Transcendental Analytic as offering two forms of constitution, those of (posited) sensibility and that of (determined) objects respectively. Both levels of constitution are allegedly types of formative acts. If so, Kant's contrast between the receptivity of intuition and the spontaneity of forms is undermined: "Concepts are based on the spontaneity of thought, sensible intuitions on the receptivity of impressions" (*CPR* A68/B93). Adorno points out that this contrast is not ultimately supported by the account of sensibility given in the Transcendental Aesthetic. The very effort to construct arguments for the apriority of space and time is possible only because of what Adorno sees as an ambiguity built into Kant's notion of intuition: intuition is passive, yet formal (it is operative only as the forms of space and time). However problematic it may be, sensibility, in Kant's view, must have an ideal and hence spontaneous basis. That, of course, leaves us with the difficulty that Adorno identifies: we are to think of intuitions as pure (that is, as a priori)—lest they be empirical—but experiential in some sense. But by thinking of them as experiential we contradict the very idea of pure form. For Adorno, these aporias within Kant's idealism are debilitating. Since for Adorno Kant's is perhaps the most rigorous statement of constitutive subjectivity, this failure, in Adorno's view, has implications a fortiori for the entire tradition that follows.

5 The Antinomy of the "I think": Adorno's "Anthropological-materialist" Critique

The "I think" is the central concept in Kant's transcendental idealism. We have already seen Kant's account of it as a logical component of experience. If it is more than this it becomes an element of subjective idealism. Adorno, as we shall see, is dissatisfied with the claim that Kant can sustain a purely transcendental "I think." Ultimately he argues that if the "I think" is effectively to guarantee the continuity of our experience it cannot be simply a logical condition or a question of "validity," as Sartre puts it.[14] And as soon as it is acknowledged that it must be more than this condition further questions about its relation to objects may be raised.

Adorno's strategy for reading the "I think" might be called—to borrow one of his own terms—an "anthropological-materialist" critique.[15] This anthropological-materialist critique has two main lines. First, it holds that claims for the reality of the "I think" are incoherent since they are irrevocably committed to the mistaken belief that the "I think" is an individual entity, even though it does not conform to the conditions that make the indexical "I" appropriate. Second, it attempts to demonstrate that the alleged transcendental reality of the "I think" involves an irreparable separation of transcendental and empirical aspects of the self. This results in the impossibility of our being able to explain key features of the empirical world. I would say that this part of Adorno's critique of Kant is particularly acute in that it relies on a relatively uncontroversial assumption about Kant's project. It neatly presses the question of what the "I think" is without necessarily assuming the questionable Hegelian view that Kant is committed in some way to a subjective idealism. Rather it analyzes the idea of the "I think" in terms that are recognizable within contemporary Kant scholarship and yet also manages to arrive at (what I regard as) devastating conclusions about the fundamental possibility of transcendental idealism.

Adorno's anthropological-materialist critique involves, then, tracing all alleged transcendental qualities or conditions back to those of material experience: the point of their origin. As will be seen, this strategy reveals a *critical antinomy* in Kant's position: *either* the "I think" can be identified as a pronominal indexical—it is phenomenal—thus representing nothing beyond the empirical, and it thereby fails to be intelligible as an a priori condition of empirical consciousness; *or* the "I think" is beyond the empirical—it is noumenal—in which case it would appear to stand in no explanatory relation to the empirical. (Interestingly, Adorno's *The Concept of the Unconscious*, as we have seen, had already registered disagreements with Kant to the effect that the transcendental made sense only if it was understood as empirically grounded.)

5.1 The "I Think" Is Phenomenal

Kant's views about the phenomenality of the "I think" are quite confusing. The main reason for this is that the "I think" is given diverging functions in the Analytic and the Paralogisms. In the latter, the "I think" is defined, perhaps, with too much stress upon its distinction from the *Cogito*. Indeed, Kant's tentativeness here in relation to what he will allow regarding knowledge of the "I think" is at odds with statements that he makes earlier in the first *Critique*. Thus, in the Paralogisms, the "I think" is almost always referred to as a proposition. Specifically, it is an empirical proposition: "The 'I think' is ... an empirical proposition and contains within itself the proposition 'I exist'" (*CPR* B422n). And, "The proposition, 'I think' or 'I exist thinking,' is an empirical proposition" (*CPR* B428).

This claim may seem to be a relatively uncontentious rejection of the Cartesian conception of mind. From a strictly Kantian point of view, however, it is deeply problematic. The first problem is that if the reality to which the proposition "I think" refers is phenomenal then it must have some appearance. But if it is perceivable then it can no longer be part of the combinate form—the synthetic unity—that gives rise to empirical or phenomenal consciousness. This is because precisely as perceivable it is thereby already part of that phenomenon of consciousness. To put it another way, a phenomenal "I think"

The Critique of Kant

could hardly be distinguished from an empirical self, at least not to any extent that could allow it to act as a ground of empirical consciousness. A phenomenal "I think" would contradict the idea of the transcendental unity of apperception. Since all phenomenal objects are in some sense produced by the transcendental unity of apperception it would be contradictory to claim that the "I think," which is part of that unity, is itself phenomenal: it would be aporetically part of the same givenness which its priority is supposed to explain. Adorno states this problem in the following way: "It [the 'I think'] must obviously not be the spatio-temporal, empirical and already constituted [*bereits konstituierte*] subject. Otherwise the necessary condition for the concept of givenness would be precisely what, in the wake of the entire tradition since Hume and Kant, turns out to be a structure of the given" (*ME* 147/142). Adorno argues that as soon as we are able to identify the "I think" in empirical terms its status (as the ground of experience) is denied as a consequence.[16] He writes: "That the I is an entity is implicit even in the sense of the logical 'I think,' which should be able to accompany all my representations,' because the sequence of time is a condition of its possibility and there is no sequence of time save in temporality. The pronoun 'my' points to a subject as an object among objects and again without this 'my' there would be no 'I think'" (*ND* 184–185/183).[17]

The issue here is how an "I" can be given the sort of privileged particularity that relegates everything considered to be "non-I." Adorno develops a reply to this position by proposing that the very linguistic assertion of "I" implies a context that denies the privileged utterance. As he puts it: "It is unfathomable why 'my' individual consciousness should take precedence over anything else. By using the pronoun 'my' the speaker of the moment supposes the linguistic generality he would deny by the priority of his particularization" (*ND* 132/126).[18] What is at stake here, in Adorno's view, is whether we can use terms like "my" without already committing ourselves to an implicitly anti-idealist position. That is, in using "my" I have to be aware—if I am to understand that pronoun properly—that it can be used similarly by others.

Adorno is denying the possibility of excluding the constitutive subject from material conditions: once its status as an entity is established, it thereafter becomes an object among others. There are interesting similarities to this thought in Ernst Tugendhat's Wittgensteinian theory of indexicals. Tugendhat defines his thesis straightforwardly, as follows:

> [I]t is constitutive for the use of *I* that someone who says *I* knows, first, that this person can be addressed as "you" and be designated as "she" or "he" by other speakers, and, second, that he thereby picks out an individual person among others whom he can designate as "they." If this connection did not exist, *I* would not be capable of designating an entity. It therefore also pertains necessarily to the use of the word *I* that everybody who employs it knows that others can refer to the same entity he refers to as "I" as "he" or "she." . . .[19]

Thus it lies in the nature of pronominal indexicals that they cannot be used to designate a privileged field. They are incapable of coherent employment in an extraempirical context. Adorno makes the further point that unless we have a way of employing the concept of "I" in this transcendental context as intelligible also as a potential component of a "we" that "I" "has no meaning" (*KK* 229). And speaking of Husserl, though in a way that is pertinent to Kant, Adorno argues: "If the variant, 'pure ego' [the 'I think'] is always supposed to remain a variant of 'my ego' [empirical self] and draw its evidence from self-experience, then it is necessarily bound to a determinate life of consciousness [*bestimmtes Bewußtseinsleben*], viz. that which is called 'I.' It is thus mundane or irrevocably referred back to the mundane. Otherwise the loaded term, which Husserl repeatedly employs, is strictly incomprehensible" (*ME* 229/228). The conclusion that follows from the unavoidably "mundane" conception of the "I think" is that it is circular, since it is both the cause (as part of the constitutive unity of apperception) and the effect (as phenomenal) of itself.

It might be suggested that Adorno reached this kind of indexical theory through an appropriation of a Hegelian idea. What I have in mind is Hegel's view that particulars always refer beyond themselves. We could say that Hegel's analysis of indexicals semantically deprives them of exclusive reference to one "I," "this," "here," or "now," and so forth. In the *Phenomenology*, he writes: "The 'I' is merely universal like 'Now,' 'Here,' or 'This' in general; I do indeed *mean* a single 'I,' but I can no more say what I *mean* in the case of 'I,' than I can in the case of 'Now' and 'Here.' When I say 'this Here,' 'this Now,' or a 'single item,' I am saying all thises, Heres, Nows, all single items. Similarly, when I say 'I,' this singular 'I,' I say in general all 'Is,' everyone is what I say, everyone is 'I,' this singular 'I' " (*PhS* 62). What Hegel does with these indexicals is a question which can only be answered by telling the story of *Geist*. His point at this stage of the *Phenomenology* is to establish that empiricism and sensualism in general are aporetic in that they deal with particulars but rely upon terms that cannot capture that particularity: language cannot express sheer experience. For this reason Hegel proceeds to examine universality since it seems to him to be the proper subject of philosophy. This is decisively different from the direction in which Adorno takes his indexical theory. For Adorno philosophy will have to capture the structure that makes the particulars intelligible, in contrast to Hegel who believes, as we have seen, that only the universal is intelligible. Nevertheless, a materialistic transformation of this part of Hegel's philosophy may seem to provide Adorno with concepts that enable him to argue that certain particular referents are incapable of denoting unique objects.

There is a second problem, which can be expressed in the form of a question: how could this phenomenal self interact with its own constitutive acts? Since these latter acts are not in any sense acts of the phenomenal world (since they are in some sense productive of it) they must be widely divergent from the thinking acts of a phenomenal "I think." This means, then, that there is a critical lacuna between the constitutive and phenomenal levels.

5.2 The "I Think" Is Noumenal

That the "I think" is noumenal seems to be Kant's most sustained view. Patricia Kitcher argues that this view arises merely out of Kant's desire to accord apriority to that aspect of the self that is responsible for the moral law; namely, its spontaneous, undetermined aspect.[20] Regardless of that possible extraepistemological motivation, its contrastive relation to the idea of the phenomenality of the "I think" gives it some sense (albeit, as Adorno's criticisms reveal, at the price of a few alternative mysteries). Here the "I think" is to be identified as noumenal because it is *spontaneous*; that is, free of the causal determinism of the phenomenal world. This must be necessary for the overall success of transcendental idealism if it is to resolve the epistemological difficulties of receptive empiricism:

> All the manifold of intuition has, therefore, a necessary relation to the "I think" in the same object in which this manifold is found. But this representation is an act of spontaneity [*Aktus der Spontaneität*], that is, it cannot be regarded as belonging to sensibility. I call it pure apperception, to distinguish it from empirical apperception, or, again, original apperception, because it is that self-consciousness which, while generating the representation "I think" (a representation which must be capable of accompanying all other representations, and in which all consciousness is one and the same), cannot itself be accompanied by any further representation. (*CPR* B132)

The idea here is that this "I think" is spontaneous because if it were not then all knowledge and experience would be explained as the product of sensibility would leave no place for the consciousness of this knowledge or experience. This claim for the spontaneity of the "I think" entails that the "I think" is nonphenomenal. If it is active and nonphenomenal, it must be considered as noumenal. But the question about interaction arises again. What relation can hold between a noumenal self and the constitutive acts of the forms of intuition and the categories? The constitutive acts themselves are quite complicated from this point of view. What seems to be the case, however, is that they produce data that, after combination with the acts of the "I think," can become available to consciousness. How is this interaction between a noumenal self and sensible data possible? This, the second side of the antinomy, is more acute. Adorno addresses the question forcefully. The point of his criticism is that a self devoid of empirical content is unable to perform acts that have influence upon the empirical world. The key issue he raises is that of how the given could be affected by a nonphysical and a priori subject. According to Kant, sensibility is produced through the a priori modes of space and time, and thereafter *given* to the transcendental self. Adorno attacks the assumptions that sustain this position:

> But certainly nothing can be given to a "pure" transcendental subject. For that subject is a determination of thought, a product of abstraction, which

The Critique of Kant

is certainly not to be straightaway brought to a denominator with the immediate. It is not a concrete ego possessing concrete contents of consciousness. The transcendental subject itself is supposed to be cut off from the given by the ontological difference which should disappear in the construction of the subject. The sense-perceptible does not exist immediately for the supersensual [*Unsinnliches*]; rather, it exists only by the concept which "is" not sense-perception, but means [*meint*] and therefore sublates it.... No subject emancipated from anything empirical can ever be a form for the given; to no such subject can something be given (referring to "it" as "it" or "him" is already problematic); none can receive such content in whatever manner. (*ME* 147/142)

And in another place Adorno makes the accusation that the "I think"—understood as transcendental and nonphenomenal—is nothing other than an abstraction which entirely distorts the phenomenology of our experience: "The concept of the transcendental or all the moments through which something like experience appears to be realized—the so-called constitutings of our consciousness—are not as the sense of the 'Deduction of the Pure Concepts of the Understanding' would like it to be, as immediately known to us. But rather they are mediations, they are abstractions of a determinate moment of experience—and this moment is hypostatized in the *Critique of Pure Reason*" (*KK* 236). Given that for Kant the "I think" is inseparable from the categories—it is, in fact, the function of the applications of the categories, as Paul Guyer argues[21]—this remark by Adorno has the clear intention of locating the transcendental in its material origins.

Here, again, we see the twofold nature of the "anthropological-materialist" critique. Adorno exploits the indexical incoherence of a nonempirical self. He points out that no indexical is appropriate to it and therefore the term "I" has no significance in its transcendental employment. And he also argues that a gulf exists between the transcendental-noumenal and empirical self. As a nonempirical entity this form of the "I think" can neither have anything given to it, nor can it, as something "emancipated from everything empirical," claim any sort of identity or parallel with the empirical subject.

Adorno's objections, in fact, anticipate the famous criticisms of Strawson, who speaks, congenially, of "the imaginary subject of transcendental psychology."[22] Indeed Adorno himself refers to Kant's efforts as falling within the "peculiar no man's land of knowledge between psychology and logic" (*KK* 40). Strawson also, like Adorno, notes the huge problem surrounding pronominal reference to a transcendental subject. As he writes: "We have to ask what *we* human beings, Kant's readers, can unambiguously understand by 'us' and 'we' and 'our' when these expressions are so easily and loftily used to convey the doctrines of transcendental idealism."[23] Strawson's criticisms are specifically concentrated on Kant's assumptions regarding a relationship between the transcendental and the empirical self. His arguments resemble those of Adorno in that his emphasis is on the implicit ontological claims for the transcendental subject. For Strawson there is a semantic cleft between the two aspects of Kant's subject. Kant's mistake is to think that a nonempirical self could be spoken of according to normal empirical conventions: "Repeated like spells, these pronominal incantations are as inefficacious as spells. In the dictum regarding knowledge of oneself (empirical self-consciousness) the identity which has to be explained—the identity of the empirically self-conscious subject and the real or supersensible subject—is simply assumed without being a whit more intelligible. If the appearances of x to x occur in time, they cannot be assigned to the history of the transcendental, supersensible subject, for that being has no history."[24] And, bluntly, "[W]hat has the non-history of the transcendental subject to do with us?"[25] This is not answered in the first *Critique*. This, indeed, is the insoluble aporia that Adorno addresses.[26] In short, no such interaction is possible. The basic problem is that Kant has set up the need for an answer to the question of interaction by dividing the self into different functions and ultimately, thereby, into different realities. As Adorno notes, "[t]he concept of what 'is there' means nothing but what exists, and the subject as existent comes promptly under the heading of 'object.' As pure apperception, however, the subject claims to be the downright Other of all existents" (*SO* 754/148). But this merely gives rise to an antinomical theory of the subject: in so far as it is subject to empirical conditions it is nonconstitutive—but if it is constitutive it then has a status outside the limits of justification.

We have seen Adorno's reasons for holding that the "I think" cannot be considered "transcendental": the "I think" has no defensibly special

The Critique of Kant

status that would allow it to be separated from the conditions of material reality. Adorno goes on to argue that Kant must be forced to concede that the constitutive "I think" is nothing more than an abstraction from the subjective moment of experience. In his lectures on the *Critique of Pure Reason* Adorno paid quite a lot of attention to the question of whether the transcendental elements of experience really could be understood to be independent of experience. He considered Kant's claim in the introduction to the *Critique* in the following way: "*[A]ll our knowledge begins with experience, but does not [all] arise from experience.* However, I would like to say to you that this crass opposition between the two moments . . . has truly something dogmatic about it. That is to say, when something begins with a matter [*Sache*] that matter also has something to do with the origin of the something" (*KK* 48–49). This idea informs Adorno's thoughts on the unsustainability of the "I think." The "I think"—allegedly a priori—simply cannot be separated from material conditions without becoming little more than an abstraction which is hypostatized above all experience.[27] Adorno writes: "The definition of the transcendental as that which is necessary, a definition added to functionality and generality . . . provides a legal basis for abstraction, which we cannot do without, for abstraction is the medium of self-preserving reason" (*ND* 180/179).[28] The conclusion Adorno draws is that if we do not lose sight of the experience from which the theory sets out then we will not be left with an "I think" that resides in the *Zwischenreich* of antinomical possibilities.[29]

We have already noted Adorno's remark that transcendental philosophy operates in a "peculiar no man's land." That location is the reason why transcendental philosophy falls into antinomy. In spelling itself out it commits itself to positions that can be expressed only in terms taken from both sides of the no man's land: it thereby tears itself in two. Officially the "I think" is merely a condition, and not to be confused with the *Cogito*. But when Kant spells out what this "I think" is in ways that make it plausible that it can have the efficaciousness he claims for it the answers fall into the antinomical commitments entailed in the distinction between the phenomenal (material, spatiotemporal) and the noumenal (spontaneous). It leaves this no man's land at the price of theoretical incoherence.

Adorno adds that this peculiar "*Zwischenreich* is the realm in which the *Critique of Pure Reason* plays itself out and through which it earns itself the title of a transcendental investigation" (*KK* 40). It maintains its theoretical integrity—acquires its distinctive program—only when it is allowed to remain within its unique *Zwischenreich.*

The "anthropological-materialist critique" undermines the key commitments of the transcendental enterprise. Experience, Adorno concludes, is grounded in materiality. No other explanations can cohere since they move beyond the conditions in which they can be expressed. The conditions are, of course, what we have already seen in the previous two chapters. The critique of Kant refines what we are to understand by those conditions and why Adorno sees them as compelling.

5
Adorno on Husserl and Heidegger

Kant and Hegel are, as we have seen, quite troubling presences in Adorno's negative dialectic. Their influence is so marked at times that there appears to be no discernible difference between some of their concepts and Adorno's use of them. It really is impossible to understand the arguments and structure of the negative dialectic unless one has an adequate account of the nature and extent of Adorno's critical appropriations of these figures. And yet Adorno at other times does not spare them from radical critique: the alleged metaphysical components of Kant and Hegel are thoroughly criticized and rejected. But curiously it is not Kant and Hegel who, in terms of the number of pages written, have received most attention from Adorno. That compliment (I say without irony) goes, in fact, to the twentieth century philosophers Edmund Husserl and Martin Heidegger.

As I noted in the previous chapter, the young—very young—Adorno submitted a doctoral thesis to the Faculty of Philosophy at the University of Frankfurt and he wrote and almost presented for the *Habilitation* examination a work we looked at in the previous chapter, *The Concept of the Unconscious in Transcendental Psychology*. (In the end it was an entirely new *Habilitationsschrift* on Kierkegaard [1931] that earned him his *venia legendi*.) But Adorno returned to Husserl throughout the 1930s, '40s, and '50s: in Oxford in the 1930s it was his "DPhil" topic; in the United States during the '40s he published (in English) a piece on Husserl's idealism; and then in 1956 his major work on Husserl, the

Metacritique of Epistemology,[1] appeared. Only in the last decade of his career was Husserl not an important concern for Adorno. With regard to Heidegger, we can see from "The Actuality of Philosophy"—Adorno's programmatic and ambitious inaugural lecture of 1931—that he regarded Heidegger as the key philosopher of his time. Adorno's paper, "The Idea of Natural History," the following year, attempted to develop a critique of fundamental ontology. In writing his *Habilitationsschrift* on Kierkegaard, Adorno was keen to undermine some of the key concepts of existential philosophy, which was then primarily associated by Adorno and others with Heidegger. But in the 1960s Adorno gave ever greater attention to Heidegger, marked by the appearance of the book *The Jargon of Authenticity* (1964), a critique of the existentialist linguistic usage popular in conservative German theologico-philosophical circles. Although Heidegger is not, as we can see from Adorno's text, by any means the worst "jargonizer," he is the most important. But, for reasons we shall see in sections 3–6 of this chapter, it is the sixty or so pages of Adorno's magnum opus, *Negative Dialectics*, on the critique of fundamental ontology that are especially important in establishing Adorno's position in relation to Heidegger.

What Adorno will conclude essentially is that both Husserl and Heidegger are committed to principles that are rationally unsustainable. But more significant from the point of view of the possibility of critical theory is Adorno's allegation that phenomenology in both its Husserlian and Heideggerian forms cannot provide a basis for the idea of a critical subject. Far from it, indeed, in Adorno's view: Husserl's theory of objectivity requires a subject who must passively register objective validities which are entirely subject independent, whereas Heidegger's account of *Dasein* undermines the conditions in which a critical subject—a subject that is engaged in a conceptual understanding of its environment—can be articulated.

I used the word "compliment" above for a good reason: Adorno did not waste his time with philosophy he considered unimportant. But what is the criterion of importance here? For Adorno, an important philosophy is one that shares some aspect of his own conception of the task of philosophy. So Husserl's philosophy—at least that part we will be considering here—is driven by the aim of recovering objectivity, whereas Heidegger is clearly interested in turning philosophy away from subjectivism and towards experience. Both Husserl and Heidegger are, obviously enough, outstanding exponents of their respective projects, and that is why Adorno strives to understand them, to see whether they really do represent coherent alternatives to the subjectivist tendencies of modern philosophy. It will not, I expect, spoil the conclusion to say that Adorno finds serious flaws in the positions set out by Husserl and Heidegger. He subjects them to transcendental criticism—or immanent critique—demonstrating the incompatibility of their commitments with their aims—aims that, in various respects, Adorno shares. The task of this chapter is to examine, in turn, Adorno's treatments of Husserl and Heidegger.

1   The Critique of Husserl

Adorno's reading of Husserl in the *Metacritique of Epistemology* falls into two main parts: a critique of Husserl's notion of subjectivity, and, in effect, a critique of Husserl's notion of objectivity. I have already given a great deal of consideration to Adorno's critique of subjectivity both in chapter 3 and in the chapter on Kant, and much of what we find in those chapters applies equally to Husserl's views of subjectivity. It therefore seems most expeditious to focus in this half of the present chapter on Adorno's critique of Husserl's concept of objectivity. Adorno's approach, as we shall see, will be to raise questions about the assumptions behind and implications of Husserl's famous rejection of psychologism. The particular text with which Adorno deals is the *Prolegomena to Pure Logic* (in volume 1 of *Logical Investigations*). In the *Prolegomena* Husserl sets out his reasons for rejecting psychologism, and having demonstrated to his own satisfaction the explanatory dead ends of psychologism he proposes instead a "logical absolutism"—a position that holds that logical validity is pure, since it is irreducible to psychological processes or lived experiences. The essence of Adorno's criticism of this part of Husserl's philosophy is that in committing himself to certain quasi-Platonic ideas of objectivity, in which something remains pure and unaffected in its constitution throughout its apprehension, Husserl's position suffers the inevitable difficulties of any position that diminishes the contribution of subjective agency to objectivity. Because it is detached from human beings, in the manner of a quasi-Platonic reality, it is, Adorno argues, impossible to justify. This critique of Husserl provides us with an opportunity to explore what Adorno sees as a particular kind of mistake; that is, to attempt to affirm objectivity (in this case, as we shall see, the laws of logic) outside the structure of mediation. In the previous two chapters we looked at the converse and debilitating problems that stem from placing the subject outside the object (as in idealism). To examine Adorno's argument in its context I want in this section to consider briefly the motivations and reasons behind Husserl's rejection of psychologism. The real business will then be to see what Adorno makes of these reasons.

Dallas Willard has pointed out that there are seemingly irreconcilable tendencies in our efforts to describe the nature and origin of logic. He sees a certain paradox arising between the two following tendencies: (1) "[T]he non-normative statements made by logicians engaged in their business both are about, and draw their evidence from the examination of the particular conceivings, assertings, and inferrings of particular persons—a range of facts commonly thought to belong ultimately to the science of psychology alone."[2] Yet (2) "[T]hey nonetheless, as Husserl, Frege, and others have shown, do *not* draw their evidence from the examination of such events."[3] In one respect logical processes, inferences and so on, can quite reasonably be understood as psychological activities. But from the point of view of validity it must be denied that these processes are *reducible* to psychological activities. Husserl's position is broadly aligned with the view that validity is suprapsychological (tendency 2 above). And in his commitments to this view he obviously must reject the psychologistic claim that logic is nothing more than the psychological processes of its assertion.

What I want to consider here are Husserl's exact arguments against the idea that logical truths can be grounded in psychological attributes. And that will lead us into Adorno's examination of Husserl's logical absolutism. Adorno, as we shall see, will argue, quite ingeniously, that logical absolutism threatens to invalidate truth. Why? Because it actually detaches objectivity from the subject, claiming that objectivity means the absence of subjective interference. And crucially that places it outside the structure of mediation (mediation, as we have seen, being for Adorno the only possible explanation of objectivity).

One of Husserl's arguments against the doctrine of psychologism is that it leads to relativism. Husserl never wavered from the conviction that relativism was both a bad thing and quite simply false. This conviction carried the attendant belief about the possibility of absolute truth of some kind. In any case, if relativism is true then logic as Husserl conceives it is denied. Husserl sees logic as follows (to cite David Bell):

> The science of logic studies "the laws of rational thought," but, according to Husserl, this entails neither that it is a mere empirical science resulting in contingent generalizations about how rational thought in fact proceeds, nor that it is at bottom a practical discipline resulting in normative laws governing how rational thought should proceed. Rather, Husserl claims, logic is a purely formal science whose subject matter comprises abstract, non-spatio-temporal entities, and whose results are *a priori*, timeless, and entirely general truths.[4]

This conception of logic clearly emphasizes above all the notion of validity—the conditions of the operation of logic are not considered to be relevant to the very nature of validity.

According to Husserl relativism is produced by psychologism through its principle that logic arises from purely contingent genetic factors—the psychology of the thinker. That effectively places validity on a relativist footing since the psychology of the thinker is in no way necessary. (In this regard Adorno notes that contingency was Husserl's "*horror intellectualis*" [*ME* 89/82].) Even if it could be shown that certain features of our psychology are necessary (Kant) such a position would nevertheless undermine objectivity by placing it within a subjective framework, however generalized. Husserl writes: "Psychologism in all its subvarieties and individual elaborations is in fact the same as relativism, though not always recognized and expressly allowed to be such. It makes no difference whether, as a formal idealism, based on a 'transcendental psychology' (Kant), it seeks to save the objectivity of knowledge, or whether, leaning on empirical psychology, it accepts relativism as its ineluctable fate" (*LI* 145). Husserl offers a number of reasons in support of this claim, all of which appear to assume that the absence of absolute objectivity leads necessarily to the presence of relativism. A middle ground between these two—some kind of historicism—is effectively no part of his position. It is this radical opposition between absolute objectivity and relativism to which Adorno gives particular attention, as we shall see, in his effort to reveal the metaphilosophical implications of Husserl's doctrine.

The principal claim of the psychologistic logicians is that logic is part of psychology. Since all of the processes that we describe as logical activities—inferring, deducing, affirming, denying, and so on—are more fundamentally psychological activities logic has no separate sphere of operation. Logical acts are just one sort of psychological act. And the implication to be drawn from this is that logical validity—the paradigmatic form of objectivity for Husserl—far from being pure in some Platonic sense—that is, subsisting separately from human beings and their mental activities—must be referable back to psychological processes. This view is obviously empiricist in that it traces all objectivity to observable processes. Husserl, in fact, takes direct issue with the claims of empiricist methodology that it can explain what he sees as self-evidently true of logic (its absolute validity). He raises three objections against the empiricist reduction of logic to psychology.

He argues, first, that if logical processes are simply particular cases of psychological processes, then the laws of logic and the laws of psychology ought to be the same in character. But obviously they are not, since empirical laws are never exact, quite unlike the laws of logic. He writes: "If psychological rules lack exactness, the same must be true of the prescriptions of logic.... But precisely the laws which are pointedly called 'logical,' which as laws of proof make up the real core of all logic—the logical 'principles,' the laws of syllogism, the laws of many other kinds of inference, as, e.g. equational inferences, the Bernoullian argument from n to $n + 1$, the principles of probability-inferences etc.—are of absolute exactness" (*LI* 98–99). The second objection utilizes the well-known contrast between the necessity of logical laws and the mere probability of inductively identified laws: "Induction does not establish the holding of the law, only the greater or lesser probability of its holding.... Nothing, however, seems plainer than that the laws of 'pure logic' all have *a priori* validity" (*LI* 99). The laws of psychology are inductively established and are of course revisable. The laws of "pure logic" are not.

Husserl's final objection focuses on the comparative content of psychological and logical laws. Psychological laws are "laws for mental states" (*LI* 104) and are psychological in content "by presupposing or implying the existence of such states" (*LI* 104). By contrast no "logical law implies a 'matter of fact,' not even the existence of presentations or judgments or other phenomena of knowledge. No logical law, properly understood, is a law for the activities of mental life, and so not a law for presentations (as experiences), nor for judgments (experiences of judging), nor for our other mental experiences" (*LI* 104). This third objection consolidates the idea, then, that the laws of logic are independent of any anthropological conditions. Of course, psychologism would reply to this that the laws of logic imply the existence of entities who assert, deny, deduce, and so on.

Given the failure of psychologism, as Husserl sees it, to account for the specific character of logic—its absolute validity—it seems an entirely obvious step (for Husserl) to make claims for the position he denotes as logical absolutism. Logical absolutism is the thesis that the laws of logic have validity and existence, both of which are irreducible to any empirical condition. It is important to point out that Husserl does not see himself as proposing a position that is simplistically the reverse of psychologism. Interestingly, he believes that he has discovered the possibility of a *third way*—"where truth lies in the middle" (*LI* 96)—in which psychology can be seen to be part of logic to the extent that logical validity is useful to beings with certain kinds of psychologies. But this is not, as psychologism would fallaciously see it, the basis of validity. Use and assertion play no part in validity. Logical laws and judgments are just not the same. But that is not to deny that logical laws are *expressed through* judgments. As he puts it, "[T]he laws, as '*contents of judgment*' have been confused with the *judgments* themselves" (*LI* 102). Willard argues that what Husserl is really doing here is emphasizing the "characters of acts"—their validity, truth claims, and so on—as opposed to the psychological activities that are required to judge at all.[5] If this is so then Adorno's accusations of Platonism are difficult to sustain. Adorno objects nevertheless: "But how could one assert a complete divergence between legitimization of logical propositions and the factical legitimization of logical operations if the two permeate each other in one and the same consciousness?" (*ME* 71/64). In other words, the separation of the character of valid arguments from the assertion of valid arguments is a separation that Adorno wants to undermine. Adorno's objection may seem rather naive, even simplistic, in its rejection of what is a reasonable looking distinction. But the argument he goes on to provide is sophisticated, as we shall see. What I want to consider in the next section is Adorno's implicit investigation of what Husserl sees as the "gap" (*LI* 96) that creates the space for a possible third way. Adorno, however, continually argues that, far from finding a third way, Husserl's philosophy contains the debilitating weakness that it cannot relate acts of logic to empirical entities. And that means, put plainly, that Husserl's "third way" is nothing more than the absolutist hypostatization of logic (the second way above) in disguise.

2 Adorno's Response

There are two quite different aspects to Adorno's consideration of Husserl's move toward logical absolutism. First, he argues *metaphilosophically* that Husserl could never have regarded logical absolutism as the necessary consequence of the refutation of psychologism had he not already been committed to certain presuppositions about the character of objectivity. Second, Adorno proposes a *philosophical* critique based on the idea that logical absolutism is committed to a concept of truth that it cannot deliver. The reason it cannot deliver it is because it operates outside the conditions of intelligibility: namely, mediation. Husserl, to be more precise, fails to recognize that assertions of validity are possible only within judgments. Once again the judicative structure of experience that we have seen in previous chapters plays an important role in Adorno's philosophical criticisms. This second part of the response to Husserl picks up something I discussed earlier: Adorno's transcendental critique. This is the form of critique—also applied to Kant, as we saw in the previous chapter—that holds that the conditions of experience are the conditions of intelligibility. The conditions of experience are explained as subject-object mediation. Because Husserl's logical absolutism is at odds with this structure—emphasizing instead an independent, non-mediated/immediate object—it consequently deprives itself of the ability to express itself coherently. Indeed Adorno's criticism of Husserl is probably the outstanding case of this form of criticism in all of Adorno's work. Before looking at this, however, I will examine the first aspect (mentioned above) of Adorno's reading of Husserl.

2.1 The Metaphilosophical Critique

Adorno's metaphilosophical critique of Husserl's logical absolutism is conducted by identifying the key motivations that lead Husserl to conclude that the falsity of psychologism entails the truth of logical absolutism. It is clear from Husserl's text that he effectively takes these positions to be mutually exclusive and he supposes that the key principles of logical absolutism are largely justified by way of the refutation of psychologism. Adorno argues, however, that Husserl simply fails to consider alternative conditions that might serve to explain logical validity. He writes,

> Husserl makes things easy on himself in his polemic against the genetic interpretation of logic, because he confines himself to "psychologism." The genetic interpretation of logical laws must supposedly turn to the processes of consciousness in the psychological subject, the single human individual, as its ultimate substratum. That, of course, allows him to present the difference between psychological foundation in individual conscious acts and the objectivity of logical content. (*ME* 82–83/76)

But what alternative is there? Adorno's position is that logic has its genesis in what we might call sociality: it emerges within the context of human projects and needs. As he writes (directly following the above passage): "But the implicit genesis of the logical process is certainly not psychological motivation. It is a sort of social behavior. According to Durkheim, logical propositions contain a deposit of social experiences such as the order of generation and property relations which claim priority over the being and consciousness of the individual" (*ME* 83/76). In a discussion of the law of noncontradiction Adorno underlines the social nature of logic by characterizing it as a principle of organization. In a manner reminiscent of Nietzsche's "evolutionary" explanation of rationality, Adorno claims that the law of noncontradiction is simply a way of organizing our experience:[6] "Genetically logic presents itself as an attempt at integration and the solid ordering of the originally equivocal—a decisive step in demythologization. The law of non-contradiction is a sort of taboo which hangs over the diffuse. Its absolute authority, which Husserl insists upon, directly originates in the imposition of the taboo and in the repression of powerful counter-tendencies. As a 'law of thought,' its content is prohibition: Do not think profusely" (*ME* 87/80). Now it is obvious that Adorno's efforts to propose an alternative account of the genesis of logic are quite problematic. He accepts that psychologism is false but proposes a kind of, what we might call, "sociologism" in its place. What he is saying is that no feature of logic—understood as a realm of pure validity—can be understood as independent of its sociogenesis. And his procedure here is little different from that of psychologism. It means explaining the processes of logic—its laws or rules—in terms that effectively disregard the special activities of logic and instead explain it in terms of something more general: in Adorno's case, as part of the social process. Like the procedure of psychologism Adorno's is reductionist—it presupposes, in this case, the priority of sociality and attempts to explain all experiences through this principle. The laws or rules of logic may no doubt have a very eminent place within the social process, Adorno would perhaps allow, but they are nonetheless part of it and nothing more, he seems to say. Adorno provides little support for this. And curiously in the later *Negative Dialectics* (1966) he makes a remark that entirely excludes the sociologism of the *Metacritique* (1956). He writes that only "a childish relativism would deny the validity of formal logic and mathematics and treat them as ephemeral because they have come to be" (*ND* 50/40). So Adorno opposes Husserl's logical absolutist account of logic with his sociologist one. What a metaphilosophical reading of Husserl merely achieves is to reveal Adorno's competing metaphilosophical assumptions.

Adorno looks at further aspects of Husserl's assumptions in an effort to explain the absence of sociality in Husserl. He believes that Husserl has certain metaphilosophical commitments to individualism. What this individualism consists in is the view that the intellectual constitution of the individual is independent of sociality. Adorno writes: "Husserl is blinded by individualism, and the only consciousness he knows belongs to monads" (*ME* 66–67/60). And on that basis sociality is not considered as a condition of any feature of the rational world. It therefore cannot serve to explain the origin of logic. The consequence of this individualism, according to Adorno, is that it places the search for the genesis of logic entirely outside the individual. Since, as the critique of psychologism has shown, the origin of logic cannot be explained by the individual's abilities and cognitive equipment its objectivity must be explained otherwise. At first sight this may sound anti-individualist, given that it does not explain logic through the individual. But not at all, in Adorno's view, since it is the failure to consider sociality that is, in fact, the defining characteristic of individualism. Adorno develops this point by making a number of supporting arguments that help to defend his sociologism. He argues that Husserl's "reasoning is possible only because he [Husserl] isolates monadologically the consciousness of different individuals at different times. Collective unity in the execution of acts of consciousness, the social moment of the synthesis of thought, never enters his mind" (*ME* 66/59). Husserl's individualism, then, assumes the monadic operations of intelligences—none can influence another and none belongs to a greater substance. For that reason Adorno argues that if "thought in fact belonged just to monads, then it would be a miracle that all monads would think according to the same laws, and theory would have no way out other than to appropriate this miracle through Platonic realism of logic" (*ME* 66/59).

In line with his own sociologistic position Adorno sees the development of this quasi-Platonic position as explicable in terms of the sociological phenomenon of reification. In full-blooded critical theory mode Adorno discerns parallels between Husserl's view of the status of logic and those of "vulgar economic thought" (*ME* 72/65). (1) Both logical absolutism and vulgar economic thought see an intrinsic significance in some particular thing—logical validity and the value of goods respectively—failing to realize that these significances have social origins (*ME* 72/65). (2) There is also the residuum parallel. In just the same way as the "value" of a commodity is what remains once all of the production costs are subtracted pure logical validity is what remains once the agency of subjectivity is factored out (*ME* 76/70). These are provocative connections, and curiously

Adorno is tentative about claiming the classic Marxist thesis that economic structures have causal influence on the presuppositions implicit in intellectual production. But the suggestion is there (and it really can be called no more than a suggestion) as another aspect of Adorno's metaphilosophical account of Husserl's motivations.[7]

We saw above Husserl's arguments against a certain form of relativism: logical absolutism is developed specifically to provide an alternative explanation to logic other than the relativistic version proposed by psychologism. But Adorno makes the interesting suggestion that logical absolutism and relativism sustain each other: "[A]ll relativism lives off the consistency of absolutism" (*ME* 94/87), he writes. His point is a useful one. If something is to be *absolutely* true, that is, true "independently of further qualification," then it is placed (by Husserl) outside the conditions of validation (since it is unconditional). That is, Husserl is accused of refusing to justify the validity of logic on the basis that because it is simply valid in itself nothing further need be said. To attempt to validate logic by reference to processes in which it is employed runs the risk of falling into psychologistic explanation. But if Husserl can be allowed to maintain this position then, according to Adorno, he actually provides the possibility of relativism. If absoluteness means that no validation is required, then entirely contingent dogmatic theses are permissible: this is the very relativism Husserl had sought to avoid. Of course we have to remember that Husserl is speaking only of logic (including mathematics, which for him is a branch of logic), not of any other knowledge. But in so far as logic is presented by Husserl as knowledge that requires no support, Adorno's observation is clearly challenging.[8]

2.2 The Philosophical Critique

As I mentioned above, Adorno's philosophical critique of logical absolutism is conducted by means of transcendental critique, or immanent critique, to use the term found in Adorno. (In chapter 1, section 1.2 I have explained what I see as the relationship between transcendental and immanent critique.) He takes his description of subject–object mediation as the basic structure of experience. And positing that structure as constitutive of the limitations of what philosophy can coherently assert, he questions Husserl's effort to establish that logical validity is in some respect a thought-object that has no constitutive relation to a subject. In the *Metacritique* in particular Adorno uses the term "dialectic" to describe the inevitable incoherence within systems that have no basis in nonreduced experience (as described in subject–object mediation). When a system is criticized through a revelation of its incoherence the criticism simply identifies the inner "dialectic"—a debilitating tension—within or "immanent" to the system. Adorno sees Husserl as in some respects a victim of his own virtues. In his rigorous and consistent commitment to certain principles the impossibility of his position is correspondingly pronounced. Its "dialectic" or incoherence is a direct result of Husserl's unwavering commitment to principles that defy the only rationally articulable version of experience. As Adorno writes: "Any dialectic in his philosophy occurs in spite of itself, and can be extracted from it only with the force of its own consistency" (*ME* 56/49).

This "dialectic," Adorno argues, takes the form of a central antinomy—it falls into incompatible commitments as, classically, arguments that blithely ignore transcendental conditions must. Since a central thesis of logical absolutism is that subjectivity has no role to play in the notion of logical validity, logical absolutism in a sense proposes a model of knowledge or experience that is at odds with that put forward by the thesis of subject–object mediation. Adorno contends that the insistence on subject-free validity can be achieved, and achieved at best superficially, only at the price of ineluctably antinomical implications.

The antinomy of Husserl's position is: (a) the laws of logic are reasonable to thought, and (b) the laws of logic are not validated according to any criterion of reasonableness—they are valid in themselves. The first side (a) of the antinomy is described as follows:

Consciousness confronts logic and its "ideal laws." If consciousness wishes to substantiate the claim of logic as founded and not crudely assume it, then logical laws must be reasonable to thought. In that case, however, thinking must recognize them as its own laws, its proper essence. For thinking is the content of logical acts. Pure logic and pure thought could not be detached from each other. The radical dualism between logic and consciousness would be sublated, and the subject of thought would enter along into the foundation of logic .... (*ME* 80/73)

Adorno's point here is this: the assessment of what is reasonable is an activity of "thought." The laws of logic too can be assessed in this way. But in order to assess, "thought" must have some criterion or criteria of what it takes as reasonable. Now if among the criteria of what is reasonable there are such principles as "a phenomenon cannot be contradictory" then it seems to follow that the laws of logic—in particular the notion of validity—are already available to consciousness. They are not simply "out there" awaiting passive endorsement: they have no subject-free subsistence. And as soon as we recognize that our rational judgments *already* operate with certain logical criteria of reasonableness then the separation that is proposed by logical absolutism simply does not work.

Before considering (b), the alternative, it is worth pointing out, I think, that a conclusion very much in Husserl's favor might be drawn from Adorno's very own argument. The fact, explicitly acknowledged by Adorno, that the laws of logic are already available to consciousness suggests, at least, that they have some kind of apriority. They are not, so to speak, produced by the utterance of a valid argument, but are presupposed as certain kinds of rules of what can count as a reasonable—say noncontradictory—utterance. True, the idea that validity is some kind of Platonic *eidos* would be problematic, but Husserl is not obviously committed to that notion. Validity can, in a sense, be a property of arguments and is unintelligible when divorced from that context. The question is whether Husserl actually engages in such a divorce or hypostatization. Again, it is by no means clear that he does so. However what he does not commit himself to—and here, I think, we find a way in for Adorno's criticism—is the idea that validity is a property of propositions or judgments. It cannot, as such a property, be considered to be in-itself. Through judgment—judgment used in argumentation—we assess validity or otherwise.

In any case, the alternative is (b), that is (according to Adorno) the alternative to seeing the laws of logic as already presupposed, is to see the laws of logic as appearing phenomenally to thought, that is (in contrast to (a)) as appearing before subjectivity and being accepted without evaluation. In some sense this avoids the difficulty of (a) in that it does not attribute logical validity to the laws of thoughts and thus, prima facie at least, allows the idea of the separation of the two to be maintained. But it brings its own peculiar difficulties. If the laws of logic were given "phenomenally"—in full and without any question of being *accepted* by us simply because their subject-free validity would thereby be compromised—then our acceptance of them would be entirely *noncritical*. And in that case the laws of logic would have dogmatic authority simply because *we could not* evaluate them: "If it were merely registered and accepted as a higher order 'phenomenon,' the purity of the logical *a priori* may indeed be saved. Yet logic then also forfeits the character of unconditioned validity which is just as inviolable for logical absolutism as ideal purity. Its laws would then be valid only in the framework of its 'appearing.' They would remain dogmatic, unproven and contingent" (*ME* 81/74). In essence, the elimination of the subject from the story of logical validity leads to the impossibility of our accounting for why it is that we regard logic as the discipline whose central concept is validity.

Adorno's criticism of logical absolutism—that is, that it is based on an inexpressible model of objectivity, something in which the subject necessarily has no agency—should not be divided from the theoretical framework that Adorno uses to support it. Adorno, it has to be remembered, does not see himself primarily as a contributor to the venerable literature of Husserl scholarship. Rather, it is his intention to persuade us of his subject–object model by way of demonstrating the impossibility of the alternatives. Husserl's philosophy, he writes, is the "occasion" and not the "purpose" of the *Metacritique* (*ME* 9/1). What Husserl's position highlights are the transcendental constraints within which philosophical rationality is possible. As Adorno contends: "Since no thinking can break out of the subject–object polarity, nor ever even establish it and determine either distinct moment independently of the other, the object which had been ejected in the hypostatization of pure logic returns within it" (*ME* 76–7/69).

Adorno's argument is that Husserl's commitment to a number of dualities—genesis/validity, subject/object—leads inevitably to incoherence. By attempting to explain experience without subjectivity Husserl is faced with the problem of explaining how the object—the laws of logic as presupposed by logical absolutism—can be justifiable to subjectivity. As he writes: "The thesis that what matters is not how experience is generated but rather what content it would have to have to become objectively valid experience, ignores the fact that the content of experience is itself a 'generating' in which subjective and objective moments are chemically united, so to speak" (*ME* 81/75). The failure of Husserl's logical position, Adorno is saying, should encourage us to see experience as a process in which the *mediation* of subject and object is the vital element. A separation of genesis and validity denies precisely that point, according to Adorno.

But in what way, we must ask, is the genesis/validity relation similar to the subject/object structure? Needless to say, it must be understood as similar if the transcendental critique offered by Adorno is to be convincing. Otherwise the genesis/validity separation would not introduce the same incoherence as that which Adorno has carefully shown to emerge from the subject–object separation. It has to be said that nothing we have found in Adorno's thoughts about subject/object prepares us explicitly for the genesis/validity entailment. However, it is worth returning to an already discussed distinction in the introduction to Hegel's *Phenomenology*, because there we can actually see a plausible way of connecting the subject/object issue with the genesis/validity issue. Hegel describes the object as "the true," but emphasizes that, in order for the object to become an item of knowledge, it has to be captured by concepts. This conceptual activity is where the role of subjective agency can be recognized. Our concepts attempt to grasp what is true, but since it is only through concepts that the object can be captured (become knowledge) concepts have a determinative role to play—they are not attachments but ways of expressing the true, the object. Subject and object are both present to consciousness, but in different ways: the object as that which is to be specified, the subject's conceptuality as what specifies. In this model we can see quite easily, I think, the connection between the subject/object issue and the genesis/validity issue. Concepts can be understood as the *genesis* of the object in so far as the latter only becomes an item of knowledge through concepts. Objects, as "the true," represent a certain kind of *validity*, but they cannot be intelligible as pure validity since without concepts objects are not yet articulated as knowledge. The unity of concept and object in a judgment is, then, the only way in which validity can be asserted. Put this way, genesis and validity can stand for the logically isolable elements of the activities of the subject–object relation. But their logical separation is no grounds for an actual separation. As Adorno remarks: "Logic is not being, but rather a process which cannot be reduced purely to either a 'subjectivity' or an 'objectivity' pole. The consequence of the self-critique of logic is the dialectic" (*ME* 81/74).

Now what Husserl's position does in direct contrast with the Hegelian model is to see the object as being both *the true* and the *known* despite the elimination of the conceptualizing agency of the subject. But without this agency even truth could not be asserted since it stands outside any conditions of possible articulation. By denying an active subject Husserl is left with a purely passive subject who must simply register the facts. This will not work, says Adorno, as "it ultimately undermines the very concept of truth" (*ME* 62/55).

Adorno suggests that for Husserl truth is a "residue"—what remains of the "object-in-itself" once all of the factors involved in its being known are taken away. Adorno, in fact, uses this view to criticize Husserl's attempt to identify an objective content to thought to which the mind simply attaches itself: "By suppressing the subjective moment, thinking, as the condition of logic, Husserl also conjures away the objective, the subjective matter of thought which is inscrutable in thought" (*ME* 74/67). In other words, Husserl makes the mistake of thinking that objectivity is achieved by the withdrawal of the subject. Husserl assumes that the interference of subjectivity has to be suppressed in order for objectivity to be uncovered or revealed: "For the sake of mastery, subjectivism must master and negate itself. Just to avoid mistake—since that is how they promote themselves—they [philosophers of foundation] abase themselves and at best would like to eliminate themselves. They use their subjectivity to subtract the subject from truth and their idea of objectivity is as a residue.... Truth is supposed to be the leftover ..." (*ME* 23/15). This "unreachable ideal," as Thomas Nagel put it, is the illusion against which Adorno also argues in his attempt to establish the mediational basis of thought. Adorno's endeavor, as we have seen, takes the apparently paradoxical form of retrieving subjectivity from subject philosophy, or the idealist self from idealism. What subject philosophy offers, in Adorno's view, is the idea that there is an irreducible subjective function. If mediation is true then the idea of subject-free mediation is exposed as the fallacy of unmediated subjectivity: "[O]nce cut off from the subject, [truth] becomes the victim of sheer subjectivity" (*ME* 78/72). That is, if we think that there is no subjective element in objectivity then we mistakenly assume that the object is known in its pure *in-itself*. But since this is impossible (according to the principle of the mediated priority of the object) then what actually happens when we think that we have deleted the subjective perspective is that our idea of the object *in-itself* is merely our personal object.[9] Adorno's critique therefore entails not only that the view from nowhere is impossible, but that whatever truths it may seem to produce—being unfounded—are the result of purely private perspectives. His term for the view from nowhere is the idea of "truth as residue." The "truth as residue" thesis fails to appreciate the contribution of human interests to knowledge. By withdrawing the subject there is the fallacy that somehow bare objectivity might remain. But what remains is still part of the structure of human knowledge. As such it is not a residue but the product of mediation.

Adorno also dismisses Husserl's efforts to avoid the pitfalls of a subject-free objectivity. According to Adorno, Husserl devises a concept that attempts to bridge the gap between detached purity and psychologism, namely, the concept of evidence—Husserl's third way, perhaps. This concept is supposed to satisfy the obvious need for a subjective component in our recognition of logical laws. In evidence, it is claimed, phenomena are given to consciousness. If the concept of evidence said only that, it might seem to be commonsensical. However, it has a further stipulation. Evidence means that logical truths are simply present in their totality to consciousness; that is, they, logical truths, are "given" without any subjective activity. Adorno explains: "The central role [of the concept of evidence] in all of Husserl's thought is explained by the fact that evidence promises to cover the contradictory demands of foundation through recourse to the subjective and of observation of irreducible 'absolute' states-of-affairs" (*ME* 63–64/57). But what, in the conventional understanding of the word "evidence," can such evidence be if it is something located in consciousness apparently without mediation; that is, without any possibility of a discursive justification? Since evidence is normally supported by arguments of various kinds, evidence as proposed by Husserl is, according to Adorno, "nothing more than the incantation of evidence" (*ME* 64/57).

As in the critique of Kant, Adorno also provides a materialist reading of certain principles in which the apparently metaphysical elements of Husserl's logical absolutism—those parts that are somehow supposed to lie outside both the structure of subject-object mediation and the experience it grounds—are retraced to material conditions. He does so by examination of another significant argument in Husserl's *Prolegomena*. There is, according to Adorno, a vagueness in Husserl's language that enables him to proceed with this separation of genesis and validity. This vagueness is located in Husserl's concept of the "logical object." Husserl is reported by Adorno to remark that the validity of logical objects "has nothing to do with an object, simply because it concerns all objects" (*ME* 73–74/66). Husserl tries to move away from involvement with the contingent object of experience and turns to a notional object, "object in general," that appears to be cleansed of all individual determinations. But in so doing he concedes at the very least the need for an object in some form. In other words, the necessity for matter and content within the activity of logical judgment is established. What ought to follow, but does not, is the recognition of objects in particular, given that no object in general exists: "Thus the talk of logic as an in-itself is strictly not permissible. Its very possibility depends on existents, the propositions, with all that this existence involves . . ." (*ME* 74/67). Logic cannot simply be validated as an in-itself. And this, in Adorno's view, returns logic to material reality: "Logical propositions can only be 'experienced' at all as related to some sort of entity" (*ME* 63–64/58). Since, finally, it is part of material reality it must be intelligible within subject-object mediation.

It is a curious feature of Husserl's intellectual odyssey that his own unease with the detached entities of his logical absolutism led him to reframe his account of the relationship between logical-mathematical principles and human beings. The motivation behind the *Prolegomena* was, as we saw, the hope that a pure logical foundational for the theoretical sciences might be protected from the apparently relativistic tendencies of psychologism. The price paid for such a thoroughgoing defense of the thesis of logical absolutism—with its commitments to validity in-itself—is a dualism that arose between the concrete scientific motivations and activities of human beings (genesis) and logic-mathematical principles (validity) that in their very character seemed to have little connection with these activities. This, indeed, led to Husserl's notion of the "crisis" in the sciences. It is interesting to consider—albeit rather briefly—the way in which Husserl attempted to address this, in that it may be that the new direction overcame the dualism of genesis and validity that Adorno so stridently criticizes.

In Husserl's late project *The Crisis of European Sciences* (1934–1937) it is argued that the scientific project since Galileo has created idealizations of nature—hypostatized entities—by forgetting that these entities have their origins in our intuitive engagement with the world. Geometry, for instance, was initially developed as technology for land surveying, and in that original context it has an immediate relevance: "Immediately with Galileo, then, begins the surreptitious substitution of idealized nature for pre-scientifically intuited nature."[10] Geometry and the science of idealities, as a science without genesis, loses its relation to life. The task of philosophy, Husserl claims, is to reintegrate the activities of science into the realm of human values. It is this latter claim that gives rise to the notion of the *Lebenswelt* (lifeworld). Insofar as the *Lebenswelt* pertains to human values and their everyday practices—such as surveying, to give Husserl's instance—it inevitably appears to contain some notion of historicality. A recent commentator expresses the general view in this way: "[in] *The Crisis of European Sciences* Husserl shows a much greater appreciation of historical, or what he called 'historico-genetic' explanation. Husserl became more urgently aware that the conditions of the natural attitude and indeed the scientific attitude were not merely static universal states of humankind but were historically constituted."[11] If so then Husserl himself seemed to think that the *Lebenswelt* might be the mediating point between genesis and validity.

However, an important question here is whether the historico-genetic explanation can be made equivalent to historical explanation. In the context of Husserl's philosophy it seems that we must be careful about preserving that distinction. The following passage from the *Crisis* is revealing: "The supposedly self-sufficient logic which modern mathematical logicians think they are able to develop, even calling it a truly scientific philosophy, namely, as the universal, *a priori*, fundamental science for all objective sciences, is nothing but naiveté. Its self-evidence lacks scientific grounding in the universal life-world *a priori*, which it always presupposes in the form of things taken for granted, which are never scientifically, universally formulated, never put in the general form proper to a science of essence."[12] If we are to understand from this passage that the *Lebenswelt* is thoroughly historical then we see that science is merely a historical product whose grounds lie entirely within the compass of the *Lebenswelt*. Thus understood the *Lebenswelt* resembles the notion of social totality proposed by Adorno, and indeed the *Lebenswelt* of Gadamer's hermeneutics, and in that respect the disconnection of genesis and validity that emerged from the *Prolegomena* is formally addressed, if not resolved. In this respect the *Lebenswelt* would generate various intellectual devices as it needed them and would, under rules peculiar to that *Lebenswelt*, as a historically specific place, see logical validity, for instance, as its own particular convention.

Whatever we might think of the merits of such a position it is not ultimately the one offered by Husserl. The *Lebenswelt* may explain the historico-genesis of logico-mathematical entities, but it does not give them over to any kind of historical relativity. As Edo Pivčević notes: "The language in which Husserl's exhortations about the *Lebenswelt* are phrased is, however, somewhat misleading."[13] What is misleading is that ultimately the *Lebenswelt* has invariant transcultural features. And for that reason Husserl's sense of the "historical" is extremely attenuated: it refers to the point of origin, not the origin itself (unlike, say, Hegelianism in which historical arrangements generate ideas). In the *Crisis* he writes:

[T]he life-world does have, in all its relative features, a *general structure*. This general structure, to which everything that exists relatively is bound, is not itself relative. We can attend to it in its generality and, with sufficient care, fix it once and for all in a way equally accessible to all. As life-world the world has, even prior to science, the "same" structures that the objective sciences presuppose in their substruction of a world which exists "in itself" and is determined through "truths in themselves" ... these are the same structures that they presuppose as a priori structures and systematically unfold in a priori sciences, sciences of the *logos*, the universal methodical norms by which any knowledge of the world existing "in itself, objectively" must be bound.[14]

The account of the *Lebenswelt* serves to deepen, rather than broaden the foundations of scientific activities. It is certainly not a historically oriented analysis of knowledge in any familiar sense of the term "history." And for that reason it is not easy to imagine that this account of the historico-genesis of logical and mathematical entities could easily satisfy the objections raised by Adorno in his critique of logical absolutism. The idea of the *Lebenswelt* in its deepened account of the basic rational concepts used by science is far from retracting the claim that these notions can only be defended as atemporal and a priori. In other words, the relation between genesis and validity remains dualistic, from an Adornian perspective at least. It is a matter that we cannot now pursue as to whether, indeed, the notion of the *Lebenswelt*, as this deepened foundation of phenomenology, might open up new paths for phenomenology. What remains in place, I would suggest, however, is that insofar as Adorno's objections to logical absolutism attack the notion of validity in-itself they remain historically significant as a specific response to the position of Husserl's *Prolegomena* and also have possible relevance for the position that Husserl attempted to develop in the *Crisis*.

Adorno's critique of the aprioristic aspects of Husserl's philosophy is clearly pretty powerful in places. Furthermore, it serves to affirm the position that we have seen Adorno more or less committed to throughout. Of particular significance is the illustration of the impossibility of explaining experience without subjective agency. The problem entailed here is the impossibility of a nonjudicative assertion of truth or validity. For a criticism of an existentially oriented phenomenology we turn now to Adorno's views of Heidegger.

3 Heidegger and the Problem of Epistemology

There can be no doubt that Adorno is difficult to read and sometimes harder to understand. It is perhaps no surprise that many of Adorno's readers have found it easier to fit Adorno into the well-established framework of some other philosopher than to wade through the endlessly qualified and recast concepts we find throughout his texts. This approach sometimes starts out for illustrative purposes, but often ends with the conclusion that few differences exist between Adorno and the philosopher with whom he is being compared. It is easy to lose control of Adorno's texts. The result is a loss of distinctiveness: the very ideas that this book has given so much attention to are buried under exciting similarities with other postidealist philosophers. As an instance of this Adorno's negative dialectic has lately been "recognized" as a precursor to deconstruction.[15] Martin Jay has described the temptations behind such tantalizing likenesses: "Adorno's 'negative dialectics' and Jacques Derrida's deconstruction have ... earned frequent comparisons because of their common rejection of totalizing philosophies of identity, distrust of first principles and origins, suspicion of idealist ideologies of sublation, and valorization of allegorical over symbolic modes of representation."[16] That such general similarities have lead many into a virtual "mind meld" of Adorno and Derrida says much about the lack of detailed attention that Adorno's texts receive. And yet these superficially plausible comparisons have at least reawakened interest in Adorno's work.

Prior to the comparison with Derrida various commentators detected deep similarities with Heidegger, and this is a far more serious matter. There are profound difficulties in aligning Adorno with Heidegger, given the weight that Adorno places on his critique of the latter's fundamental ontology. It can appear, at times, that Adorno uses Heidegger as little more than a foil, an "occasion" par excellence for Adorno's own agenda: Heidegger's role is that of the paradigmatic subjectivist and irrationalist to be heroically opposed by Adorno's reconstructed subject–object theory. Regardless of Adorno's exaggeration of the distinction between his philosophy and that of Heidegger, significant theoretical differences nevertheless remain. That is not to deny the interesting, sometimes beguiling parallels. For instance, both philosophers criticize certain fundamental assumptions about the modern philosophy of the subject. Furthermore, both reject the claims of empiricist epistemology on the grounds that it fails to capture what they take to be a wider notion of the objectivity of experience. Not surprisingly, then, this leads many to questions about the rational and systematic basis of the apparent parallels between Adorno and Heidegger.[17] From the point of view of understanding Adorno's philosophy this is a vital issue, in my view, for an important part of the subtlety of his position lies precisely in those aspects of it that lead him into opposition to Heidegger's version of antiepistemological philosophy. This opposition could be fatally embarrassing were Adorno's position to become ultimately indistinguishable from what he takes to be the failed categories of fundamental ontology.

So, what are we to make of the points of parallel? It is my view, as I shall argue here, that those points are coincidental. By examining Adorno's critique of Heidegger we can see that Adorno and Heidegger reach their respective conclusions about the limitations of traditional epistemology by very different means and out of concerns for very different philosophical problems. Broadly put, the difference between Adorno and Heidegger can be characterized as a difference between *critical* and *phenomenological* versions of transcendental philosophy. By this I mean that Adorno's philosophy tends to emphasize a particular rational structure of experience, a structure missed by traditional philosophy. Heidegger, by contrast, constructs a different model by elaborating a phenomenological account of existing. In essence, this latter is a phenomenological description of the conditions of experience.

Once we appreciate the particular sensitivity to philosophical concepts with which both Adorno and Heidegger operate we will be able to separate the different routes by which they reach their respective conclusions from the conclusions themselves. If we fail to acknowledge this then our interpretation will be guided by a fallacious hermeneutic that confuses a superficial lack of incompatibility with programmatic similarity. Read in that way, the exceptional vehemence of Adorno's critique of Heidegger suggests a case of fraternal rivalry and a consequent "protesting too much." In my view, a major difficulty with Adorno's critique of Heidegger is not that it obscures similarities, but rather that Heidegger is sometimes misrepresented beyond recognition. It is undoubtedly the case that the animus that Adorno feels toward Heidegger's philosophy leads him to act more like a prosecutor than a critic. And that animus may have cultural roots, arising as it does partly from the clash of the different worlds of prewar Frankfurt and Freiburg.

I will, as in my examination of Adorno's other philosophical critiques, attempt to adjudicate on the accuracy of Adorno's reading of Heidegger. But it is not enough to understand Adorno's criticisms and the exegetical limits of those criticisms. A further issue here is whether Heidegger's position has better claims to the conclusions that Adorno wants to reach. From a Heideggerian point of view it might be possible to consider Adorno's philosophy as simply abstract and negative: arguably it is abstract in that it identifies subject and object as the basic concepts for discussion. It may also be merely negative in that it operates primarily by delimiting the potential of epistemological analysis. If these can be shown to be problems in Adorno's position then the possibility that Heidegger's phenomenological version of transcendental philosophy can analyze experience without abstraction or negation represents a serious challenge. In this light, *Being and Time* may, in part, be understood as an attempt to establish a materialist yet antiempiricist philosophy. Heidegger, in rejecting scientistic thought and what he would understand as deforming epistemology, seems to go a considerable way toward presenting a model of experience that is neither abstract nor reductive. This is the basic position from which Adorno has to distinguish himself. Adorno, however, differentiates himself from Heidegger through critique. Before assessing the justification of that differentiation it is necessary to understand the relevant terms of Heidegger's philosophy (even if this exposition might initially be somewhat familiar).

4 Epistemology and "Being-in-the-world"

For Heidegger, the starting point for philosophy is crucial and much of his labor in the early parts of *Being and Time* can be seen as efforts to find that point. His analysis of the form of being characteristic of human beings is taken, to a large extent, from the point of view of what he terms "everydayness" (*Alltäglichkeit*). Even though, during the course of *Being and Time*, Heidegger's analyses extend into facets of human being that are by no means "everyday"—for example, the feeling of *Angst*—the focus is always in opposition to the supposed special viewpoints of epistemology. Thus human existing does not primarily take the form of rationalistic categorial performance—as seems to have been assumed by Enlightenment treatments of human nature—but is discovered, more fundamentally, in the prereflective hermeneutic practices of everyday existence. The idea of practices suggests a nontraditional philosophical picture of human existence. It deliberately contrasts with the modern epistemological model of the subject that takes the subject to be separate in some way from the epistemic situation in which it finds itself. Heidegger's "concrete" enquiry argues that, in contrast to the epistemological idea of an instrumental and contemplative subject, the subject is part of its practices and not external to them. In this connection Heidegger famously employs the term *Dasein* for individual human existence as it captures the appropriate concrete or material sense of existence. Because of his radically different views about the relation of the subject to its practices, Heidegger distinguishes his enquiry from what he sees as the available problematic alternatives. His way of explaining this is as follows: "Philosophical psychology, anthropology, ethics, 'politics,' poetry, biography, and historiography pursue in different ways and to varying extents the behavior, faculties, powers, possibilities, and destinies of Da-sein. But the question remains whether these interpretations were carried out in as original an existential manner as their existentiell originality perhaps merited" (*BT* 16). For Heidegger, then, a "new" philosophy will be a matter of outlining the fundamental structures of *Dasein* that are either superficially captured or entirely missed by other disciplines.

Already at this point an important difference with Adorno can be noted. Adorno does not set out to describe or reveal structures or essential features of the being of human beings. Indeed Adorno expresses disagreement with the anthropological essentialism that, he suspects, might be the result of Heidegger's program *malgré lui*. This possibility emerges, he thinks, from a philosophy based on the historical entity, *Dasein*. He writes: "The more concrete the form in which anthropology appears, the more deceptive will it come to be, and the more indifferent to whatever in man is not at all due to him, as the subject, but to the de-subjectifying process that has paralleled the historic subject formation since time immemorial" (*ND* 130/124). Adorno's interest is rather with the structure of experience, the structure of the determinative relation between subjects and objects. This marks a different question. The difference might be stated as follows: although Adorno and Heidegger are both engaged in attempting philosophical regeneration, their respective fields are primarily radicalized epistemology and ontology.

The issue, however, goes some way further than this. Included within Heidegger's ontological analysis is an existential "category," the category of "being-in-the-world." Even though this is an ontological term—it describes a mode of being of *Dasein*—it is also a term with significant epistemological implications. Traditional epistemology, as Adorno also argues, operates with a dualistic terminology that establishes a relationship of knower against the world. For Heidegger, the idea of being-in-the-world is intended to oppose this very claim and to underpin a completely different model of the subject-object relationship. It is intended, indeed, to bypass precisely the difficulties of idealism that are set up by subject-object dualism. This obviously involves a reevaluation of the role of epistemology. For Heidegger it appears to be taken as given that epistemological and ontological conditions are different. Epistemological descriptions fail to capture the reality of what happens in *Dasein's* being-in-the-world: "[S]ubject and object are not the same as Da-sein and world" (*BT* 60). In contrasting epistemology with concrete experience, the program offered by Heidegger in so far as it is concerned with a critique of subjective immanence may seem quite close to Adorno. Both reject that model of subjectivity that sees subjectivity as self-constituted or independent of the world (Heidegger) or object (Adorno). Heidegger's consequent critique of subject–object dualism (presented in the form of an antinomy) could hardly be disputed by Adorno:

> The more unequivocally we bear in mind that knowing is initially and really "inside," and indeed has by no means the kind of being of physical and psychic beings, the more we believe that we are proceeding without presuppositions

in the question of the essence of knowledge and of the clarification of the relation between subject and object. For only then can the problem arise of how this knowing subject comes out of its inner "sphere" into one that is "other and external," of how knowing can have an object at all, and of how the object is to be thought so that eventually the subject knows it without having to venture a leap into another sphere. (*BT* 60)

By contrast, the idea of being-in-the-world underwrites what Heidegger sees as a more unified, indeed holistic, relationship: "The compound expression 'being-in-the-world' indicates, in the very way we have coined it, that it stands for a *unified* phenomenon. This primary datum must be seen as a whole" (*BT* 53). This relationship is further characterized as one that underlies the conditions of the possibility of knowledge. It follows that knowledge cannot be explained as "instrumentalism," a model founded on an inside/outside distinction, that is, the essential separation of subject and object. Typically, Heidegger finds another compound expression for this epistemological aspect of being-in-the-world: "[K]nowing itself is grounded beforehand in already-being-in-the-the-world [*Schon-sein-bei-der-Welt*]" (*BT* 61).

From the foregoing, then, we can see that Heidegger proposes an analysis of traditional epistemology that appears to be quite compatible with Adorno's conclusions. Clearly, fundamental ontology denies that traditional epistemology can give an accurate account of our relation to the world. Further, it grounds philosophy in an existential concreteness—a materialism—that consciously contrasts itself with the dualizing tendencies of the modern representationalist tradition.

5 Subject–object in Heidegger: Adorno's Critique

There is no surprise in the tendency of the history of philosophy to produce similar philosophical positions from diverse sources. One could see how Heidegger's existential-pragmatist reading of phenomenology[18] and Adorno's materialization of German Idealist philosophy might coincidentally produce parallel lines. But it is important, nevertheless, to investigate their differences for the simple reason that, as I have said, Adorno criticizes and rejects Heidegger's proposed solution to the central problem of modern philosophy.

Adorno on Husserl and Heidegger

The critical issue separating Adorno from Heidegger is that of the subject-object relationship. Heidegger may not intend that fundamental ontology contain the categories of phenomenological reduction, *epoché*, or Cartesian introspection. Adorno argues, however, that Heidegger's philosophy retains the key features of immediacy so remarkably exploited by the "phenomenological Husserl" (i.e., the Husserl of, for example, *Ideas* or *Cartesian Meditations*). In this regard there is a passage in *Being and Time* that proposes a particular way of dealing with the problem of subject-object. Significantly, it is a passage that reveals a very deep philosophical disagreement with Adorno. In relation to the philosophical value of dialectics Heidegger boldly announces: "The possibility of a *more radical conception* of the problem of being grows with the continuing development of the ontological guideline itself, that is, with the 'hermeneutics' of the *logos*. 'Dialectic,' which was a genuine philosophic embarrassment, becomes superfluous" (*BT* 25, my italics). This radical view is more than just rhetoric: it makes a programmatic announcement regarding the relationship of subject and object. Adorno contends that the dismissal of the "dialectic," in the name of something "more radical," must produce a fall back into a position of sheer immediacy—one in which the rational mediation of subject and object is denied. He writes that Heidegger "pursues dialectics to the point of saying that neither the subject nor the object are immediate and ultimate; but he deserts dialectics in reaching for something immediate and primary beyond subject and object" (*ND* 112/106). Adorno's version of subject–object theory establishes a relation founded upon a "dialectic" of immediacy (or identity) and mediation (or nonidentity). But if that structure is to be abandoned, as Heidegger seems to be implicitly suggesting, then we are left, by the very nature of the subject-object structure established by Adorno, with the options of either immediacy or radical dualism: the subject–object relationship cannot be set up in any other way once mediation has been excluded. Since Heidegger is attempting to overcome what he sees as the dualism of subject and object it appears that what remains after his rejection of the "dialectic" of "immediacy and mediation" must be "immediacy." At least that is what Adorno wants to establish. A look at the lines of Adorno's argument is thus required.

In a way, Heidegger, in the above passage (regarding dialectic) has given prima facie credibility to Adorno's charge (although Adorno regrettably does not cite it). By attempting to step outside the subject–object relationship Heidegger will appear to Adorno to have committed the "error" of immediacy. It is undoubtedly this stance that gives Adorno reason to place Heidegger's effort within the subjectivistic excesses of so-called constitutive phenomenology. Adorno lays two main charges against Heidegger on the basis of the latter's particular rejection of a subject–object account of experience. First, Heidegger is accused of privileging a prereflective form of experience that leads him to irrationalism. Second, fundamental ontology is alleged not to contain the conceptual resources that would enable it to overcome idealism, the key position in the philosophical tradition that Heidegger criticizes so strongly. Even without examining any particular philosophical arguments it is by no means obvious that both such critical claims can be sustained at the same time. Modern irrationalism, it is true, is subjectively immanent in that it gives authority to the subjectivity of experience; that authority is granted at the expense of what it sees as the inhibitions of reason. Epistemological idealism, on the other hand, is not a disposition but an explanation; that is to say, it is not a normative activity (whereas irrationalism is, prescribing as it does ways of achieving immediate access to certain truths).

Given that, as Adorno claims, the subject-object relation is the basis of thinking and thus the basis of any conceptual knowledge of the world it would seem, *from this assumption*, that Heidegger has committed himself to *irrationalism*. Heidegger short-circuits the categories of reflection and appeals, instead, to an immediacy that supersedes such categories: "One of the motives of dialectics is to cope with that which Heidegger evades by usurping a standpoint beyond the difference of subject and object—the difference that shows how inadequate the *ratio* is to thought. By means of reason, however, such a leap will fail. *We cannot, by thinking, assume any position in which the separation of subject and object will directly vanish, for the separation is inherent in each thought; it is inherent in thinking itself.* This is why Heidegger's moment of truth levels off into an irrationalist *Weltanschauung*" (*ND* 92/85, my italics). Adorno distinguishes himself from Heidegger by the differing attitude that he takes to epistemology. They might both reject the subject–object divide of modern epistemology, but the conclusions they draw from that rejection are quite different. An alternative account of experience does not have to be—as Adorno accuses Heidegger of proposing—a process of nonrational immediacy. Rather, experience, for Adorno, contains an irreducible subject–object relation. And it is the task of a new philosophy—in effect, Adorno's negative dialectic—to capture that relationship rationally without reduction. Without both aspects of that program philosophy will either become reductive (empiricism and idealism) or irrational (Heidegger). As Adorno puts it: "When we believe we are, so to speak, subjectlessly clinging to the phenomenality of things, are original and neorealistic and at the same time doing justice to the material, we are in fact eliminating all determinations from our thought, as Kant once eliminated them from the transcendental thing-in-itself. Determinations would be equally offensive to us as works of mere subjective reason and as descendants of a particular entity" (*ND* 86/79). The pressing immediacy of the world allegedly eliminates, it seems, the need for rational reflection, a move that gives Adorno grounds for his charge of irrationalism against Heidegger.

But we really must ask, how true is it that Heidegger's rejection of subject–object analysis aligns him with modern irrationalism? The passage from *Being and Time* regarding dialectic (cited above) certainly causes difficulties. Heidegger's proposal for something "more radical" seems to make Adorno's case relatively easily. Heidegger's other important work from the period of *Being and Time*, *The Basic Problems of Phenomenology* (often considered a useful companion volume to *Being and Time*), however, gives us reason to think that Heidegger's "radical" conception might be fairly construed in a way that does not demand what Adorno would see as irrationalist immediacy. Rather, indeed, it might refer to that level of experience that Adorno himself is also attempting to explain: concrete nonreified experience. If this is so, then a defense of Heidegger might (sloganistically) be put as follows: the *pre*epistemological does not imply the *anti*epistemological. *Basic Problems* should cause us to be cautious about suggesting that Heidegger has *irrationally* abandoned subject–object philosophy. It seems that Heidegger's critique of the subject–object relationship is not intended, contrary to the assumptions of Adorno's arguments, to bring thought back to a dogmatic premediational level. Were it intended to, then Heidegger would have to accept Adorno's division of the philosophical territory and concede that he had given himself no option but irrationalism. But Heidegger's program is independent of Adorno's.

Heidegger refers to the preepistemological attitude as the "mode of primary self-disclosure" by which the self is known.[19] "The self," he writes, "is there for Dasein without reflection and without inner perception before all reflection."[20] Clearly, Heidegger is attempting to capture the nature of preepistemological self-apprehension. The object of criticism is the epistemological subject as conceived both by empiricism and idealism. Heidegger's claim is that the obvious but nontrivial order of self-apprehension is existentially more relevant than epistemological description: "The Dasein does not need a special kind of observation, nor does it need to conduct a sort of espionage on the ego in order to have the self; rather, as the Dasein gives itself over immediately and passionately to the world itself, its own world is reflected to it from things. This is not mysticism and does not presuppose the assigning of souls to things. It is only a reference to an elementary phenomenological fact of existence, which must be seen prior to all talk, no matter how acute, about the subject–object relation."[21] This passage challenges Adorno's critique of Heidegger, for it suggests that Adorno's critique is a misconception of the project of fundamental ontology. In it we can see that Heidegger is contrasting the indubitable ordinary experience that we have of ourselves with epistemological explanations of self-consciousness. Crucially, Heidegger is not saying that we should (irrationally) abandon conceptual analysis in favor of the sheer immediacy of experience. Rather he is proposing—contrary to the assumptions of the epistemological tradition—that our ordinary experience has an authoritative priority, and that the "in the world" reality of our subjective life is not reached by idealistic constructions. Thus Heidegger is not engaging in an antirational analysis of the kind that, in Adorno's view, must lead him to step back from conceptual philosophy.[22]

But there is another way in which Adorno's "irrationalist" charge attempts to gain some purchase on Heidegger. Irrationalism in its strict philosophical form—the rejection of conceptualization in certain experiences—may not be accurately applied to fundamental ontology, as we have seen. But if the task of philosophy—as Adorno thinks—is one of generating a new version of rationality that has transformative capacities, then Heidegger in this specific sense lacks the version of rationality Adorno regards as necessary. The product of Heidegger's eschewal of traditional discussion of the subject–object relation deprives him of an account of a critical subject in the sense that Adorno thinks is required. Adorno writes: "By the demand which Husserl set forth and Heidegger tacitly adopted, on the other hand, that mental facts be purely described—that they be accepted as what they claim to be, and as nothing else—by this demand such facts are so dogmatized as if reflecting on things of the mind, re-thinking them, did not turn them into something else" (*ND* 88/81). The claim here, then, is that the contributing agency of subjectivity is replaced by a noncritical intelligence that merely accepts things "as what they claim to be." The idea that reflection has transformative capacities is excluded. What Adorno is expressing in this latter criticism is a disappointment for critical theory with the apparently conservative tendencies of fundamental ontology. The element of irrationalism that may be discerned here, then, is in Heidegger's exclusion of that moment—an exercise of rationality, as Adorno sees it—in which the subject can critically differentiate itself from its environment by subjecting it to rational evaluation.

6 Heidegger's Idealism?

A further criticism Adorno makes of Heidegger is that fundamental ontology has an idealist commitment that is entirely antithetical to Heidegger's stated efforts to overcome the traditional options of modern epistemology. This surprising charge becomes intelligible from within the framework of Adorno's philosophy. Adorno's subject–object theory commits him to the view that, if a philosophical position implicitly rejects his construction of subject–object relations, then it is necessarily committed to immediacy and identity.[23] As set out in chapter 2 above, the failure to work within what Adorno proposes in his account of subject–object mediation means that it will be difficult to explain the real role of the object as prior to the subject. Consequently, implicit rejection of Adorno's epistemology means reverting to a "predialectical" position. (Within the present terms of philosophy there cannot be a "postdialectical" philosophy.) For Adorno, quite simply, a premediational philosophical position amounts to the endorsement of unmediated subjectivity: a subject that is not explained by reference to objects. In view of this, Heidegger's radicalism must amount, as Adorno nicely puts it, to "an escape into the mirror" (*ND* 91/84). This is a paradoxical conclusion; that is, that the escape from subjectivity by nonepistemological means finds itself enmeshed in subjectivity: "Heidegger's realism [*Sachlichkeit*] turns a somersault: his aim is to philosophize formlessly, so to speak, purely on the ground of things, with the result that things evaporate for him. Weary of the subjective jail of cognition, he becomes convinced that *what is transcendent to subjectivity is immediate for subjectivity*, without being conceptually stained by subjectivity" (*ND* 86/79, my italics). The move to a sheer being-in-the-world, then, that attempts a move away from subjectivity, is incoherent, Adorno argues, in that it contains a commitment to immediacy: objects are immediate to the subject and as such cannot be construed as in any respect nonidentical with the object. It is no longer explicable within those terms required by Adorno to affirm its priority. Adorno takes this to amount to Heidegger's alignment with idealism.

In this regard Adorno gives particular attention to Heidegger's concept of "project" (*Entwurf*). He argues that the concept of project is "idealist" in that it sees worldhood as a projection of subjectivity. As an explanation of experience it thus leaves no room for the idea of nonidentity, for something that is part of experience, yet irreducible to the activities of the subject. In *Basic Problems* Heidegger explains "project" as follows: "The world is something 'subjective,' presupposing that we correspondingly define subjectivity with regard to this phenomenon of world. To say that the world is subjective is to say that it belongs to the Dasein so far as this being is in the mode of being-in-the-world. The world is something which the 'subject' 'projects outwards,' as it were, from within itself. But are we permitted to speak here of an inner and an outer?"[24] There is something curious about the question raised in that passage about "inner" and "outer."

The holistic account of experience he offers (the idea of being-in-the-world) would seem to move beyond the problematic relations of inner states and outer objects. However, Adorno's position seems to be that Heidegger cannot assert that the inner–outer distinction is no longer meaningful on the grounds that he has overcome subjective idealism. Rather, such a claim arises from Heidegger's alleged reduction of the relationship between subject and object to subjectivity. It may therefore not seem to be an accident that Heidegger's attempt to account for the non-I resembles in character the Fichtean hypothesis that the object is objective only by virtue of subjectivity:

> But even if we grant the legitimacy of starting not with an isolated subject but with the subject-object relation it must then be asked: Why does a subject "require" an object, and conversely? For an extant entity does not of itself become an object so as then to require a subject; rather, it becomes an object only in being objectified *by* a subject. A being is without a subject, but objects exist only for a subject that does the objectifying. Hence the existence of the subject-object relation depends on the mode of existence of the subject. But why? Is such a relation always posited with the existence of the Dasein? The subject could surely forego the relation to objects. Or is it unable to? If not, then it is not the object's concern that there exists a relation of a subject to it, but instead *the relating belongs to the ontological constitution of the subject* itself. To relate itself is implicit in the concept of the subject. In its own self the subject is a being that relates-itself-to.[25]

The significant omission from this passage is any expression of a belief in the possibility that subjectivity might be in any way shaped, caused, or determined by its relation to objects. Heidegger often appears to claim that the subject-object relation is merely a mode of *Dasein*, and Adorno takes this to be synonymous with subjectivity. Again it cannot be that Heidegger is actually recommending idealism. It is rather that the structures of fundamental ontology do not provide the appropriate distinction between subject and object.

In "The Idea of Natural History" (1932)—one of the earliest of his mature works—Adorno was already suspicious of the Heideggerian idea of "project." He understood Heidegger's thesis to be that history is a mode of human beings (*IN* 350/114). The basis of our historical dynamic lies in "project," the horizon of our possibilities. What of nature though? According to Adorno, Heidegger's account of the world assumes that as history is a mode of human beings then all facticity—the actual world—can be explained through "project." Significantly, this concept of facticity, Adorno claims, also includes nature. In this way there is no basis on which we might contrast nature and history. It is this, however, that gives Adorno the grounds for the charge of idealism: if nature is nothing more than history—conceived through the idea of "project"—then there is no way of identifying any external limits to the subject. If we conceive history as project we are precluded from explaining the complexity of the phenomenon, in that, as Adorno thinks, it contains aspects—accident and contingency—that cannot be explained by reference to the concept of project. That, at least, is Adorno's assertion. As a way out of this difficulty, ontology sets up the category of "contingency," and in so doing attempts to demonstrate that what does not fit within the project is nevertheless a feature of the historical (*IN* 351/115). In a sense, then, the category of contingency, according to Adorno, is a category that attempts to master the contingent. The resistance of the world to transparency is given ontological significance, and thereby schematized within the ontological project. History is reduced to ontology by Heidegger. The complex and contradictory character of history is given a role within the project of life. In that way, it is alleged, ontology follows the classical ambition of encompassing all of reality.

A defense of Heidegger might be that a philosophy that takes life as its material can hardly be idealistic since it assumes that life is prior to the construction of the self. This was indeed one of the principles that made Heidegger such an influential critic of the Cartesian project.[26] However, Adorno's counter is that regardless of the phenomenon of life—the nonrational, something that is not reducible to categories—Heidegger assumes that an exhaustive structural-ontological interpretation of the world is possible. In distinguishing himself from Heidegger he makes this clear: "It makes ... an enormous difference whether irrational contents are inserted into a philosophy that is founded on the principle of autonomy, or if philosophy no longer assumes that reality is adequately accessible" (*IN* 352/116).

Recently William Blattner has argued that Heidegger can be construed as a particular kind of idealist. His claim that Heidegger explains "time" as mode of Dasein is suggestive of Adorno's claim that Heidegger reduces "history" to a mode of Dasein. A large part of Blattner's argument is developed by demonstrating connections between Heidegger's fundamental ontology and certain claims found in Kant's transcendental idealism. He writes:

> What I have called Kant's "epistemological standpoint" is the reflective posture of the mind as it works through the conditions for the possibility of its *a priori* knowledge. We find a correlative standpoint in Heidegger, what we may call his "phenomenological standpoint," his stance as he puts into words the sense and ground of all phenomena, their ontological framework. Time is assigned to the conditions of sensibility [Kant]/ontological frameworks [Heidegger] from the epistemological/phenomenological standpoint. So far, then, Heidegger and Kant are both transcendental idealists. They both take time to be transcendentally ideal, or dependent upon the human mind/Dasein, when considered from the transcendental standpoint. Heidegger is, in considerable detail, a Kantian, transcendental idealist about time.[27]

If this is so—and Blattner's arguments are impressively comprehensive—then it might be used to support Adorno's claim that Heidegger's position is idealist. We can see, interestingly, that the charges Adorno lays against Heidegger are similar to those he laid against Kant. He has criticized Kant for failing to supply an account of experience that can accommodate the notion of nonidentity: both the Transcendental Aesthetic (concerning the forms of space and time intuition) and the Transcendental Deduction failed, according to Adorno, to explain the role of objectivity in the operations of experience. Either they relied on terms that had no application at the transcendental level or they simply failed to explain the experience of particularity. (Our examination of Adorno's critique of the "I think" suggested that Adorno's reading of Kant could not be accepted without reservation.) And interestingly, parallel charges were brought against Heidegger by Adorno in that his account of Dasein allegedly either illicitly employs notions at the transcendental level—"project," "history," or "contingency"—or fails to explain experience without reference to independent objects. However, it is the absence of detailed argument that is an issue in the success of Adorno's criticism. Unless he can show—and ultimately he does not—that Heidegger's considerations of Dasein's role in "worldhood" are equivalent to the discussion in epistemological idealism about the role of the agent in the constitution of objects, we are left with an open question about the effectiveness of Adorno's critique.

What remains significant here are the position-defining distinctions that Adorno makes between his version of transcendental philosophy and Heidegger's. Adorno develops a rational epistemology in an attempt to demonstrate that the structure of experience is an irreducible subject–object relation, whereas Heidegger establishes ontological concepts while still operating firmly within the domain of phenomenological experience. Certainly, this distinction is made sharper by exaggerating, to an extent, Heidegger's commitment to a form of phenomenological immediacy. And quite obviously there is more to Heidegger's position than Adorno is prepared to admit. For instance, Heidegger's account of readiness-to-hand (*Zuhandenheit*), with all its existential-pragmatic implications, provides an analysis of experience that, in terms of detail, is sorely missing from Adorno's account of dialectics. This concept, indeed, might serve Adorno's purpose very well in that it acknowledges the pragmatic role of a thing "for me," without ever reducing the thing to a mere thought entity. Adorno is adept at situating isolated elements of fundamental ontology within the critical framework of his negative dialectic. Inevitably, that selectivity is not to Heidegger's advantage. As I suggested, arguing that Heidegger fails to conform with the thesis of mediation presupposes that thesis. Nevertheless, Adorno's critique does give us some grounds for questioning the radicalism that Heidegger claims for his fundamental ontology. It also, I think, presses us to think about the ability of fundamental ontology to conceive of a subject that is not constitutively immersed and effectively lost in its environment. Again, it is not necessarily the case that Heidegger thinks criticism is impossible: it is just that—as against Adorno's way of defending this notion—Heidegger's philosophy simply does not support it. The distinctive contribution of Adorno's "new philosophy" is highlighted in this perhaps most important of contrasts.

Conclusion

I have argued that Adorno's negative dialectic is a coherent and largely defensible position. My aim has been to set out the numerous dimensions and implications of Adorno's efforts to generate a critical philosophy, one that might return us to the possibility of experience. To make this case, I have had to reconstruct, to a certain degree, some of Adorno's unfinished arguments. Nevertheless, all of the views I attribute to Adorno have a basis in Adorno's own texts. As a final way of assessing whether Adorno's position has the coherence (and indeed strengths) that I attribute to it—that is, whether it really can give philosophical support to the idea of a critical experiencing agent as required by the broader program of critical theory—I want to test it against two key and potentially damaging objections.

The first of these is from Jürgen Habermas. Habermas's central objection to Adorno's philosophy has been quite influential in two major ways: first, it has generated a particular picture of Adorno that became authoritative in German philosophical circles, and, second, Habermas himself has been able to define his own position as a resolution of some of the issues with which the so-called first generation Frankfurt School (primarily Adorno) became, on his account, so abysmally confused. Indeed a significant tranche of the history of recent philosophy takes its orientation from Habermas's view of Adorno.[1] Habermas argues that Adorno is committed to a model of subjectivity that actually excludes the possibility of the new version of the subject-object relation (mediation) that Adorno himself attempts to develop in his theory of experience. He writes: "The fear of a fall back into metaphysics is appropriate only so long as one moves within the horizon of the modern philosophy of the subject. The idea of reconciliation cannot plausibly be accommodated in the basic concepts of the philosophy of consciousness from Descartes to Kant; and in the concepts of objective idealism from Spinoza and Leibniz to Schelling to Hegel, it can only be given an extravagant formulation. Horkheimer and Adorno know this, but they remain fixated on this conceptual strategy in the very attempt to break its spell."[2]

Habermas believes, then, that Adorno's philosophy employs a "conceptual strategy" that entails: (a) that it can be positioned "within the horizon of the modern philosophy of the subject" and (b) that it also lies within "the basic concepts of the philosophy of consciousness."[3] His argument is that Adorno is locked within some theory of subjectivity that undermines the possibility of a "reconciliation" of subject and object. This is potentially a quite devastating critique of Adorno in that if true it aligns him with a tradition of philosophy that he himself has attempted to refute in various ways. Furthermore, this tradition is criticized by Adorno precisely on the grounds that its version of subjectivity is a parody of the critical subject proposed by and defensible from within Adorno's own theory of subject–object mediation. It is the case, as we have seen, that Adorno pays a great deal of attention to the subject–object relation, attempting to devise a structure that gives appropriate value to the role of objects in experience (and here Adorno likes to contrast himself with all of those philosophers with whom Habermas associates him). For Adorno the limits of our conceptualization are revealed in the nonidentical component of experience.

To put it in "transcendental terms," the very possibility of subjectivity assumes the possibility of experience, and in experience there is always this nonsubjective component. There is no question as to how the subject connects with or engages in the nonsubject: there is no foundational commitment to subjectivity—as there may be in Kant, according to Adorno and to Heidegger's more famous criticism—which leaves the philosopher, like some reincarnated early German Idealist, attempting to make "the non-ego result from the ego as the web from the spider," to use Schopenhauer's scornful phrase.[4] The thesis of mediation, as we have seen, is a thesis about the interdetermination of subject and object. Adorno offers an extensive range of ideas on the role of the object—ideas that exclude the possibility of philosophy taking the position of the philosophy of the subject. Subject–object language certainly has its roots in the tradition that appears to unnerve Habermas, but Adorno's version of the subject–object relationship represents a critical evolution from the problematic representationalism of the eighteenth and early nineteenth centuries.

There is a wider agenda lying behind Habermas's objection: whether critical theory in the form proposed by Adorno can deliver the kind of critique of rationality needed for social transformation. Clearly, Habermas believes the answer to be no. And of course, Habermas's conclusion is that the linguistic turn in philosophy—that is, the turn to language and the turn away from epistemology—should be exploited in the effort to achieve a theory of social transformation. I have disputed that Adorno's position suffers the incoherence attributed to it by Habermas. As a contribution to critical theory the "negative dialectic" provides an account of how we might criticize the irrationality of contemporary society. It takes seriously the Hegelian idea of "experience" in which a "consciousness" confronted by a body of data that does not cohere with its concept of knowledge must revise its concept. Thus, a comprehensive evaluation of the contemporary notion of "liberal democracy" might reveal strains between, say, the notions of freedom and individuality. And that revelation might lead to a more "self-conscious" notion of liberty. Or the reality of reification might become knowledge to an individual struck by the inability of her concepts to determine adequately some given object. In each of these cases, the rational response is to develop a sophistication of conceptual framework. (One might imagine the utopian situation in which a flexible and complex consciousness would spontaneously critically examine the assumptions behind any putative validity claim.) Adorno approaches the question of the possibility of critical rationality through epistemological considerations. This necessarily deprives it of a certain specificity. But its strength lies in its capacity to defend a notion of rational experience (contrasted with "withered" experience). Again and again his critiques of the key positions of contemporary philosophy are conducted through an enquiry into what conditions must pertain if experience is to be possible. And finding these positions problematic he charges not simply that they make philosophical errors, but that they operate under erroneous models of rationality, models that, in various ways divide subject and object, rather than expressing their mutual mediation. In the course of his treatment of subjectivity Adorno demonstrates, I think, that "unencumbered" constitutive subjectivity—which, as a basic belief of critical theory holds, is the philosophical expression of bourgeois subjectivity—can be shown to be aporetic. Habermas, nevertheless, finds this unsatisfactory. He claims that in Adorno the "critique of instrumental reason, which remains bound in the conditions of the philosophy of the subject, denounces as something that it cannot explain in its defectiveness because it lacks a conceptual framework sufficiently flexible to capture the integrity of what is destroyed through instrumental reason."[5] In this book I have tried to show that Adorno, in fact, does go a considerable distance in showing us what it is that is "destroyed by instrumental reason" and reification; namely, Adorno's account of the possibility of "full unreduced experience, in the medium of conceptual reflection."

Adorno's position—as an epistemological treatment of the issues of concern for critical theory—does not take the linguistic turn followed by Habermas. Habermas's position has moved considerations of validity from epistemology (Habermas would prefer to say "philosophy of consciousness") to an examination of the rationality implicit, although not always realized, in communicative norms. What Habermas's version of critical theory moves toward—in self-conscious contrast with Adorno (his negative justification for the move)—is "linguistically established subjectivity,"[6] as opposed to the alleged effort of Adorno to develop out of the isolated consciousness a socially relevant rationality. He positively justifies this move in the following way:

If we assume that the human species maintains itself through the socially coordinated activities of its members and that this coordination has to be established through communication—and in certain central spheres

Conclusion

through communication aimed at reaching agreement—then the reproduction of the species *also* requires satisfying the conditions of a rationality that is inherent in communicative action.[7]

And further,

[A] subjectivity that is characterized by communicative reason resists the denaturing of the self for the sake of self-preservation. Unlike instrumental reason, communicative reason cannot be subsumed without resistance under a blind self-preservation. It refers neither to a subject that preserves itself in relating to objects via representation and action, nor to a self-maintaining system that demarcates itself from an environment, but to a symbolically structured lifeworld that is constituted in the interpretative accomplishments of its members and only produced through communication.... The utopian perspective of reconciliation and freedom is ingrained in the conditions for the communicative sociation of individuals; it is built into the linguistic mechanism of the reproduction of the species.[8]

The move from "consciousness" to "communication" is supposed to provide an entirely different model of subjective agency to the instrumental model inherent in modern philosophy. Insofar as Adorno remains within the earlier model he is left, the charge goes, with a self-defeating task.

It is not easy to imagine how Adorno would respond to the complex position offered by Habermas. He might reply that all experience contains the potential for "reconciliation" of subject and object, that indeed all experience is made possible only because there is a relation of mediation that philosophy and conventional social rationality has simply failed to recognize. In that respect the solution to the problem of reconciliation is implicit in the very structure of experience (just as for Habermas it is implicit in communicative action). But he might further suggest that if the ideological assumptions of modern society are a barrier to the recognition of what might be then they stand in the way, a fortiori, of Habermas's hope for a critical theory based on "a rationality that is inherent in communicative action." It is impossible—and self-evidently unnecessary—to set out the details of Habermas's position in this context. Furthermore, it would be too great an undertaking to compare the comparative merits of the two models of critical theory offered by Adorno and Habermas.[9] Undoubtedly the history of philosophy will find in Habermas's writings a significantly more comprehensive and sophisticated version of critical theory. However, I think that it is simply unfair to deny that Adorno's critical theory has manifest achievements even though it operates outside the sort of linguistic analysis provided by Habermas. The line of thought that I emphasize in Adorno—his epistemological strategy—certainly provides only a limited contribution to the complex and detailed questions raised by the second generation of critical theory—it is, after all, quite abstract in its procedure. But it is by no means incoherent.

The second key objection comes from Michael Rosen. His objection to Adorno's theory of the components of rational experience relates to Adorno's idea of objects. Whereas Habermas alleges that we cannot overcome subjectivity by means of Adorno's crypto-subjectivist philosophy, this second objection charges that we cannot understand objects in Adorno's sense—as having some identifiably independent role in the reciprocality of subject-object mediation—unless we see Adorno's position as more idealist than he really wants to allow. Either the object is intrinsically meaningless or indeterminate, and thus infused *idealistically* by intentional relations or determinations, or it is intrinsically meaningful, a postulate incompatible with Adorno's avowed materialism. Again, the essence of the objection is that Adorno is unable to achieve his philosophical aims except, inconsistently, with concepts that he has claimed to replace. As Rosen states it: "As a materialist Adorno denies that natural processes are intrinsically meaningful because nature has a purpose—a *telos* towards which it strives. So what can he mean when he says that history is 'sedimented' in phenomena? How can a materialist say that an object literally 'bears in itself' anything other than a causal natural history? . . . . It is at this point that we see the fundamental equivocation in Adorno's theory. Instead of answering the question of how meaning processes can have this quasi-natural 'objectivity' in relation to individuals, he slips back into an Idealist terminology that conceals the dilemma."[10] Rosen holds here (1) that Adorno is a materialist, (2) that he denies that nature is intrinsically meaningful, (3) that he claims that objects are "sedimented history." From what we have seen in this study it is fair to say that each of Rosen's points captures a discernible aspect of Adorno's philosophy.

Conclusion

The conclusion Rosen draws is that (1) and (3) simply exclude each other, and that fatally undermines the realization of Adorno's philosophy. I think that this conclusion forces us to consider just what exactly Adorno's materialism is, since it is precisely this concept that is at stake in Rosen's criticism.

It is true that Adorno's materialism denies—as we have seen—the inherent conceptuality of objects. It might seem reasonable to extend this idea and to claim that Adorno therefore regards nature—the sum total of all objects—as intrinsically meaningless. But this is not what Adorno actually holds. For Adorno, nature is the world of objects, and objects are conceptualized only through the processes of the social totality. They are thereby, as we have seen and as Rosen notes, their "sedimented history." (Indeed, some Marxist philosophers who also hold this view of nature term nature, in this sense, "second nature," distinguishing it from the concept of nature assumed in the natural sciences.) The social totality and the individual are not of course identical: the individual is faced with meanings that have been produced through the social totality, and obviously enough, these meanings are irreducible to any individual (and this reality, for Adorno, undermines the possibility of subject-oriented philosophies). The object can in this respect be coherently described as independent of the subject.

But how is this materialist? It is worth rehearsing the main ideas once again. Adorno's version of materialism is of course nothing like the well-known thesis that matter is ultimate and spirit (or mind) is either dependent on it or illusory. (He is no La Mettrie, no Churchland.) More precisely this materialism originates from the standard Marxist rejection of Hegel's idea that society and history are guided by the extramaterial forces of *Geist.* Famously, the Young Hegelians reread theology as the concealed history of humanity. Marx applied this to Hegel to reveal that the world of *Geist* is nothing more than the world of society. Furthermore, society does not move forward by means of the self-developments of spirit. It moves because of the activities of human beings. This is a materialist conception in that it sees the world as explicable entirely in terms of human beings attempting to understand and order their experience. Consistent with that is the further characteristic that materialism rejects the

Conclusion

concept of an inherently meaningful reality. The idea of a meaningful reality could only be justified by appeal to some metaphysical, Hegelian conception of the nature of reality. Such a conception would exclude the fundamental role of human agency. Only if we take Adorno to be offering a traditional, let us call it mechanistic materialism, does his claim for the sedimented historical nature of objects seem problematic.

I have also discussed a further sense in which Adorno can be considered as a materialist. The account of experience in Adorno is not, as we have seen, simply "conceptualist": it does not hold that each component of experience is ultimately conceptual. The very idea of nonidentity expresses the materialistic or naturalistic relation of subject to object, and in this moment of nonidentity the particularity of the object is experienced. This nonidentical moment arises paradigmatically in our physical relation to objects. Adorno would indeed be guilty of an inconsistency were he to claim that this nonidentical moment conveys the conceptual qualities of the objects. The nonidentical moment is part of the meaning of the experience, as indeed are the conceptual qualities of the object as they have come to be in their sedimented history. The discussion of this in chapter 2 showed, I think, that Adorno sees experience as containing a vertical moment expressed within the relation of concept to object in judgment. And this vertical moment is essential as an element of experience—as a dimension of subject–object mediation.

Habermas and Rosen are surely right to be concerned by Adorno's employment of idealistic looking concepts in the name of what are often anti-idealistic theses. Adorno may run the risk that his use of originally idealistic terminology actually obscures his largely anti-idealist commitments. As I think chapter 1 shows, Adorno, idiosyncratically no doubt, sees the German Idealist tradition as a mine of potentially revolutionary concepts. But what that mine yields is fashioned in ways that would have been the cause of grievous consternation to Kant and Hegel.

I have not attempted to disguise the fact that from certain perspectives Adorno's negative dialectic contains some limitations. But it is my view too that the interpretation that I have made of

Conclusion

Adorno reveals the particular strength of his position, which is that of revealing the hidden commitments and structures of contemporary philosophy. Contemporary philosophy operates with a version of rationality that ultimately prevents it from offering a viable description of the real. As Adorno's reading of fundamental ontology makes particularly clear, the analysis of the subject–object relationship is preparatory to whatever further account we can give of experience. By making the analysis of the subject–object relationship the center of his philosophy Adorno can be aligned (as I have argued) with that transcendental tradition that seeks to describe not the historical nature of meaning and experience, but rather the necessary structures and conditions of our experience. That is not to say that Adorno has nothing to say about historical matters: his various critiques of culture are replete with historical specificity. But negative dialectics deals with experience in its general structure. It is, after all, attempting to give philosophical foundation to the very practice of critical theory, to the very possibility of a rationality that lies latent—although not always recognized—within experience itself. Because philosophy is ultimately a matter of how we are to understand our world, it is important to appreciate the structural conditions of our interrelation with the world. The ultimate importance of Adorno's negative dialectic, it seems to me, is its successful encouragement of a deeper awareness of the subject–object structure of our philosophical commitments.

Notes

Preface

1. See J. M. Bernstein, "Introduction" to Theodor W. Adorno, *The Culture Industry: Selected Essays on Mass Culture* (London: Routledge, 1991), ed. J. M. Bernstein, in which the presuppositions behind Adorno's use of empirically specific aspects of society are concisely laid out.

2. See *MM* 93–96/85–87. For a fuller treatment of this issue, "The Essay as Form" (*EF*) in its entirety is indispensable.

3. Rüdiger Bubner, "Adornos Negative Dialektik," in *Adorno-Konferenz 1983* (Frankfurt am Main: Suhrkamp Verlag, 1983), eds. Ludwig von Friedeburg and Jürgen Habermas, p. 35.

Introduction

1. Jürgen Habermas, *Theory of Communicative Action*, volume 1 (London: Heinemann, 1984), trans. Thomas McCarthy, p. 390.

2. Rüdiger Bubner in this regard offers the conventional criticism that "Precisely in the name of dialectic, it cannot be permitted to break off at one place, which is characterized only by private opinions and convictions which allow of no justification. The point at which, as it were, the tablets of the law announce 'Thus far and no further' is not, as Adorno suggests, where dialectic begins but where it abruptly comes to an end" (Rüdiger Bubner, *Modern German Philosophy* [Cambridge: Cambridge University Press, 1981], trans, Eric Mathews, p. 180).

3. The arguments are not always laid out in the most helpful ways: at times, in fact, as Herbert Schnädelbach points out, Adorno seems to eschew the need for argument. See Herbert Schnädelbach, "Dialektik als Vernunftkritik: Zur Konstruktion des Rationalen bei Adorno," in *Adorno-Konferenz 1983* (Frankfurt am Main: Suhrkamp Verlag, 1983), eds. Ludwig von Friedeburg and Jürgen Habermas, pp. 77–78.

Notes

4. I therefore agree entirely agree with Anke Thyen's observation that *"Negative Dialectics* can be read as a theory of experience." *Negative Dialektik und Erfahrung: Zur Rationalität des Nichtidentischen bei Adorno* (Frankfurt-am-Main: Suhrkamp Verlag, 1989), p. 213.

5. Cf. J. M. Bernstein, "Why Rescue Semblance: Metaphysical Experience and the Possibility of Ethics," *The Semblance of Subjectivity: Essays in Adorno's Aesthetic Theory* (Cambridge, Mass./London: MIT Press, 1997), eds. Tom Huhn and Lambert Zuidervaart, pp. 180–183.

6. For a helpful discussion of the specific *rationality* of Adorno's position see Schnädelbach, "Dialektik, also Vernunftkritik" pp. 67–69; also Helga Gripp, *Theodor W. Adorno: Erkenntnisdimensionen negativer Dialektik* (Paderborn: Verlag Ferdinand Schöningh, 1986), pp. 12–15.

7. Jürgen Habermas has given an excellent taxonomy of positivism, largely supportive of Adorno's critique of it. In *Knowledge and Human Interests* (London: Heinemann, 1972), trans. Jeremy J. Shapiro, pp. 74–77, he has attempted to reach a definition of positivist philosophy. The essential criteria, he argues, are (1) the emphasis on sense certainty; (2) methodological certainty; (3) precision; (4) utility of knowledge; and (5) relativity.

8. Confronted by what he takes as the prevailing scientism Adorno suggests an alternative; what in those early days he called "philosophy as interpretation." Interpretation would be *the* philosophical approach, the approach that acknowledges from the start that experience is irreducible to either subject or object: ultimately the complex relation of subject-object would be the philosophically justifiable account of experience. Adorno begins to make his case by distinguishing philosophy from science in the following way: "Plainly put the idea of science [*Wissenschaft*] is research; that of philosophy is interpretation" (*AP* 334/31). Philosophy is the activity of engaging in an understanding of experience—interpretation reveals the dynamic qualities of experience. The hard sciences, by contrast, according to Adorno, "accept their findings, at least their final and deepest findings, as indestructible and static" (*AP* 334/31). A perhaps more important point is that philosophical reflection is committed to an idea of objects that are complex, whereas science allegedly assumes that they are fully reducible to the findings of research. Some commentators have argued, indeed, that Adorno's philosophy is usefully considered as a form of hermeneutic theory, precisely because of Adorno's remarks that philosophy has an interpretative objective. Ulrich Müller sees the negative dialectic as a "critical hermeneutics" (Ulrich Müller, *Erkenntniskritik und Negative Metaphysik bei Adorno* [Frankfurt: Athenäum, 1988], p. 116). Michael Rosen makes a similar connection. See Michael Rosen, *Hegel's Dialectic and Its Criticism* (Cambridge: Cambridge University Press, 1982), pp. 164–166. Hauke Brunkhorst also points out—in a different though interesting way—the hermeneutic dimension of Adorno's negative dialectic. See Hauke Brunkhorst, *Theodor W. Adorno: Dialektik der Moderne* (Munich/Zurich: Piper, 1990), pp. 232–242.

9. In *Capital* Marx had also remarked on this reduction of the social dynamic to a quantitative comparison: "It is nothing but a social relation between men themselves which assumes here, for them, the fantastic form of a relation between things" (Karl Marx, *Capital 1* [Harmondsworth: Penguin, 1976], trans. Ernest Mandel, p. 165).

Notes

10. "Introduction," in *The Positivist Dispute in German Sociology* (London: Heinemann, 1976), trans. Glyn Adey and David Frisby, p. 25; "Einleitung zum *Positivismusstreit in der deutschen Soziologie*," in *Gesammelte Schriften*, volume 8 (1972), ed. Rolf Tiedemann, p. 306.

11. Karl Marx and Friedrich Engels, *The Communist Manifesto*, in *Karl Marx: Selected Writings* (Oxford: Oxford University Press, 1977), ed. David McLelland, p. 222.

Chapter 1

1. De facto identity and de jure identity are, we might suggest, closely related in that they are the two historical strands of representationalism: de facto identity corresponds to representational idealism and de jure identity corresponds to empiricism. In order to overcome identity (in its different forms) Adorno proposes what he sees as a necessarily rational strategy: to remain within the terms of philosophy while demonstrating their limitations: "[Philosophy] must strive by way of the concept to transcend (*hinausgelangen*) the concept" (*ND* 27/15). He does not propose to bypass concepts in the attempt to describe a different form of relationship between subject and object, one that would make the object the exclusive component of cognition. (We have already seen in "The Actuality of Philosophy" Adorno's reasons for rejecting irrationalism).

2. Michael Rosen, *Hegel's Dialectic and Its Criticism* (Cambridge: Cambridge University Press, 1982), p. 162.

3. Elsewhere I have argued that there are up to four possible versions of the concept of mediation in Hegel's work. The different versions hold that (i) mediation is the intellectual mechanism by which we proceed from contingency to necessity; (ii) the process of knowledge cannot be coherently explained without reference to a non-immediate element (and that element is mediation); (iii) the possibility of content is determined by the form of judgment, and that must include mediation; and (iv) that since a necessary precondition of any fact is its historical production it is, in this sense, mediated. See Brian O'Connor, "The Concept of Mediation in Hegel and Adorno," *Bulletin of the Hegel Society of Great Britain*, 39/40 (1999) for a fuller discussion of these issues.

4. Cornelius was the author of, among (many) other things, *Einleitung in die Philosophie* (Leipzig: B. G. Teubner, 1903), *Transcendentale Systematik: Untersuchung zur Begründung der Erkenntnistheorie* (Munich: Ernst Reinhardt, 1916, second edition, 1926), *Das philosophische System: Eigene Gesamtdarstellung* (Berlin: Junker Duennhaupt, 1934), *Kommentar zu Kants Kritik der reinen Vernunft* (Erlangen: Verlag der Philosophischen Akademie, 1926).

5. This is the influential interpretation argued for by Henry Allison, *Kant's Transcendental Idealism: An Interpretation and Defense* (New Haven, Conn./London: Yale University Press, 1983), and earlier by Graham Bird, *Kant's Theory of Knowledge: An Outline of One Central Argument in the* Critique of Pure Reason (London: Routledge and Kegan Paul, 1962).

6. Adorno, then, is by no means a Kantian in any orthodox sense. As we shall see in chapter 4, he argues that what is missing in Kant is a way of positively accounting for objects such that we can understand their role in the epistemic process. We shall see

Notes

that for Adorno the problem with the thing-in-itself is not, as it was for Kant's immediate successors, that it is incompatible with idealism. Rather the problem is that it is an empty and therefore nonviable concept of an object. Kant's strategy is, in effect, to demonstrate the limits of subjectivity, and that limitation leaves space for objects. However, because objects *in themselves* are what is on the other side of a limit, they are characterized as entirely other than the objects that can be apprehended by a subject. As we shall see, Adorno offers a certain picture of Hegelian philosophy in order to give objects conceptual quality, something which Kant, it seems, cannot. This conceptual quality is essential if we are to take Kant's insight into the limits of subjectivity into a comprehensive subject-object epistemology. As it stands, it provides some of the necessary conditions, but not all of them.

7. Heidegger, of course, rejects the idea that the Refutation of Idealism really does overcome the idealist dualism of mind and world.

8. Graham Bird, "Kant's Transcendental Arguments," in *Reading Kant: New Perspectives on Transcendental Arguments and Critical Philosophy* (Oxford: Basil Blackwell, 1989), eds. Eva Schaper and Wilhelm Vossenkuhl, p. 24.

9. In the literature on this section I have found no satisfactory account that both explains what kind of objects Kant means and at the same time acknowledges the success of the argument.

10. Though he would have had the opportunity to do so in the Transcendental Doctrine of Method, chapter 1, section 4 (*CPR* A782/B810ff) when he discusses the idea of "transcendental proofs."

11. Another possible way of illustrating the difference between the external and internal versions of antinomy is as follows. When Kant asks the following series of questions his intention is to show that only transcendental philosophy can yield the answers without contradiction. "The questions which naturally arise in connection with such a dialectic of pure reason are the following: (1) In what propositions is pure reason unavoidably subject to an antinomy? (2) On what cause does this antinomy depend? (3) Whether and in what way, despite this contradiction, does there still remain open to reason a path to certainty?" (*CPR* A421/B449). The answer to (1) is metaphysical propositions. (2) reveals that human speculation might be naturally unbounded—that is, we make claims that lie outside our experience—if we do not understand what is entailed in the constitution of our experience. Question (3) is answered with the justification of critical philosophy. Adorno's particular claim is that once we identify extraexperiential entities as the explanation of concrete experience we are left with an aporia. In practice this works out as follows: an aporetic principle is one that attempts to provide a *ground to consequence* type explanation. This means that the principle in question—for example, a transcendentally constitutive subject—is somehow to be the cause of experience. To pursue the example, an explanation with this structure, however, cannot account for experience as it is, in fact, antinomical: either the principle remains extraexperiential and fails to explain experience (as it does not connect up with experience) or it translates into experiential propositions and thereby loses the explanatory value it had attempted to attain (since the principle is merely a part of experience).

12. In the *Encyclopaedia of Philosophical Sciences* Hegel specifies that a dialectical thought is a necessary succeeding second moment of thought. What happens in that moment is that the apparently "fixed determinations" established by the abstractive

Notes

understanding in the first grasp of knowing something become complicated in a certain way. That is, when we first judge that S is p we find on further consideration of the matter, that p may be inappropriate as a characterization of S (perhaps it is too limiting). This is an experience common to anyone involved in abstract thought, from jurisprudence (where one might try to fit a principle to an instance) or literary criticism (where a coherent interpretation must always be determined by the text of the literary work) to physics (where general laws are confronted by specific hypotheses). Dialectic—also termed by Hegel "the negatively rational" (*EL* §79)—recognizes the limitation of the first moment of thought—the judgment made in that moment—and forces us to realize that the concept applied to that object in fact contradicts the object: "The dialectical moment is the self-sublation of these finite determinations on their own part, and their passing into their opposites."

13. I have argued elsewhere that this idea of "unthinking inertia" is the basis of Adorno's theory of ideology. See the introduction to *The Adorno Reader* (Oxford/Malden, Mass.: Blackwells, 2000), ed. Brian O'Connor, pp. 11–15.

14. Jon Elster, *Making Sense of Marx* (Cambridge: Cambridge University Press, 1985), p. 40.

15. Ibid.

16. Michael Oakeshott, *Experience and Its Modes* (Cambridge: Cambridge University Press, 1933), p. 19.

17. A formal way of thinking about how a purely internal standard is possible is to think about the experience of contradiction. To recognize a contradictory judgment and to reject such a judgment as invalid is the most fundamental activity of rationality. Now a contradictory judgment, say X is a not-x, can be analyzed in Hegel's terms in the following way: the concept (not-x) does not concord with the object (X). What happens is that the standard, the concept, is, in fact, dismissed because it does not coherently specify the object. If X is not a not-x then our standard, in effect, must be revised.

18. In his recent book, *Adorno: Disenchantment and Ethics* (Cambridge: Cambridge University Press, 2001), J. M. Bernstein reconstructs and develops this implicit ethical position of negative dialectics. The case is definitively made. My aim here is simply to acknowledge that there are practical implications while demonstrating primarily the evident epistemological approach of Adorno's position. This is a process of scrutinizing the epistemological structure of Adorno's thought.

Chapter 2

1. Anke Thyen, *Negative Dialektik und Erfahrung: Zur Rationalität des Nichtidentischen bei Adorno* (Frankfurt-am-Main: Suhrkamp Verlag, 1989), p. 204.

2. To repeat the definition: de facto identity posits the independent meaningfulness of concepts. No claim is made with respect to the identity of object and concept, but since concepts alone are explained as the meaning element of the relationship it follows, de facto, that the object is meaningful only insofar as it is conceptualized. The object is thereby identical with its concepts, from the point of view of meaning.

3. Adorno's rejection of Kant's official transcendental idealism is based on this principle. When Kant, in the Aesthetic and Deduction, argues that every act of knowledge involves subjective investment he fails to realize that these subjective acts must also, as Adorno puts it, "adjust to a moment which they themselves are not" (*ND* 142/138).

4. Aristotle, *Metaphysics* (Cambridge, Mass.: Harvard University Press, 1993), trans. Hugh Tredennick, Book A, 988a18–993a10 (Aristotle's criticism of his predecessors).

5. As Ralph C. S. Walker notes of the starting point of transcendental arguments in general: "To be capable of formulating thoughts at all he [the skeptic] must be aware of his experiences (though certainly it may be a more complex matter whether he must be aware of himself as their subject). It is not that it would be impossible to deny this—in a sense it is possible to deny anything; but it would be remarkably perverse, and would take him beyond the reach of serious argument" (Ralph C. S. Walker, "Transcendental Argument and Scepticism," in *Reading Kant: New Perspectives on Transcendental Arguments and Critical Philosophy* [Oxford: Basil Blackwell, 1989], eds. Eva Schaper and Wilhelm Vossenkuhl, p. 58).

6. See Eckart Förster, "How are Transcendental Arguments Possible?" in Schaper and Vossenkuhl, *Reading Kant*, pp. 11ff.

7. Another famous contemporary version of this type of proof is Jean-Paul Sartre's so-called ontological proof, as presented in *Being and Nothingness* (New York: Philosophical Books, 1956), pp. x–xii, trans. Hazel E. Barnes. The conclusions of this argument again amount to nothing more than the idea that there is extra-mental reality. There can be no sense in which this proof can, by itself, reach the distinctly Adornian claim that objects have determinations.

8. Interestingly, Adorno seems sometimes to assume that objects have integrity, an idea not suggested by their being the sum total of their parts. They are therefore not contingent bundles, the sum total of what *a subject* happens to think of them. In *EF* 11/94 Adorno refers to the "object's expression in the unity of its elements," suggesting again the idea of the "substantiality" of the object.

9. Norbert Rath brings some of these ideas together rather nicely. He writes: "The negative dialectic remains materialist in that it couples the concept of mediation to the 'priority of the object'; mediating thought has not to supply an external communication between object and recipient, but has to demonstrate the mediations in themselves. Adorno sees in this the possibility of a connection of the idealistic critique of knowledge with a materialist theory of society: a dialectical materialism must conceive the moment of mediation as constitutive for knowledge in general" (Norbert Rath, *Adornos Kritische Theorie: Vermittlungen und Vermittlungsschwierigkeiten* [Paderborn/Munich/Vienna/Zurich: Ferdinand Schöningh, 1982], pp. 137–138).

10. Actually there is another view of nonidentity proposed by several commentators. Herbert Schnädelbach sees it as a "concept symbol," a "cipher," or a "logical metaphor" (Herbert Schnädelbach, "Dialektik als Vernunftkritik: Zur Konstruktion des Rationalen bei Adorno," in *Adorno-Konferenz 1983* [Frankfurt am Main: Suhrkamp Verlag, 1983], eds. Ludwig von Friedeburg and Jürgen Habermas, p. 70). Birgit Sandkaulen also uses the term "cipher" (see Birgit Sandkaulen, "Adornos Ding an sich: Zum Übergang der Philosophie in Ästhetische Theorie," in *Deutsche Vierteljahrsschrift für Literaturwissenschaft und Geisteswissenschaft* [Sonderheft, 1994], p. 393 and passim). The "cipher" interpretation is attractive in that it can accommodate a great amount

Notes

of the indeterminacy from which the idea of nonidentity seems to suffer. But it is also for just that reason hard to accept; it simply shifts the questions elsewhere. What is the "cipher" a cipher of? (Schnädelbach, by the way, also makes the incredible suggestion that Adorno's idea of nonidentity is ultimately Platonic in that nonidentity is always—allegedly—beyond the reach of concepts ["Dialektik," p. 76].)

11. Ralph C. S. Walker, "Synthesis and Transcendental Idealism," *Kant-Studien*, volume 76 (1985), p. 25.

12. Anke Thyen notes quite rightly that "non-identity is not simply the opposite of identity, the other of identity" (Thyen, *Negative Dialcktik*, p. 198), and that for Adorno "every experience in the medium of reflection encounters something irreducible which cannot be taken in by concepts alone" (ibid., p. 218).

13. However, he adds that "the insight that philosophy's conceptual knowledge is not the absolute of philosophy ... is again due to the nature of the concept" (*ND* 23/11–12). I shall reserve discussion of this solution for a later section. The result, however, of undermining the idea that concepts are logically primitive is, for Adorno, the end of the identity thesis, for without hypostatized concepts it becomes possible to consider the contribution of the objects to meaning: "A basic philosophy, πρώτη φιλοσοφία, necessarily carries with it the primacy of the concept; whatever withholds itself from the concept is departing from the form of allegedly basic philosophizing.... Once we dismiss such identity in principle, the peace of the concept as an Ultimate will be engulfed in the fall of identity. Since the basic character of every general concept dissolves in the face of distinct entity, a total philosophy is no longer to be hoped for" (*ND* 140/136).

14. And further in this regard: "[The] judgment that a thing is such and such is a potential rebuttal to claims of any relation of its subject and predicate other than the one expressed in the judgment" (*ND* 30/19).

15. In a certain respect what Adorno is attempting here can be usefully compared with Frege's delineation of the elements of the proposition. Frege notes that "the singular definite article always indicates an object, whereas the indefinite article accompanies a concept word" (Gottlob Frege, "On Concept and Object," in *Translations from the Philosophical Writings of Gottlob Frege* [Oxford: Basil Blackwell, 1970], trans. P. Geach and M. Black, p. 45). But how do these elements of concept and object combine? Adorno, as we have seen, at one point hastily takes meaning to be a matter of particularity alone (as was suggested by the passage on the arbitrariness of words, in relation to their objects). When he discusses the more sustainable line that judgment is the basic unit of meaning he sees judgment as containing an inherent tension between object and concept. What he seems to be working toward is an account of the object-concept relation that allows a meaning-bearing asymmetry. Frege's view of the same relationship is instructive: "A thought always contains something reaching out beyond the particular case so that this is presented to us as falling under something general" (Gottlob Frege, *Posthumous Writings* [Oxford: Oxford University Press, 1974], trans. P. Long, R. White, and R. Hargraves, p. 174. Cited in Wolfgang Carl, *Frege's Theory of Sense and Reference: Its Origins and Scope* [Cambridge: Cambridge University Press, 1994], p. 60). Likewise Adorno has expressed that idea that "[n]o concept would be thinkable, indeed none would be possible without the 'more' that makes a language of language" (*ND* 112/106). Frege shares the idea that something must be incomplete in order for us to explain the very function of judgments: "[N]ot all the parts of a thought can be complete; at least one must be unsaturated or predicative"

Notes

(Frege, "On Concept and Object," p. 54). Concepts, then, are unsaturated when compared with "completed" objects.

Chapter 3

1. See Zoltan Tar, *The Frankfurt School: The Critical Theories of Max Horkheimer and Theodor W. Adorno* (New York: John Wiley, 1977), chapter 2, for a very helpful discussion of all of the background issues here.

2. See Lambert Zuidervaart, *Adorno's Aesthetic Theory: The Redemption of Illusion* (Cambridge, Mass./London: MIT Press, 1991), pp. 23–26.

3. Hauke Brunkhorst, *Theodor W. Adorno: Dialektik der Moderne* (Munich/Zurich: Piper, 1990), p. 243.

4. And: "In the unreconciled [antagonistic] condition, non-identity is experienced as negativity" (*ND* 41/31).

5. See Herbert Marcuse's "The Concept of Negation in the Dialectic," *Telos*, No. 8 (summer, 1972), pp. 130–132, for a similar view expressed by a fellow Frankfurt-Schuler.

6. And: "To proceed dialectically means to think in contradictions, for the sake of the contradiction once experienced in the thing, and against that contradiction. A contradiction in reality, it is a contradiction against reality" (*ND* 148/144–145).

7. Novalis, *Novalis Schriften; die Werke Friedrich von Hardenbergs* (Stuttgart: W. Kohlhammer Verlag, 1960/1975), eds. P. Kluckhohn and R. Samuel, volume 2, p. 106, cited in Manfred Frank, "Philosophical Foundations of Early Romanticism," in *The Modern Subject: Conceptions of the Self in Classical German Philosophy* (New York: State University of New York Press, 1995), eds. Karl Ameriks and Dieter Sturma, p. 74.

8. J. G. Fichte, *The Science of Knowledge* (Cambridge: Cambridge University Press, 1982), trans. Peter Heath and John Lachs, p. 38.

9. See *ND* 193–194/192–194 for the section entitled "Passage to Materialism."

10. A useful way of thinking about this shift of object perception can be found in J. J. Valberg's *The Puzzle of Experience* (Oxford: Clarendon Press, 1992).

11. Peter Smith and O. R. Jones, *The Philosophy of Mind: An Introduction* (Cambridge: Cambridge University Press, 1986), p. 52.

12. As a point of clarification, it might be thought that Adorno is implicitly proposing a Gestaltist alternative. Gestalt theory's "laws of organization" are opposed to the empiricist theories of perception. It could be suggested that this would have been a lesson taught to Adorno by his reading of phenomenology. In the *Metacritique of Epistemology* Adorno writes that, "the ostensible ultimate data are already not a conglomerate but rather—as Gestalt theory has already proved *ad nauseam*—are structured and more than the sum of their parts" (*ME* 100/94). Adorno's approval of this central tenet of Gestalt theory seems as wholehearted as it is ill informed. (Gestalt theory never proved these structures.) Nevertheless this is not the full story.

Adorno, in fact, argues that Gestalt theory falls ultimately into the same problem as empiricism; namely, it atomizes experience. He writes: "But if Gestalt theory correctly objects to Hume and the psychology of association that 'there are' no such things as unstructured, more or less chaotic 'impressions' isolated from one another at all, then epistemology must not stop there. For data of the sort that epistemology [i.e., phenomenology] cites Gestalt theory as appropriately describing simply do not exist. Living experience is just as little acquainted with the perception of a red 'Gestalt' as it is with the ominous red percept. Both are the product of the laboratory" (*ME* 163–164/159).

13. Manfred Frank has argued from within the framework of German Idealist philosophy of the subject that physicalism relies on certain incoherent assumptions about the nature of our mental experience. It would be mistaken to align his considerations here with those of Adorno given that Frank rather daringly founds his position on a theory of subjectivity—the German Idealist apperceptive model—which, as we have seen, Adorno rejects. However, another part of Frank's difficulty with physicalist philosophy of mind is more congenial in that it argues that the reduction of the subject—what he exaggerates in all cases of physicalism as the elimination of the subject—would undermine the very possibility of philosophy. The subject is, he argues, the vehicle of philosophical reflection. See Manfred Frank, "Is Subjectivity a Non-Thing, an Absurdity [*Unding*]? On Some Difficulties in Naturalistic Reductions of Self-Consciousness," in Karl Ameriks and Dieter Sturma (eds.), *The Modern Subject: Conceptions of the Self in Classical German Philosophy* (Albany, N.Y.: State University of New York Press, 1995).

14. Thomas Nagel, "What is it like to be a bat?" in *Mortal Questions* (Cambridge: Cambridge University Press, 1979), p. 166.

15. Nagel, *The View from Nowhere* (Oxford: Oxford University Press, 1986), p. 31.

16. Ibid., pp. 32–33.

17. See, for instance, John Foster, "The Succinct Case for Idealism," in *Objections to Physicalism* (Oxford: Clarendon Press, 1993), ed. Howard Robinson.

18. See John Searle, *The Rediscovery of the Mind* (Cambridge, Mass./London: MIT Press, 1992), pp. 111–126.

19. Ibid., p. 122

Chapter 4

1. Carl Braun provides an uncompromising account of Adorno's reading of Kant. He traces Adorno's allegations back to those Kantian texts in which the offences supposedly took place, and ultimately finds little to substantiate Adorno's position. This is a useful exercise, but it takes place under something of a misapprehension about Adorno's claims to be a Kant interpreter. The balance that we, Adorno's readers, have to strike between assessing his critique and evaluating his philosophy will be discussed later in this chapter. See chapter 5 of Braun's *Kritische Theorie versus Kritizismus: Zur Kant-Kritik Theodor W. Adornos* (Berlin and New York: Walter de Gruyter, 1983), *Kant-Studien*, supplementary volume 115.

Notes

2. These works are both republished in Adorno's *Philosophische Frühschriften, Gesammelte Schriften*, volume 1 (Frankfurt: Suhrkamp Verlag, 1973), eds. Gretel Adorno and Rolf Tiedemann.

3. Rolf Tiedemann, "Editorische Nachbemerkung," in Adorno, *Philosophische Frühschriften, Gesammelte Schriften*, p. 382.

4. Ibid.

5. The full bibliographical information is *Transcendentale Systematik: Untersuchung zur Begründung der Erkenntnistheorie* (Munich: Ernst Reinhardt, 1916, 2nd edition, 1926). This book, by the way, is an impressive neo-Kantian epistemology, that, over 250 pages or so, pays particular attention to the nature of knowledge and the components of experience.

6. The book Adorno is referring to is Hans Cornelius, *Kommentar zu Kants Kritik der reinen Vernunft* (Erlangen: Verlag der Philosophischen Akademie, 1926).

7. However, another line of interpretation suggests that Kant argues that there is some kind of awareness of these acts of the "I think." This reading of Kant certainly makes more plausible the subsequent Fichtean development of Kantian idealism precisely as a form of Kantianism. In the *Science of Knowledge*, Fichte writes of intellectual intuition: "The intellect as such *observes itself*; and this self-observation is directed immediately upon its every feature. The nature of intelligence consists in this *immediate* unity of being and seeing" (J. G. Fichte, *The Science of Knowledge* [Cambridge: Cambridge University Press, 1982], ed. and trans. Peter Heath and John Lachs, p. 17). This interpretation has in recent times been powerfully put forward by Dieter Henrich. Henrich claims, "Kant articulated this idea and occasionally discussed it: he conceives the self as that act in which the knowing subject, abstracting from all particular objects, turns back into itself and in this way becomes aware of its constant unity with itself" (Dieter Henrich, "Fichte's Original Insight," in *Contemporary German Philosophy 1* [University Park, Penn.: Pennsylvania State University Press, 1982], trans. David R. Lachterman, p. 19) and "[t]hat self-consciousness does perform this act of turning back can easily be inferred, Kant thinks, from its structure. 'The expression 'I think (this object)' already shows that I, in respect to the representation [of 'I'], am not passive.' The word 'I' refers to someone who is performing an act. Now if this subject is itself the object of its own knowledge, then it is so precisely in virtue of its active subjectivity" (ibid.). The passage that Henrich's interpretation relies on suggests that we have the ability to be aware of our constitutive-synthetic acts in the course of their operation; an ability to experience our own constituting activity. The controversial passage falls into two parts, as far as this issue is concerned. It moves from our knowledge of the bare identity of the thinking *I*, or indeed of a unified selfhood, to a claim for the awareness of this thinking *I*'s activity (I have divided the passage accordingly): "[a] The original and necessary consciousness of the identity of the self is thus at the same time a consciousness of an equally necessary unity of the synthesis of all appearances according to concepts, that is, according to rules, which not only make them necessarily reproducible but also in so doing determine an object for their intuition, that is, the concept of something wherein they are necessarily interconnected. [b] For the mind could never think its identity in the manifoldness of its representations, and indeed think identity *a priori*, if it did not have before its eyes, the identity of its act, [*denn das Gemüt konnte sich unmöglich die Identität seiner selbst in der Mannigfaltigkeit seiner Vorstellungen und zwar a*

Notes

priori denken, wenn es nicht die Identität seiner Handlung vor Augen hätte . . .] whereby it subordinates all synthesis of apprehension (which is empirical) to a transcendental unity, thereby rendering possible their interconnection according to *a priori* rules" (*CPR* A108). (Frederick Neuhouser's analysis of Fichte's attempts to validate, by proof, the idea of the Absolute Ego has been very useful. Fichte, as Neuhouser rightly observes, employs both the argument from intuition [equivalent to the argument from acquaintance] and a transcendental method. My own view is that Fichte's argument must fail since intuition is an inappropriate route to a ground. It is also inaccurate to call Fichte's other approach transcendental, since it is merely an inference from experience. See Frederick Neuhouser, *Fichte's Theory of Subjectivity* [Cambridge: Cambridge University Press, 1990], especially pp. 87 ff.) The relationship between [a] and [b], which is set up as an inference, appears to be quite without foundation. Its only possible basis is an apperception or direct awareness that Kant surprisingly assumes. Unless we commit Kant in general to a precritical philosophical psychology—that is, Cartesian introspection—we cannot properly accommodate this view. From the point of view of the context of the *Critique of Pure Reason* as a whole it would be unfair to commit Kant to that position. The problems, however, are unfortunately as much philosophical as exegetical. It is difficult to dismiss this argument on the basis that it is only occasionally employed. Part [b] above is frankly a claim for a form of self-consciousness that relies on the possibility of some deep intuition; "before its eyes the identity of its act."

8. This will confirm that Kant's constitutions take place purely mechanically—that is, that different levels of the object's empirical reality must be traced back to some faculty of the subject.

9. The figure of speech used by Adorno is not actually "square circle," but rather the idiomatic "hölzernes Eisen."

10. Indeed the same tension is carried through to the later *Selbstsetzungslehre* of the *Opus Postumum*. See Eckart Förster, "Kant's *Selbstsetzungslehre*," in *Kant's Transcendental Deductions* (Stanford, Calif.: Stanford University Press, 1989), ed. Eckart Förster.

11. The exact relation between these concepts of positing and determination is never clearly laid out by Kant. In his reading of this central question for Kant's idealism Heidegger is surely correct when he remarks that this is "a problem that lies virtually hidden in the Kantian thesis" (Martin Heidegger, *Basic Problems of Phenomenology* [Bloomington, Ind.: Indiana University Press, 1982], trans and ed. Albert Hofstadter, p. 76). Heidegger's exploration of the problem, however, is quite helpful in that he clarifies the respective fields of "being" in which *positing* and *determination* are effective. His analysis is focused on Kant's criticisms of the ontological argument. He writes: "A hundred thalers do not differ in their what-contents whether they be a hundred possible or a hundred actual thalers. Actuality [*Wirklichkeit*] does not affect the *what*, the reality [*Realität*], but the *how* of the being, whether possible or actual" (ibid., p. 43). Heidegger then develops this by linking the *reality* of a being (whether possible or actual) with determination, and its *actuality* with positing. This is a very convincing schema of what is at issue in Kant's idealism: without positing (the argument of the Aesthetic) there could be no sensibility, and without sensibility there could be no *actual* determination by the categories (the argument of the Deduction). The categories actually *determine* a sensibility that has been *posited*. Without positing, though, categories are free to determine possible realities. The relation between *Setzen* and *Bestimmen* is never thematized in this way by Kant, but it is quite probable that this is the relation that actually exists between them in the first part of the first *Critique*.

Notes

12. That there might ultimately be no distinction is a point which was extensively exploited by post-Kantian German idealism.

13. Immanuel Kant, *Critique of Practical Reason* (New York: Macmillan, 1956), trans. Lewis White Beck, p. 103 (*Akademie*, 101–102).

14. J.-P. Sartre, *The Transcendence of the Ego* (New York: Octagon Books, 1972), trans. F. Williams and R. Kirkpatrick. Interestingly Sartre's reading of Kant denies the ground of the kind of criticism proposed by Adorno, describing it as a mistake to make "into a reality the conditions, determined by Criticism, for the possibility of experience" (pp. 32–33).

15. The passage in which this term occurs is worth citing in full: "Fichte hypostatized the 'I' that had been abstracted, and in this respect Hegel adhered to what he did. Both Fichte and Hegel skipped over the fact that the expression 'I,' whether it is the pure transcendental 'I' or the empirical, unmediated 'I,' must necessarily designate some consciousness or other. Giving an *anthropological-materialist* turn to this polemic, Schopenhauer had already insisted on that in his critique of Kant" (*DSH* 263/15–16, my italics).

16. Gilles Deleuze identifies this problem in quite similar terms. He writes: "The problem is as follows: how can a subject transcending the given be constituted in the given? Undoubtedly, the subject itself is given. Undoubtedly, that which transcends the given is also given, in another way and in another sense" (Gilles Deleuze, *Empiricism and Subjectivity: An Essay on Hume's Theory of Human Nature* [New York: Columbia University Press, 1991], trans. Constantin V. Boundas, p. 86).

17. Adorno claims elsewhere that without an "individual consciousness"—by which he means ordinary nontranscendental consciousness—the "I think" would be unintelligible: "Without an 'I,' and moreover a thoroughly individuated 'I,' there is not at all the 'I think' which accompanies all my representations" (*KK* 230).

18. One might be struck by the Wittgensteinian look of this position. However, I can find no evidence that Adorno was aware of the later work of Wittgenstein. He certainly addressed the *Tractatus*, which he read as the credo of hard logical positivism.

19. Ernst Tugendhat, *Self-Consciousness and Self-Determination* (Cambridge, Mass./London: MIT Press, 1986), trans. Paul Stern, p. 62.

20. Patricia Kitcher, "Kant's Real Self," in *Self and Nature in Kant's Philosophy* (Ithaca, N.Y.: Cornell University Press, 1987), ed. Allen W. Wood, p. 122.

21. Paul Guyer, "The Transcendental Deduction of the Categories," in *The Cambridge Companion to Kant* (Cambridge: Cambridge University Press, 1992), ed. Paul Guyer, p. 152.

22. P. F. Strawson, *The Bounds of Sense* (London: Methuen, 1966), p. 32.

23. Ibid., p. 247.

24. Ibid., pp. 248–249.

25. Ibid., p. 249.

Notes

26. One further though closely related parallel between Adorno's position and that of Strawson should be mentioned. This arises from their common approach to the problem of noumenal interaction. As Strawson writes: "The point of contact, in the way of identity, between a man as a natural being and himself as a supersensible being is to be found, then, in the man's consciousness of his own possession and exercise of the power of thought, of the faculties of understanding and reason.... Any such self-consciousness must, it seems, belong to the history of, and must be conscious of some episode belonging to the history of, a being which *has* a history and hence is not a supersensible being ..." (ibid., p. 248).

27. Adorno is also prepared to connect this failure with certain historical misconceptions about subjectivity: "The deepest and most penetrating idealist theorems, e.g. the Kantian theorems of the schematism of pure reason and the synthetic unity of apperception, lie furthest from the cognitive activities of men performed and exhibitable at a time, whereas they are most efficient at turning away theoretical contradictions. Simple concepts, untenable in harmonious foundation, such as Locke's sensation and reflection, may more closely describe the procedural modes of thinking than the 'I think,' which in truth already no longer expresses real acts of thought so much as an historical constellation of subject and object removed from individual activity" (*ME* 214/211–212).

28. It is clear, by the way, that Kant would not wish to propose the idea that the "I think" is an abstraction from empirical reality. "Empirical universality," he writes, "is only an arbitrary extension of a validity holding in most cases to one which holds in all ..." (*CPR* B4). An empirical analysis of consciousness can yield no "I think" since, "No fixed and abiding self can present itself in this flux of appearances. Such consciousness is usually named *inner sense,* or *empirical apperception. What has necessarily to be represented as numerically identical cannot be thought as such through empirical data.* To render such a transcendental presupposition valid, there must be a condition which precedes all experience, and which makes experience itself possible" (*CPR* A107, my italics).

29. It may be possible that the question which has created the problems Adorno identifies has been misguided. Perhaps Adorno's question about the nature of the "I think" makes the very category mistake that Kant himself had identified in the Paralogisms: it considers the "I think" as a thing. What Adorno should have done, it might be argued, is consider the "I think" from the point of view of its function. Although Kant does have certain things to say about the phenomenality and noumenality of the "I think" he need not be bound to these views: rather than asking about the epistemologico-ontological status of the "I think," perhaps we might alternatively consider the seemingly less demanding question of the *function* of the "I think." What "thinking" does this "I think" perform? Perhaps it is the case with the "I think," like the other transcendental concepts, that, as Wilfrid Sellars puts it, we "are not able to give a non-functional definition" (Wilfrid Sellars, "... this I or he or it (the thing) which thinks ...," in *Proceedings and Addresses of the American Philosophical Association,* volume 44 [1970–1971], p. 11). Indeed Adorno too at one point seems to think of the appropriate consideration of the "I" in terms of its functionality: "Only if the I on its part is also not I does it react to the not-I. Only then does it 'do' something. Only then would the doing itself be thinking" (*ND* 201/201). So is a functional account a way around the difficulty? There are here two possible answers to this question, but again we can identify the same antinomy. [1] The "I think" is an aspect of the self, and its "thinking" *is not* thinking in the sense familiar to ordinary consciousness. But in that case the activity of the "I think" is beyond understanding since the only sense

Notes

in which we know of thinking is experiential. (The idea that computers think is merely metaphorical, and easily translated into other terms.) The activity of the "I think" can be explained only by the supposed analogy with empirical thinking, but since this analogy cannot be translated it cannot serve as an explanation of the function. It therefore remains unintelligible. [2] The "I think" is an aspect of the self, and its "thinking" *is* thinking in the sense familiar to ordinary consciousness. This thinking would have to be differentiated from ordinary thinking. Perhaps that could be done by making it a feature of certain types of thoughts; deeper, more abstract, and so on. There might be other ways. This, however, would not work as the distinction would always have to be an empirical one. The function of the "I think" would be decided merely by the type of thoughts it had. On this basis it would be impossible to describe it as transcendental in any sense.

Chapter 5

1. "*Against Epistemology*" is actually the name given to the published English translation.

2. Dallas Willard, "The Paradox of Logical Psychologism: Husserl's Way Out," in *Husserl: Expositions and Appraisals* (Notre Dame, Ind.: University of Notre Dame Press, 1977), eds. Frederick A. Elliston and Peter McCormick, p. 10.

3. Ibid.

4. David Bell, *Husserl* (London: Routledge, 1990), p. 85.

5. Willard, "The Paradox of Logical Psychologism" p. 16.

6. Nietzsche, in *The Will to Power*, takes on the challenge offered to his position by the mandatory law of noncontradiction. He contends that there are two possible interpretations of the axioms of logic: either they are "adequate to reality or they are a means and measure for us to *create* reality, the concept 'reality,' for ourselves" ([New York: Random House, 1967], trans. Walter Kaufmann and R. J. Hollingdale, paragraph 516, p. 279). Nietzsche holds that if one is to argue that the axioms of logic are adequate to reality then one must have a prior, nonaxiomatic knowledge of reality; that is, one would have to know beforehand that opposite attributes cannot be ascribed to reality. Nietzsche remarks ironically that for the logician a prior knowledge is "certainly not the case," for the logician maintains the priority of the logical method in the act of apprehension (ibid.). We are therefore left with the other interpretation, that is that logic is "an *imperative* concerning that which *should* count as true" (ibid.).

7. See Friedemann Grenz, *Adornos Philosophie in Grundbegriffen: Auflösung einiger Deutungsprobleme* (Frankfurt am Main: Suhrkamp Verlag, 1974), pp. 35–42, for an account of "commodity fetishism" as developed by Adorno.

8. As a contrast to Husserl's absolutist version of truth Adorno suggests the rather metaphorical theory that such truths are "a field of force" (*ME* 79/72). Whatever we take to be true can only be justified within systems of discourse, within the mediating relations between concepts. A field of force is, then, the context alone in which objectivity can be justified.

Notes

9. Adorno has Heidegger as well as Husserl in mind at this point. He argues that the later Heidegger's effort to establish the meaning of being turns into an arbitrary concept of being simply because it has not included a notion of a critical subject.

10. Edmund Husserl, *The Crisis of European Sciences and Transcendental Phenomenology* (Evanston, Ill.: Northwestern University Press, 1970), trans. David Carr, pp. 49–50.

11. Dermot Moran, *Introduction to Phenomenology* (London/New York: Routledge, 2000), p. 179.

12. Husserl, *Crisis*, p. 141.

13. Edo Pivčević, *Husserl and Phenomenology* (London: Hutchinson, 1970), p. 89.

14. Husserl, *Crisis*, p. 139.

15. See Peter Dews, "Adorno, Post-Structuralism and the Critiques of Identity," *New Left Review*, no. 157 (1986), *Logics of Disintegration: Post-Structuralist Thought and the Claims of Critical Theory* (London: Verso, 1987), pp. 38–44, and Helga Gripp's especially useful *Theodor W. Adorno: Erkenntnisdimensionen negativer Dialektik* (Paderborn: Verlag Ferdinand Schöningh, 1986), pp. 132–144.

16. Martin Jay, *The Dialectical Imagination: A History of the Frankfurt School and the Institute of Social Research, 1923–1950* (Berkeley, Calif.: University of California Press, 2nd edition, 1996), p. xviii.

17. Rüdiger Bubner is an important instance of a critic who is unconvinced by Adorno's efforts to differentiate himself from Heidegger. He writes: "It has been shown ever more clearly, especially since the publication of Adorno's early writings, that he stood closer to his lifelong opponent, Heidegger, than he wanted to admit. The salvation of the nonidentical, which is suppressed by all identificatory system structures, bears striking parallels with *being* which, according to Heidegger, has been forgotten in the history of metaphysics, as well as in its modern continuity in technology" (Rüdiger Bubner, "Adornos Negative Dialektik," in *Adorno-Konferenz 1983* [Frankfurt: Suhrkamp Verlag, 1983], eds. Ludwig von Friedeburg and Jürgen Habermas, pp. 36–37). Hermann Mörchen's *Adorno und Heidegger. Untersuchung einer philosophischen Kommunikationsverweigerung* (Stuttgart: Klett-Cotta, 1981) is a daunting effort to make sense of the relation between the two.

18. As some see it—most famously, Hubert Dreyfus in his *Being-in-the-world* (Cambridge, Mass./London: MIT Press, 1991).

19. Martin Heidegger, *Basic Problems of Phenomenology* (Bloomington, Ind.: Indiana University Press, 1982), trans. A. Hofstadter, p.159.

20. Ibid.

21. Ibid.

22. Adorno is just as opposed as Heidegger is to explanations which presuppose preexperiential entities as the ground of experience. But if some of the results of Adorno's subject-object theory and fundamental ontology are occasionally similar it is also the case that the philosophical arguments that bring them there have to be

radically distinguished. It is fair to say that Adorno, unlike Heidegger, adheres to a quite traditional idea that epistemological considerations—considerations of the structure of experience—ought to be a matter of identifying the rational structure of experience, or at least of all talk about experience. Heidegger, by contrast, begins with experience, or rather "being" itself, and tries to establish a mode of enquiry which is uniquely suited to the task of describing the different modes of being. Adorno, however, attempts to explain the rational structure of experience so as to avoid making what he would see as simple "dogmatic" claims about it.

23. I do not know of any philosopher who has explicitly done so.

24. Heidegger, *Basic Problems*, p. 168.

25. Ibid., p. 157. And Heidegger then connects this to his concept of intentionality.

26. Jean-Luc Marion identifies unexpected connections between *Dasein* and the Cartesian *ego cogito*. Marion's reading, though perhaps forced at times, notes, like Adorno, the similarities between Heidegger and the modern idealist project. See his "Heidegger and Descartes," in *Critical Heidegger* (London: Routledge, 1996), ed. Christopher Macann.

27. William D. Blattner, *Heidegger's Temporal Idealism* (Cambridge: Cambridge University Press, 1999), p. 245.

Conclusion

1. Richard J. Bernstein, Axel Honneth, and Albrecht Wellmer have in this regard, it seems to me, taken their lead from Habermas.

2. Jürgen Habermas, *Theory of Communicative Action*, volume 1 (London: Heinemann, 1984), trans. Thomas McCarthy, p. 387.

3. Habermas seems also to say that Adorno has some commitment to "objective idealism" (the notion that the world has an ideal and internally coherent structure, a view held in different ways by Spinoza, Leibniz, Schelling, and Hegel). This may simply be an infelicity in Habermas's text. Vague and confusing as Adorno's language might be it still does not permit interpretation as a form of "absolute idealism." To say otherwise is to miss Adorno's relentless (repetitive even) criticism of Hegel to the effect that Hegel's presupposition that the world has an intelligible and rational structure—a preeminently objective idealist claim—is philosophically indefensible, as being contrary to the negativity of experience. This is said so often in Adorno's texts that one has a fair chance of finding a statement to this effect on any randomly opened page of *Negative Dialectics*, and especially, of *Hegel: Three Studies*.

4. Arthur Schopenhauer, *The World as Will and Representation*, volume 1 (New York: Dover, 1969), trans. E. F. J. Payne, §7, p. 33.

5. Habermas, *Theory of Communicative Action*, p. 389.

6. Ibid., p. 397.

Notes

7. Ibid., p. 397.

8. Ibid., p. 398.

9. For such a comparison I recommend Deborah Cook's *Adorno, Habermas, and the Search for a Rational Society* (London/New York: Routledge, 2004).

10. Michael Rosen, "Critical Theory: Between Ideology and Philosophy," in *The Need for Interpretation* (London: Athlone Press, 1983), eds. Sollace Mitchell and Michael Rosen, pp. 104–105. Cf. also Rosen's *Hegel's Dialectic and its Criticism* (Cambridge: Cambridge University Press, 1982), chapter 7, for further background to his views on Adorno's "materialist transformation" of Hegel's metaphysics.

References

Adorno

Adorno, Theodor W. *Gesammelte Schriften* (Frankfurt: Suhrkamp Verlag, 1971–1986). Edited by Gretel Adorno and Rolf Tiedemann.

Individual works cited

Schriften 1 (1973): *Die Transzendenz des Dinglichen and Noematischen in Husserls Phänomenologie* (1924); *Der Begriff des Unbewußten in der transzendentalen Seelenlehre* (1927); "Die Aktualität der Philosophie" (1931), trans. Benjamin Snow, "The Actuality of Philosophy," in *The Adorno Reader*, ed. Brian O'Connor (Oxford/Malden, Mass.: Blackwell, 2000); "Die Idee der Naturgeschichte" (1932), trans. Bob Hullot-Kentor, "The Idea of Natural History," *Telos*, no. 60 (1984).

Schriften 3 (1981): *Dialektik der Aufklärung* (1947), trans. John Cumming, *Dialectic of Enlightenment* (London: Verso, 1979).

Schriften 4 (1980): *Minima Moralia* (1951), trans. E. F. N. Jephcott, *Minima Moralia*, (London: NLB, 1974).

Schriften 5 (1970): *Zur Metakritik der Erkenntnistheorie: Studien über Husserl und die phänomenologischen Antinomien* (1956), trans. Willis Domingo, *Against Epistemology: A Metacritique* (Oxford: Basil Blackwell, 1982/Cambridge, Mass.: MIT Press, 1983); *Drei Studien zu Hegel* (1963), trans. Shierry Weber Nicholsen, *Hegel: Three Studies* (Cambridge, Mass./London: MIT Press, 1993).

Schriften 6 (1973): *Negative Dialektik* (1966), trans. E. B. Ashton, *Negative Dialectics* (London: Routledge and Kegan Paul, 1973).

Schriften 8 (1972): "Soziologie und empirische Forschung" (1957), trans. Glyn Adey and David Frisby, "Sociology and Empirical Research," in *The Positivist Dispute in German Sociology* (London: Heinemann, 1976), ed. Glyn Adey and David Frisby; "Einleitung zum *Positivismusstreit in der deutschen Soziologie*" (1969), trans. Glyn Adey and David Frisby, "Introduction," in *The Positivist Dispute in German Sociology* (London: Heinemann, 1976), ed. Glyn Adey and David Frisby.

Schriften 10.2 (1977): "Zu Subjekt und Objekt" (1969), trans. Andrew Arato and Eike Gebhardt, "Subject and Object," in *The Adorno Reader*, ed. Brian O'Connor (Oxford/Malden, Mass.: Blackwell, 2000).

Schriften 11 (1974): "Der Essay als Form" (1958), trans. Hullot-Kentor and Frederic Will, "The Essay as Form," in *The Adorno Reader*, ed. Brian O'Connor (Oxford/Malden, Mass.: Blackwell, 2000).

Kants "Kritik der reinen Vernunft," Nachgelassene Schriften, part. 4, volume 4 (Frankfurt am Main: Suhrkamp Verlag, 1995).

Philosophische Terminologie (1) (Frankfurt am Main: Suhrkamp Verlag, 1973).

Other Authors

Allison, Henry. *Kant's Transcendental Idealism: An Interpretation and Defense* (New Haven, Conn./London: Yale University Press, 1983).

Aristotle, *Metaphysics* (Cambridge, Mass.: Harvard University Press, 1933), trans. Hugh Tredennick.

Bell, David. *Husserl* (London/New York: Routledge, 1990).

Bernstein, J. M. "Introduction" to Theodor W. Adorno, *The Culture Industry: Selected Essays on Mass Culture* (London: Routledge, 1991), ed. J. M. Bernstein.

Bernstein, J. M. "Why Rescue Semblance: Metaphysical Experience and the Possibility of Ethics," in *The Semblance of Subjectivity: Essays in Adorno's Aesthetic Theory*, eds. Tom Huhn and Lambert Zuidervaart (Cambridge, Mass./London: MIT Press, 1997).

Bernstein, J. M. *Adorno: Disenchantment and Ethics* (Cambridge: Cambridge University Press, 2001).

Bird, Graham. *Kant's Theory of Knowledge: An Outline of One Central Argument in the Critique of Pure Reason* (London: Routledge and Kegan Paul, 1962).

Bird, Graham. "Kant's Transcendental Arguments," in *Reading Kant: New Perspectives on Transcendental Arguments and Critical Philosophy*, eds. Eva Schaper and Wilhelm Vossenkuhl (Oxford: Basil Blackwell, 1989).

Blattner, William D. *Heidegger's Temporal Idealism* (Cambridge: Cambridge University Press, 1999).

Braun, Carl. *Kritische Theorie versus Kritizismus: Zur Kant-Kritik Theodor W. Adornos* (Berlin/New York: Walter de Gruyter, 1983), *Kant-Studien*, supplementary volume 115.

Brunkhorst, Hauke. *Theodor W. Adorno: Dialektik der Moderne* (Munich/Zurich: Piper, 1990).

References

Bubner, Rüdiger. *Modern German Philosophy* (Cambridge: Cambridge University Press, 1981), trans. Eric Mathews.

Bubner, Rüdiger. "Adornos Negative Dialektik," in *Adorno-Konferenz 1983* (Frankfurt: Suhrkamp Verlag, 1983), eds. Ludwig von Friedeburg and Jürgen Habermas.

Carl, Wolfgang. *Frege's Theory of Sense and Reference: Its Origins and Scope* (Cambridge: Cambridge University Press, 1994).

Cook, Deborah. *Adorno, Habermas and the Search for a Rational Society* (London/New York: Routledge, 2004).

Cornelius, Hans. *Einleitung in die Philosophie* (Leipzig: B. G. Teubner, 1903).

Cornelius, Hans. *Transcendentale Systematik: Untersuchung zur Begründung der Erkenntnistheorie* (Munich: Ernst Reinhardt, 1916, second edition, 1926).

Cornelius, Hans. *Kommentar zu Kants Kritik der reinen Vernunft* (Erlangen: Verlag der Philosophischen Akademie, 1926).

Cornelius, Hans. *Das philosophische System: Eigene Gesamtdarstellung* (Berlin: Junker Duennhaupt, 1934).

Deleuze, Gilles. *Empiricism and Subjectivity: An Essay on Hume's Theory of Human Nature* (New York: Columbia University Press, 1991), trans. Constantin V. Boundas.

Dews, Peter. "Adorno, Post-Structuralism and the Critiques of Identity," *New Left Review*, no. 157 (1986).

Dews, Peter. *Logics of Disintegration: Post-Structuralist Thought and the Claims of Critical Theory* (London: Verso, 1987).

Dreyfus, Hubert. *Being-in-the-World* (Cambridge, Mass./London: MIT Press, 1991).

Elster, Jon. *Making Sense of Marx* (Cambridge: Cambridge University Press, 1985).

Fichte, J. G. *The Science of Knowledge* (Cambridge: Cambridge University Press, 1982), trans. Peter Heath and John Lachs.

Förster, Eckart. "How are Transcendental Arguments Possible?" in *Reading Kant*, eds. Eva Schaper and Wilhelm Vossenkuhl (Oxford: Basil Blackwell, 1989).

Förster, Eckart. "Kant's *Selbstsetzungslehre*," in *Kant's Transcendental Deductions* (Stanford, Calif.: Stanford University Press, 1989), ed. Eckart Förster.

Foster, John. "The Succinct Case for Idealism," in *Objections to Physicalism* (Oxford: Clarendon Press, 1993), ed. Howard Robinson.

Frank, Manfred. "Is Subjectivity a Non-Thing, an Absurdity [*Unding*]? On Some Difficulties in Naturalistic Reductions of Self-Consciousness," in *The Modern Subject: Conceptions of the Self in Classical German Philosophy* (Albany, N.Y.: State University of New York Press, 1995), eds. Karl Ameriks and Dieter Sturma.

References

Frank, Manfred. "Philosophical Foundations of Early Romanticism," in *The Modern Subject: Conceptions of the Self in Classical German Philosophy* (Albany, N.Y.: State University Press of New York, 1995), eds. Karl Ameriks and Dieter Sturma.

Frege, Gottlob. "On Concept and Object," in *Translations from the Philosophical Writings of Gottlob Frege* (Oxford: Basil Blackwell, 1970), trans. P. Geach and M. Black.

Frege, Gottlob. *Posthumous Writings* (Oxford: Oxford University Press, 1974), trans. P. Long, R. White, and R. Hargraves.

Friedeburg, Ludwig von and Habermas, Jürgen (eds.). *Adorno-Konferenz 1983* (Frankfurt: Suhrkamp Verlag, 1983).

Grenz, Friedemann. *Adornos Philosophie in Grundbegriffen: Auflösung einiger Deutungsprobleme* (Frankfurt: Suhrkamp Verlag, 1974).

Gripp, Helga. *Theodor W. Adorno: Erkenntnisdimensionen negativer Dialektik* (Paderborn: Verlag Ferdinand Schöningh, 1986).

Guyer, Paul. "The Transcendental Deduction of the Categories," in *The Cambridge Companion to Kant* (Cambridge: Cambridge University Press, 1992), ed. Paul Guyer.

Habermas, Jürgen. *Knowledge and Human Interests* (London: Heinemann, 1972), trans. Jeremy J. Shapiro.

Habermas, Jürgen. *Theory of Communicative Action*, volume 1 (London: Heinemann, 1984), trans. Thomas McCarthy.

Hegel, G. W. F. *The Encyclopaedia Logic* (Indianapolis, Ind.: Hackett, 1991), trans. T. F. Geraets, W. A. Suchting, and H. S. Harris; *Enzyklopädie der philosophischen Wissenschaften* (Hamburg: Felix Meiner Verlag, 1991), eds. Friedhelm Nicolin and Otto Pöggeler.

Hegel, G. W. F. *Phenomenology of Spirit* (Oxford: Oxford University Press, 1977), trans. A. V. Miller; *Phänomenologie des Geistes* (Hamburg: Felix Meiner Verlag, 1988), eds. Hans-Friedrich Wessels and Heinrich Clairmont.

Heidegger, Martin. *Being and Time* (Albany, N.Y.: State University of New York Press, 1996), trans. J. Stambaugh; *Sein und Zeit* (Tübingen: Max Niemeyer Verlag, 16th edition, 1986).

Heidegger, Martin. *Basic Problems of Phenomenology* (Bloomington, Ind.: Indiana University Press, 1982), trans. Albert Hofstadter.

Henrich, Dieter. "Self-Consciousness: A Critical Introduction to a Theory," *Man and World*, volume 4, no. 1 (1971).

Henrich, Dieter. "Fichte's Original Insight," in *Contemporary German Philosophy 1* (University Park, Penn.: Pennsylvania State University Press, 1982), trans. David R. Lachterman.

References

Henrich, Dieter. "The Identity of the Subject in the Transcendental Deduction," in *Reading Kant*, eds. Eva Schaper and Wilhelm Vossenkuhl (Oxford: Basil Blackwell, 1989).

Huhn, Tom and Zuidervaart, Lambert (eds.). *The Semblance of Subjectivity: Essays in Adorno's Aesthetic Theory* (Cambridge, Mass./London: MIT Press, 1997).

Husserl, Edmund. *Logical Investigations* (London: Routledge and Kegan Paul, 1973), trans. J. N. Findlay.

Husserl, Edmund. *Cartesian Meditations: An Introduction to Phenomenology* (The Hague: Martinus Nijhoff, 1969), trans. Dorian Cairns.

Husserl, Edmund. *The Crisis of European Sciences and Transcendental Phenomenology* (Evanston, Ill.: Northwestern University Press, 1970), trans. David Carr.

Jay, Martin. *The Dialectical Imagination: A History of the Frankfurt School and the Institute of Social Research, 1923–1950* (Berkeley, Calif.: University of California Press, second edition, 1996).

Kant, Immanuel. *Critique of Pure Reason* (London: Macmillan, 1927), trans. Norman Kemp Smith; *Kritik der reinen Vernunft* (Hamburg: Felix Meiner, 3rd edition, 1990), ed. Raymund Schmidt.

Kant, Immanuel. *Critique of Practical Reason* (New York: Macmillan, 1956), trans. Lewis White Beck.

Kitcher, Patricia. "Kant's Real Self," in *Self and Nature in Kant's Philosophy* (Ithaca, N.Y.: Cornell University Press, 1987), ed. Allen W. Wood.

Lukács, Georg. *History and Class Consciousness* (London: Merlin Press, 1971), trans. Rodney Livingston.

Marion, Jean-Luc. "Heidegger and Descartes," in *Critical Heidegger* (London: Routledge, 1996), ed. Christopher Macann.

Marx, Karl. *Capital I* (Harmondsworth: Penguin, 1976), trans. Ernest Mandel.

Marx, Karl, and Engels, Friedrich. *The Communist Manifesto*, in *Karl Marx: Selected Writings* (Oxford: Oxford University Press, 1977), ed. David McLelland.

Moran, Dermot. *Introduction to Phenomenology* (London/New York: Routledge, 2000).

Mörchen, Hermann. *Adorno und Heidegger. Untersuchung einer philosophischen Kommunicationsverweigerung* (Stuttgart: Klett-Cotta, 1981).

Müller, Ulrich. *Erkenntniskritik und Negative Metaphysik bei Adorno* (Frankfurt: Athenäum, 1988).

Nagel, Thomas. *Mortal Questions* (Cambridge: Cambridge University Press, 1979).

Nagel, Thomas. *The View from Nowhere* (Oxford: Oxford University Press, 1986).

References

Neuhouser, Frederick. *Fichte's Theory of Subjectivity* (Cambridge: Cambridge University Press, 1990).

Nietzsche, Friedrich. *The Will to Power* (New York: Random House, 1967), trans. Walter Kaufmann and R. J. Hollingdale.

Oakeshott, Michael. *Experience and Its Modes* (Cambridge: Cambridge University Press, 1933).

O'Connor, Brian. "The Concept of Mediation in Hegel and Adorno," *Bulletin of the Hegel Society of Great Britain*, 39/40 (1999).

O'Connor, Brian (ed.). *The Adorno Reader* (Oxford/Malden, Mass.: Blackwell, 2000).

Pivčević, Edo. *Husserl and Phenomenology* (London: Hutchinson, 1970).

Rath, Norbert. *Adornos Kritische Theorie: Vermittlungen und Vermittlungsschwierigkeiten* (Paderborn/Munich/Vienna/Zurich: Ferdinand Schöningh, 1982).

Rosen, Michael. *Hegel's Dialectic and Its Criticism* (Cambridge: Cambridge University Press, 1982).

Rosen, Michael. "Critical Theory: Between Ideology and Philosophy," in *The Need for Interpretation* (London: Athlone Press, 1983), eds. Sollace Mitchell and Michael Rosen.

Sandkaulen, Birgit. "Adornos Ding an sich: Zum Übergang der Philosophie in Ästhetische Theorie," *Deutsche Vierteljahrsschrift für Literaturwissenschaft und Geisteswissenschaft* (special vol., 1994).

Sartre, J.-P. *Being and Nothingness: An Essay on Phenomenological Ontology* (New York: Philosophical Library, 1956), trans. Hazel E. Barnes.

Sartre, J.-P. *The Transcendence of the Ego* (New York: Octagon Books, 1972), trans. F. Williams and R. Kirkpatrick.

Schaper, Eva and Vossenkuhl, Wilhelm (eds.). *Reading Kant: New Perspectives on Transcendental Arguments and Critical Philosophy* (Oxford: Basil Blackwell, 1989).

Schmidt, Alfred. "Begriff des Materialismus bei Adorno," in *Adorno-Konferenz 1983* (Frankfurt: Suhrkamp Verlag, 1983), eds. Ludwig von Friedeburg and Jürgen Habermas.

Schnädelbach, Herbert. "Dialektik als Vernunftkritik: Zur Konstruktion des Rationalen bei Adorno," in *Adorno-Konferenz 1983* (Frankfurt: Suhrkamp Verlag, 1983), eds. Ludwig von Friedeburg and Jürgen Habermas.

Schopenhauer, Arthur. *The World as Will and Representation*, volume 1 (New York: Dover, 1969), trans. E. F. J. Payne.

Searle, John. *The Rediscovery of the Mind* (Cambridge, Mass./London: MIT Press, 1992).

References

Sellars, Wilfrid. "... this I or he or it (the thing) which thinks ...," *Proceedings and Addresses of the American Philosophical Association* 44 (1970–1971).

Smith, Peter and O. R. Jones, *The Philosophy of Mind: An Introduction* (Cambridge: Cambridge University Press, 1986).

Strawson, Peter F. *The Bounds of Sense* (London: Methuen, 1966).

Tar, Zoltan. *The Frankfurt School: The Critical Theories of Max Horkheimer and Theodor W. Adorno* (New York: John Wiley, 1977).

Thyen, Anke. *Negative Dialektik und Erfahrung: Zur Rationalität des Nichtidentischen bei Adorno* (Frankfurt-am-Main: Suhrkamp Verlag, 1989).

Tugendhat, Ernst. *Self-Consciousness and Self-Determination* (Cambridge, Mass./London: MIT Press, 1986), trans. Paul Stern.

Valberg, J. J. *The Puzzle of Experience* (Oxford: Clarendon Press, 1992).

Walker, Ralph C. S. "Synthesis and Transcendental Idealism," *Kant-Studien*, vol. 76 (1985).

Walker, Ralph C. S. "Transcendental Argument and Scepticism," in *Reading Kant*, eds. Eva Schaper and Wilhelm Vossenkuhl (Oxford: Basil Blackwell, 1989).

Willard, Dallas. "The Paradox of Logical Psychologism: Husserl's Way Out," in *Husserl: Expositions and Appraisals* (Notre Dame, Ind.: University of Notre Dame Press, 1977), eds. Frederick A. Elliston and Peter McCormick.

Zuidervaart, Lambert. *Adorno's Aesthetic Theory: The Redemption of Illusion* (Cambridge, Mass./ London: MIT Press, 1991).

Index

Absolutism, 26, 27, 39, 34, 78–79
Adorno, Theodor W.
  "Actuality of Philosophy, The," 4–8, 16, 31, 41, 42, 43, 45, 46, 48, 67, 128, 176n8
  Aesthetic Theory, 19
  Concept of the Unconscious in Transcendental Psychology, The, 102, 103, 104, 118, 127
  Dialectic of Enlightenment, 18
  "Essay as Form, The," 175n2, 180n8
  Hegel: Three Studies, 186n15
  "Idea of Natural History, The," 128, 161, 162
  "Introduction," in *The Positivist Dispute in German Sociology*, 177n10
  Lectures on the Critique of Pure Reason, 20, 100, 111, 113, 120, 122, 124, 125, 126, 186n17
  Metacritique of Epistemology, The, xii, 26, 27, 29, 42, 60, 61, 87, 89, 90, 91, 92, 94, 97, 100, 112, 119, 120, 122–123, 128, 129, 131, 133–134, 135, 136, 137, 138, 139, 141, 142, 143, 144, 145, 182n12, 187n27, 188n8
  Minima Moralia, 175n2
  Negative Dialectics, ix, x, xii, 2, 3, 12, 13, 17, 18, 42, 43, 48, 50, 52, 53, 56, 58, 59, 60, 61, 62, 63, 65, 66, 67, 68, 75, 76, 77, 78, 79, 80, 81, 82, 83, 88, 91, 96, 101, 116, 119, 125, 128, 136, 153, 155, 156, 157, 159, 160, 177n1, 181n13, 181n14, 181n15, 182n4, 182n6, 182n9, 187n29
  Philosophical Terminology, 48
  "Sociology and Empirical Research," 49
  "Subject and Object," x, 20, 50, 51, 52, 53, 54, 57, 61, 63, 73, 74, 82, 83, 84, 85, 86, 87, 124
  Transcendence of the Real and Noematic in Husserl's Phenomenology, The, 102, 103, 104, 105, 106
Allison, Henry, 177n5
Antinomy, 25–28, 30, 139
Apperception, 22, 24, 85–86, 104–105, 108, 124
Aristotle, 53
Atomization, 12

Being, 5–6, 80
Bell, David, 131
Berkeley, George, 20, 21, 55
Bernstein, J. M., 175n1, 176n5, 179n18
Bird, Graham, 23, 177n5
Blattner, William D., 162–163
Braun, Carl, 183n1
Brunkhorst, Hauke, 75, 176n8
Bubner, Rüdiger, xii, 175n2, 189n17

Class, 12
Commodity exchange, 9, 137
Community, 11–12, 137
Concepts
  character of, 18, 31, 34, 35, 36, 37, 45, 50, 59, 62, 63, 64, 65–69, 72, 77, 113, 142
  concept employment, 7, 25, 29, 30, 47, 49, 89, 158, 166
Conceptualism, 34–37, 57, 59–60, 61, 64, 69, 172

Index

Concretion, ix–x, xi, 18, 74
Consciousness
 character of, ix, 53, 71, 74, 76, 83, 86, 89, 104, 167, 169
 false, x, 2, 43, 47
 Hegel's idea of, 30, 33, 34, 35, 36, 38–39
 irreducibility of, 92–98
 mind, 23, 81, 84, 87, 90, 91, 94, 95–98, 110
Cook, Deborah, 191n9
Cornelius, Hans, 19, 102, 103, 106, 177n4, 184n6
Critical Theory, ix–x, xi, 1, 18, 51, 71, 128, 137, 159, 167, 173

Deconstruction, 149
Deleuze, Gilles, 186n16
Derrida, Jacques, 149
Descartes, René, 20, 21–22, 24, 87
Determinism, 26, 75–76
Dews, Peter, 189n15
Dialectic
 Hegelian, 27, 33–34, 37, 55, 76–81
 historical, 8
 master-slave, 38–41
 negative, ix, 42, 63, 68, 75, 77, 79, 139, 143, 155
Dreyfus, Hubert, 189n18
Dualism
 concept, 84, 91, 140, 141
 mind-body, 93, 95–98, 153
Durkheim, Émile, 135

Elster, Jon, 33
Empiricism, 7, 74, 75, 88–89, 90, 91, 92, 93, 106, 131, 132, 150
Engels, Friedrich, 177n11
Epistemology, xi, 1, 2, 3, 12, 17, 20, 27, 28, 42, 47, 48, 49, 60, 61, 69, 73, 91, 97–98, 150, 151–154, 157, 163
Experience, ix, xi, 1–2, 3, 4–5, 6, 12, 15, 17, 18, 20–21, 22, 23, 24, 25, 28, 29, 30–31, 33, 34, 35, 37, 42, 43, 46, 47, 49, 50, 51, 52–53, 54–59, 62, 63, 64, 65, 69, 71, 74–81, 86, 90, 93–94, 95, 109, 111, 112, 113, 118, 123, 125, 134, 142, 151, 153, 156, 161, 163, 164, 165–166, 168, 173
 somatic, 81, 87–92

Fichte, Johann Gottlieb, 2, 85, 161, 184n7
Formalism, 6

Förster, Eckart, 180n6, 185n10
Foster, John, 183n17
Frank, Manfred, 183n13
Freedom, 26, 60, 75, 167, 169
Frege, Gottlob, 1, 130, 181n15

Gadamer, Hans-Georg, 147
Geist, 8, 171
Givenness, ix, 7, 11, 12, 27, 37, 52, 58, 60, 62, 64, 74, 88, 94, 97, 106, 112–113, 119
Grenz, Friedemann, 188n7
Gripp, Helga, 176n6, 189n15
Guilt, 42
Guyer, Paul, 123

Habermas, Jürgen, 1, 165–170, 172, 190n3
 Knowledge and Human Interests, 176n7
 Theory of Communicative Action, The, 1, 166, 167
Hegel, Georg Wilhelm Friedrich, 2, 4, 16–17, 19, 27, 29–43, 49, 55, 60, 61, 65, 66, 73, 75, 76–81, 100, 107, 117, 120, 127, 142, 143, 167, 171, 172
 Encyclopaedia Logic, The, 27, 32, 78, 178–179n12
 Phenomenology of Spirit, 29, 30, 32, 33, 35, 36, 37, 38, 40, 41, 46, 78, 80, 120–121
Hegelian-Marxism, 8
Heidegger, Martin, ix, xii, 5–6, 28, 58, 100, 127, 128, 149–164, 166
 Basic Problems of Phenomenology, 158, 160, 161, 185n11
 Being and Time, 151, 152, 153, 154, 155
Henrich, Dieter, 184n7
History, 161–162
Hume, David, 107
Husserl, Edmund, 28, 58, 100, 101, 120, 127–128, 129–148, 155
 Crisis of European Sciences, The, 146, 147, 148
 Logical Investigations, 129, 131, 132, 133, 134

Idealism
 in general form, 27, 60, 72, 73–74, 82, 92
 Hegelian, 77
 material, 22
 subjective, 19, 20, 21, 73, 74, 85, 86, 87, 99, 100, 101, 102, 107, 117, 159–163

Index

transcendental, 99, 100, 102, 103, 106, 109, 117, 122, 125, 131, 163
Identity, 17–18, 20, 24, 27, 29, 33, 34, 45, 51, 63, 66, 68, 78, 80
Ideology, 2, 9, 77
Immanent critique, 26–27, 139
Immediacy, 60, 61, 64, 80, 88, 112–113, 156–157, 160
Individualism, 136–137
Individuality. *See* Particularity
Intuition
  intellectual, 110–113
  sensible, 64–65, 85, 114, 115, 116, 122
Irrationalism, 6, 46, 149, 156–159

Jay, Martin, 149
Judgment, 16, 18, 31, 33, 35, 36, 37, 46, 47, 49, 65–69, 77, 106, 107, 113, 133, 140

Kant, Immanuel, ix, xii, 1, 3, 11, 16–17, 19–28, 29, 43, 46, 53–54, 55, 56, 58, 83, 87, 99–126, 127, 131, 145, 163, 172
  Antinomies of Pure Reason, 21, 25–28, 54
  Critique of Practical Reason, 115
  Critique of Pure Reason, 19, 20, 21, 22, 23, 24, 62, 64, 87, 107, 108, 109, 110, 111, 113, 114, 115, 116, 118, 121, 178n10, 178n11, 184n7, 187n28
  Paralogisms of Rational Psychology, 84, 93, 97, 103–104, 105, 114, 119
  Refutation of Idealism, 20–25, 83, 114, 115
  Transcendental Aesthetic, 109–113, 114, 115
  Transcendental Deduction, 107–109, 113–117, 123
Kierkegaard, Søren, 5, 100
Kitcher, Patricia, 121
Knowledge, 30, 31, 32, 35, 37, 38, 50, 64, 71, 98
Kracauer, Siegfried, 19, 101

Language, 49, 50, 68, 119–121, 123–124, 168–169
Levinas, Emmanuel, 38
Lifeworld (*Lebenswelt*), 59, 146–148
Locke, John, 90
Logic, 58, 130, 131, 132, 133, 134, 135, 136, 137, 138, 139–140, 141, 143, 145, 147, 148
Logical absolutism, 129, 130–145

Logical positivism, 7
Lukács, Georg, 4, 8–13, 55

Marburg neo-Kantianism, 6, 46
Marcuse, Herbert, 182n5
Marion, Jean-Luc, 190n26
Marx, Karl, 9, 59, 72, 171, 176n9, 177n11
Materialism, 20, 34, 72, 73, 79, 81, 84, 100, 117, 151, 170–172
Matter, 11, 34, 56, 91, 92
Meaning, 18, 45, 46, 48, 49, 56, 59–60, 67, 71, 170–172
Mediation, 17, 18–19, 46, 48, 49, 52, 54, 56, 58, 59–60, 61, 62, 71, 73, 75, 78, 82, 89, 90, 91, 92, 93, 96, 98, 100, 112, 123, 130, 131, 134, 138–139, 143, 144, 145, 155, 159, 166, 167
Metaphysics, 81
Moran, Dermot, 189n11
Mörchen, Hermann, 189n17
Müller, Ulrich, 176n8

Nagel, Thomas, 93, 85–97, 143
Nature, 72, 146
Negation, 32, 33, 37, 40, 61, 73, 74–81
Neuhouser, Frederick, 185n7
Nietzsche, Friedrich, 15, 135, 188n6
Nonconceptuality, 17, 24, 34, 35, 47, 49, 50, 57, 59, 61–65, 66, 69, 71, 91, 113
Nonidentity, 16, 20, 25, 34, 42, 43, 45, 48, 49, 61, 63, 64, 67, 68, 69, 71, 77, 78, 160, 163, 166, 172
Normativity
  epistemological, 1–2, 8, 25, 28, 32, 42, 43
  ethical, 38, 41, 42
Noumenal realm, 118, 121–124
Novalis, 85

Oakeshott, Michael, 35
Object(s), 11, 20, 22, 23, 24, 27, 32–33, 37, 42, 45, 47, 48, 49, 50, 51–54, 55, 56, 57, 59–60, 61–63, 64, 65, 66, 67, 71, 82, 83, 113, 170–172
  as historical sedimentation, 59, 74, 170–171, 172
  priority of, 16, 43, 45, 49, 51–54, 55–59, 60, 61, 63, 73, 74, 78, 82–83, 88, 144
  as thing-in-itself, 20, 24, 56, 61–64, 78, 107, 143, 144
O'Connor, Brian, 177n3, 179n13
Otherness, 38–39, 41, 57, 61, 82, 119

Index

Particularity, 17, 42, 45, 46, 47, 48, 49, 59, 66, 71–72, 80
Passivity, 75–76
Phenomenology, 26, 61, 72, 92, 129, 150–151, 154, 156
Philosophy (possibility of), 4, 10–11, 12, 152
Philosophy of mind, 90–91, 92–93
Philosophy of the subject, xi, 52, 53, 150, 166
Physicalism, 93, 96, 97
Pivčević, Edo, 147
Plato, 17, 132, 137, 140
Positivism, 7–8, 46, 77, 100
Praxis, x, 73
Predication, 65–68
Production, 9–10, 137
Psychologism, 129, 130, 131–137, 144, 146

Rath, Norbert, 180n9
Rationality
 critical, ix–x, xi, 1–2, 5, 6, 8, 10, 13, 15, 29, 30–31, 32, 33, 37, 43, 74–75, 76, 81, 100, 128, 159, 167–170, 173
 in modernity, 3, 4, 8, 9–10, 12–13, 28, 51, 55, 56, 74, 91, 167, 168
 philosophical, 25, 28
 rationalism, 11–13
Realism
 indirect, 21–22, 23, 62
 naive, 50–51, 52, 74
Recognition, 39–41, 43
Reconciliation (of subject and object), 166, 169–172
Reification, 8–11, 47, 49, 51, 55, 57, 59, 63, 94, 168
Reinhold, Karl, 85
Relativism, 131, 136, 138
Representation, 21, 22, 23, 24, 61–62, 64, 107, 108–109, 111
Rosen, Michael, 19, 170–172, 176n8

Sandkaulen, Birgit, 180n10
Sartre, Jean-Paul, 76, 117, 180n7
Schelling, Friedrich Wilhelm Joseph von, 85
Schnädelbach, Herbert, 175n3, 176n6, 180n10
Schopenhauer, Arthur, 166
Science, 53–54, 146, 148
Scientism, 7–8, 151
Searle, John, 93, 97–98, 183n18
Sellars, Wilfrid, 187n29

Sensibility, 62, 63, 69, 80, 87–91, 107, 116
Skepticism, 21–23, 25, 32, 107
Sociality, 135–137
Social totality, 59–60, 71, 74, 147, 171
Society, 8, 9, 10, 12, 51, 74
 civic, 38–39
Spinoza, Baruch, 4
Spontaneity, 29, 94, 99, 106–107, 108, 111, 114, 115, 116, 121, 122
Strawson, P. F., 56, 123–124, 187n26
Subjectivism, 45, 48, 53–54, 87–88
Subjectivity, 9, 16, 20, 24, 29, 82–83, 84–87, 152
 agency, 48–49, 50–51, 59–60, 71–81, 94, 97, 101, 130, 137, 143, 144, 148, 164
 constitutive, 21, 52, 53–54, 57, 72, 80, 85–86, 92, 99, 106–109, 110, 115, 116, 117, 168
 Dasein, 128, 152, 153, 158, 160, 161, 163
 as physical, 71–72, 81, 84–92
 transcendental, 23, 28, 102, 104, 105, 106, 107, 108, 109, 115, 117–125
Subject–object relation, x, 1, 2, 4, 6, 16–17, 18, 20, 24–25, 28, 29, 31, 34–35, 38, 41, 42, 43, 46, 47, 48, 49, 50, 51, 53, 54–58, 72–73, 76, 77, 78, 86, 87, 90, 91, 97, 100, 106, 116, 117, 134, 138–139, 141, 143, 145, 149, 154–164, 166, 172
Synthesis, 107–108, 116, 123
System, 6, 11, 27, 77

Tar, Zoltan, 182n1
Thyen, Anke, 49, 176n4, 181n12
Tiedemann, Rolf, 103
Totality, 4–5, 11, 48
Transcendental
 critique, xi, 15, 23, 25–28, 54–59, 89, 134, 135, 138, 142
 structures (of experience), 2–3, 17, 25–28, 43, 55, 96, 134, 139, 141, 150
Truth, 2, 3, 7, 8, 12, 15, 20, 35, 36, 79, 98, 131, 134, 142, 143, 144, 156
Tugendhat, Ernst, 120

Unconscious mind, 103–104

Valberg, J. J., 182n10

Walker, Ralph C. S., 62, 180n5
Willard, Dallas, 130, 133

Zuidervaart, Lambert, 182n2

www.ingramcontent.com/pod-product-compliance
Lightning Source LLC
Chambersburg PA
CBHW020654230426
43665CB00008B/433